TROUBLE IN STORE

Norman Wisdom: a career in comedy

by Richard Dacre

T. C. FARRIES
AND CO. LIMITED

792.092
WISDOM

26 NOV 1991

CEN

British Library Cataloguing in Publication Data
  Dacre, Richard 1951—
  Trouble in store: Norman Wisdom, a career in comedy.
  1. Entertainments. Wisdom, Norman 1918—
  I. Title
  791.092
  ISBN 0-948278-16-1

For my Mum and Dad

CONTENTS

Foreword.

It's been many years since I wrote 'Don't Laugh At Me' which has since become my theme song. At first sight it might seem a strange phrase coming from someone who strives for the opposite - but recall the whole line - 'Don't Laugh at Me 'Cause I'm a Fool'. In my opinion tears are as important as laughter, and the naïf but well-meaning little character I developed was able not only to create laughter, but was also able to bring a tear to the eye. Childish humour, some have claimed it to be. And why not. They said the same about Chaplin. I have endeavoured to provide fun that's meant to amuse children from about the age of 4 to 94 and if you don't possess a slightly childish sense of humour then you cannot be a very happy person.

My little character was named the Gump and has appeared in many films and on many stages, but he is not the whole story of my career. In this marvellously well-researched book, the author goes beyond the well-known films and looks at my stage and television work as well as the films that are not so regularly re-screened on television.

I have been extremely lucky in my life. And I'm still lucky in having such a good friend, Richard Dacre, to write this book. I hope you enjoy it.

Norman Wisdom

Introduction.

This book is not a biography as such, although I have included an outline of Norman Wisdom's life. The complete biography would be another project and hopefully one which Mr. Wisdom will undertake himself, for his is a fascinating tale. This is predominantly the story of the work Norman Wisdom has completed and which has entertained many of us for over four decades since he took his first tentative steps towards a show business career at the Collins Music Hall on December 17th, 1945.

Norman Wisdom will always be best remembered for his work in the cinema. Though he achieved the heights in other media - hailed for many years as Britain's top television comic, a record-breaking draw on stage, in variety, cabaret and pantomime - these are in the end ephemeral events. Hopefully, later comedians will be better served by the archivists of television's output - what would we think of Morecambe & Wise if we could only judge them by their films? Sadly, the truth is that very little has survived of television's output from the early days, and even from the 'sixties and 'seventies; preservation of light entertainment was deemed to be of low priority.

So, this book is biased towards Norman Wisdom's work in films. I have covered his career in detail outside the cinema, but in doing so I have had to rely chiefly on the fruits of research and hearsay, as Norman Wisdom achieved stardom at about the time I was born. However, I need no such excuses for his films. Though I watched and laughed at them as soon as I was old enough to go to the cinema, I do not have to rely on such distant and unreliable memories to discuss the characteristics of these immensely popular and splendidly achieved films: I can watch them all over again. I have great affection for British cinema comedy, especially for the nether regions occupied by robust, lowbrow slapstick and I have included a brief overview of this neglected tradition into which Norman Wisdom's work can be placed.

In gathering information for this book, I have used the services of the following organisations: the BBC's Data Services, the British Film Institute Library, the Enthoven Collection at the Victoria & Albert Museum, the Performing Rights Society, the National Sound Archive, the British Newspaper Library, the National Film Archive (David Meeker, Elaine Burrows) and the Library of the Performing Arts, New York. Thanks also to the following individuals: Liz Ashton Hill, Ann Brandon, Jill Craigie, Martyn

Kempson, Paul Kerr, Matti Salo, Paul Taylor, Tise Vahimagi. Above all I am grateful to Norman Wisdom who gave so much of his time to answering my questions - all uncredited quotes come from our conversations.

I would be glad to hear from any readers, especially with regards to additional Wisdom appearances in any media not listed in the appendixes. I can be reached by post at FLASHBACKS, 6 Silver Place, London W1R 3LJ.

Copyright material from the following companies has been reproduced in this book: the Rank Organisation, United Artists, Tigon, Philip Day. All the materials used for the illustrations are from the author's personal collection held in the Flashbacks Archive.

1. The Music Hall Tradition in British Cinema.

It is appropriate that Norman Wisdom should have made his first professional appearance in one of the then few surviving music halls, Collins in Islington. By this time - the end of the Second World War - live variety was to all intents and purposes dead. Many of the great halls had closed as early as the First World War, a proportion of the survivors going over to revue. Wireless had eaten into live entertainment's allure since the BBC was established in 1927 and then films accelerated the decline: even the London Palladium was tried out briefly as a cinema in 1928. But variety was hardy and the circuits held on tenaciously. When impresario George Black took over the Palladium in the year of its failure as a cinema, he turned it back into a showcase for variety and helped to feed a revival. It is only with the Second World War that terminal decline sets in. Acts were lost, theatres closed, and, significantly, soon after the war the Palladium turned to American talent to fill its auditorium. Finally, there was television; though until the mid 'fifties, with the advent of the commercial channels, its impact on variety's audience was negligible.

In the course of its history, the music halls spawned hundreds of fine comics utilising a wide range of techniques and styles of humour. The one thing they have in common is that their comedy sprang from the use of physical, facial and verbal resources - they are in what can be labelled the clown tradition of humour. Specific characters were born, and even if the comics did not write their own sketches, they reworked them so as to make them their own, bringing unique personal attributes to the material to provide the laughs. The music hall tradition in the cinema has its roots in the transfer of this form of humour to the big screen, a process which often seems to have been regarded as unproblematic, and which thus includes those films made by the truly physical clowns like Frank Randle, George Formby and Norman Wisdom as well as those clowns who applied their distinct personalities to the art of being stand-up, front-cloth comics such as Max Miller and Arthur Askey. Most of these films were unsophisticated lowbrow slapstick and were often treated with ill-concealed disdain by many critics, and even the producers and directors who made them - an attitude which lingers on with many film historians and archivists - but often these films possess a guts and excitement otherwise lacking in much of the

3

product of British studios. The more talented and adaptable of these comedians were able to shine through the usually tiny budgets, often slipshod production values, indifferent direction and inadequate scripts, to delight their fans and gain a new audience through the cinema.

The music halls should have provided British cinema with a flow of comedians to star in the silent period, but strangely enough we produced no top flight movie comics in those days, and it is not until the coming of sound that the music hall tradition in the cinema starts to take root more firmly. The coming of sound roughly coincided with the production boom caused by the Cinematograph Act of 1927, creating a lot of new work for proven talents. Entertainers could not ignore the fact that attendance at live variety was being eaten into, already many halls were undergoing conversion into cinemas, and they were pleased to embrace other outlets for their talents. Wireless was also a threat, though its history in the field of light entertainment does not really get under way in Britain until the war and many theatrical impresarios and agents, worried about the medium's effect on live entertainment, initially barred their stars from broadcasting.

Many of the great music hall performers entered the cinema via supporting or cameo roles, often in the revue-type films so popular in the 'thirties. However, the incorporation of this kind of appearance is not to confront the central problem inherent to adapting music hall humour to the cinema. Expressed in basic terms, this revolves around the difficulties in accommodating comics who may have been using a handful of routines perfected over many years in an act lasting from ten to twenty minutes and somehow adapting their talents into an hour or longer narrative feature film without losing their individuality as clowns. It is a problem which the writers, directors, producers and stars had difficulty in solving and we are faced with the evidence of a long history of disappointment and failure. Nevertheless, there were some sparkling triumphs. Amongst the most successful of the 'thirties were those who maintained an allegiance to their predominantly working-class following, those such as George Formby, Gracie Fields, Leslie Fuller, Arthur Lucan and Max Miller. There was Will Hay who utilised stronger plots than was usual with his contemporaries and who adapted his talents to the new medium with great thought, and achieved a middle-class acceptance. And there was a handful of middle-class entertainers, led by Jack Hulbert, who made films firmly within the music hall tradition.

By the late 'thirties, the larger and more powerful music hall circuits like the Moss Empires and the Syndicate Group still provided regular employment for a wide range of entertainers. To supplement the earnings from the tours and the Christmas shows there was the thriving summer resort trade, boosted with the passing of the Holidays With Pay Act of 1938 which brought the number of people with this right to about 14 million. Radio was

4

now producing important comedy shows and stars, and some, notably Arthur Askey, joined other favourites of the late 'thirties and the war years, such as the Crazy Gang and Frank Randle, to enrich the cinema's music hall tradition.

During the war the profession was fully occupied in entertaining the troops through ENSA (Entertainments National Service Association), the government sponsored body under Basil Dean, which also served to boost the morale of civilians. Revue and Variety continued to flourish in London's West End and at the seaside resorts. Nevertheless, touring was dying out and with the rise of television and the lack of venues after the war, the decline was such that by the 'fifties there were little more than third rate nudist shows left on the circuits. Just as had happened following the first war, so after the second there was a flowering of talent as people who found they had abilities to entertain, resulting from their experience in army concert parties, joined those professionals who wanted to resume interrupted careers. Live variety would be their starting point whether it be at the Collins Music Hall or the training ground of the Windmill Theatre.

Those who were to prove that they possessed the necessary abilities would, for the most part, have ambitions outside the dying theatre and would look to the still flourishing radio; keep an eye on the development of television; and perhaps hope for the film industry to notice them. In many ways, this was the last generation of comics to have the tremendous advantage of at least the remnants of a live variety circuit to use as a training ground, learning timing and perfecting presentation through experience on the boards. The process of working up from the 'wines and spirits' to top billing, perfecting single routines through repetition, is irreplaceable in developing knockabout physical comedy and verbal timing. After the war, the rise to fame could be speeded up with the additional launching pad of radio: *Henry Hall's Guest Night*, *Workers' Playtime*, *Variety Bandbox* and *Educating Archie* all provided platforms. The most celebrated of the theatres giving chances to up-and-coming comics with regular auditions was the Windmill, where the comedians were given the rather thankless task of filling-in between the nudes. The roll-call of comics who trod those particular boards is a *Who's Who* of postwar comedy, and though that theatre cannot be said ever to have launched a comedian on the road to stardom, it certainly provided a tremendous apprenticeship.

Sadly many of the people who did get to the top in radio or stage made little or no impact in the depressed cinema industry. As the 'fifties wore on, the attraction of television became more compelling. Television had started in August 1936 when the BBC beamed a variety show, *Here's Looking At You*, to the 300 homes which had sets and to the larger audience waiting expectantly at the Radio Show at Olympia. From then, the growth of British television was steady rather than spectacular: 30,000 sets at the resumption of broadcasting after the war and still only two million sets in 1952 when most of the country could receive broadcasts. Many variety agents and managements initially forbade their clients to appear on television. It was seen, correctly, as a huge risk because of its voracious appetite for material, and there was little protest from the artists themselves given the low rates the BBC could offer. Television came of age with the broadcasting of the 1953 Coronation to an estimated 20 million viewers, and a further boost was the launch of ITV in September 1954 when around 190,000 homes were able to receive the commercial broadcasts. From these lowly beginnings sprang, in Roy Thompson's celebrated phrase, 'the license to print money', and an investment of £2,500 in ATV when it opened in 1955 was worth £60,000 by 1958! By the end of the decade there were 10.5 million sets in operation. The principal casualty of the boom was the 'wireless', with the sale of television licences overtaking those for the radio in 1957, though it also made significant early inroads into the market for live entertainment and the cinema.

Most of the early comedy shows on television were in the variety format, and the leading exponent of this in the 'fifties was Norman Wisdom. Television comedy series began to emerge with some sort of narrative framework in the mid 'fifties and some of these, like the earlier equivalent radio series, were given cinema outings. But most 'fifties British film comedy was heavily influenced by the script-dependent products of the Ealing Studios, a formula which was broadened with the decline of that studio to give us the characteristic 'fifties product like *Genevieve* and the *Doctor* series. These situation comedies fall largely outside the music hall tradition and the true path of low humour was extended more notably by the marvellous ensemble playing of the *Carry On* team in a series which has lasted twenty-nine films.

The greatest television comedian of the late 'fifties was Tony Hancock whose enjoyable cinema ventures encompassed only two starring vehicles. Hancock and his collaborators changed the face of British television humour. Situation comedy suddenly became the principal acceptable format, with scriptwriters the kingmakers. After Hancock's brilliant intervention, television comedy series became dominated by essentially straight actors taking comic roles or bad comedians straitjacketed and constrained by dialogue, exemplified by the form's brilliant trailblazer, *Steptoe and Son*, created by Hancock's former scriptwriters Ray Galton and Alan Simpson. From then on television seemed to be closed to the antics of comics with the notable exceptions of Benny Hill and Morecambe & Wise, neither of which acts, sadly, made any sustained impact in the cinema.

6

The decline of the comedian on television coincided with the fall in status of the comedian in general. With the 'sixties in full swing, came the boom in the pop industry and singers and pop groups displaced comics as top-of-the-bill attractions; and in the world of film comedy, television spin-offs became the order of the day. It is true that the story of the music hall tradition in postwar British cinema makes fairly depressing reading, but there is an exception. One comedian was launched in films during the 'fifties and managed to climb to the very peak of the regular cinemagoer's affection where he remained for over fifteen years: Norman Wisdom.

2. Biographical notes.

Norman Wisdom's childhood was a loveless one of hardship and deprivation. The experiences of this period underlie much of Wisdom's humour and pathos and ground his character's reactions and emotions in a firm reality with which many of his natural audience could easily identify. Norman Wisdom was born in Marylebone, London. His father was a chauffeur and his mother a dressmaker and Norman and Fred, his older brother by two years, moved around the country in the wake of their father's employment, picking up only a meagre education in the meantime. Norman's first school was St. Luke's in Paddington's Fernhead Road. In *John Bull*, Wisdom poignantly recalls his first day there: 'It was a raw winter's morning, and I was shivering so much that the teacher, a kindly middle-aged woman with her hair done in a bun at the back, led me to the fireplace and put me in the hearth, inside a huge fireguard. Even so, I felt lonely and unhappy, and I cried. Next day, I was put inside the fireguard again, on a stool, and I kept this privileged seat throughout the cold spell.' By the time he was nine, Norman's parents split up. Their mother left home and with their father often away for weeks on end, the two children were left to fend for themselves on the Paddington streets, often reduced to stealing food for sustenance. A less risky method of obtaining food was to raise money through carrying bags for passengers at Paddington station, but these activities were cut short when the education authorities acted on their concern at the Wisdom children's sporadic attendance at school. The welfare department knew that the father was also a drinker, and the children were despatched to guardians at Roe Green, near Hatfield just north of London. This situation did not last long, and after an even shorter stay at a second home, they were placed alongside other children with guardians in Deal. Here new opportunities opened up, with the seaside railway station offering rich pickings for the bag carriers, and school life became more attractive after some bad experiences in the brief spell at Hatfield. The young Norman began to excel in painting and drawing, and in the sports: football, cricket and boxing.

At the age of fourteen, Norman left school, becoming a delivery boy with a china shop. For a time he seemed to have found that they offered a company tricycle with the job. Soon he gained a reputation as the fastest delivery boy in town, and was able to get Lipton's to bid against the rival Home & Colonial for the privilege of engaging his speedy services, upping his wages to the dizzy heights of 14 shillings a week in the process. However, technology caught up with him and he was rudely replaced by a van and found himself unemployed. The relatively lucrative period in the delivery trade gave Norman a taste for good clothes and provided him with a useful experience: 'I was in the first stages of wanting to be a grown man, and one summer's day I went along the front at Deal in [an] extravagant outfit, with the gloves turned back to show the fur. People turned and stared, and laughed, and I felt like diving behind a wall. The laughter shook me. I wanted to cry. Then I ran into one of the shopkeepers I knew in the High Street, out for a walk with his wife and he remarked, apparently quite seriously on my smartness. His kind words restored my confidence. In that short walk, I ran the gamut of perkiness, shame, fear, pleasure. In later years the experience was invaluable as comedy material.' (*John Bull.*)

A short spell serving at a milliner's followed, after which Norman decided to return to London and try his luck, inspired, prophetically enough, by the exciting sight of a film-crew photographing the Walmer lifeboat. Via the services of the local Juvenile Welfare Committee, Norman found employment as a living-in commis-waiter at the Artillery Mansions Hotel, Victoria, a post which did not survive the unfortunate experience of dropping a tray of crockery down a lift shaft! After a further job with a fall in wages as a pageboy at the London Ladies' Forum Club, Norman made a big decision. In company with a fellow pageboy, the 14-year-old decided to leave London during the holidays and become a miner. Armed with a cardboard boot-box full of food, Norman and his friend walked all but about twenty of the 160 miles from London to Cardiff to fulfil their ambition. By the time they reached Cardiff, the two youngsters had fallen out, leaving Norman alone once more. He paced the Tiger Bay dockside where sympathetic workmen gave him money and a family took pity on him and put him up for the couple of nights it took before he signed up as a cabin boy on the freighter *Maindy*, bound for Argentina. These were had days, Norman was tiny and light and found that the crew picked on him and made fun of him. It was during this voyage that the small boy started to develop his shadow-boxing skit in an attempt to deflect the sailors' cruelty and make them laugh. Impressed, they taught him the rudiments of serious boxing and were so pleased with his progress that they put the 5st. 9lb. lad into a boxing booth when they landed at an obscure port along the River Plate. Norman was badly beaten in the fight, though his shipmates made a little money out of him. The job itself was mainly hard work and toil, and on returning to Wales via the port of Rotterdam, Norman had no hesitation in signing off, spending the following Christmas isolated in a Cardiff hostel.

'There were only two other lads beside myself in the hotel, and they disappeared shortly before Christmas. On Christmas morning, I awoke in the long, cold dormitory to begin the worst day of my life. I collected my Christmas dinner from the kitchen, and looked disconsolately at the sausage and mash as I sat down at the bareboard table. This was just about the end. I sat crying for a long time.' (*John Bull.*) Before the new year had settled in, Norman had begun a series of jobs, with spells in Teddington, Taunton and back in London. None of these lasted long, and what little money he accumulated was soon spent on food, films and the Charing Cross pintables. Eventually, no more work was forthcoming and the 15-year-old was forced to sleep rough, often under the arches at the Adelphi or in his favourite spot beneath the Marshal Foch statue in Victoria. Survival was helped by a kindly cockney all-night coffee-stall owner to whom Norman would make a nightly plea between 3 a.m. and 4 a.m. when he would more often than not be rewarded with a mug of hot Bovril and a meat pie. Two weeks of this led to the owner suggesting to Norman that he get a job as a boy bandsman in the army. So Norman trooped off down to the recruiting office in Whitehall for an interview and was able to bluff his way on to the waiting list for the King George's Military Bandsmen. By now Norman was living with his grandmother in the Edgware Road, and while waiting for a vacancy to occur took a job at the Regal Cinema in Marble Arch as a pageboy. During this six weeks, he learnt a few lessons about hard work and practice from the cinema's celebrated organist, Reginald Foort.

Soon Norman was enrolled in the King's Own Regiment at Lichfield where his lack of musical skills did not go unnoticed, but luckily a sympathetic bandmaster allowed him the time to learn. At last, his life began to take on some direction. For the first time he experienced the luxuries of regular meals and sleep and he began to learn and improve the skills which were to play such an important role in his career - the sports: boxing, cricket and football; and the instruments. But he would never forget the pain and disappointments of his early life. As he remarked in the early 'sixties: 'When I put on that ill-fitting suit and cap, I'm back to those childhood days again.'

During a period of leave, Norman was reunited with his mother whom he had not seen since she ran away in his early childhood. They got on well, and arrangements were made to buy the youth out of the army for the princely sum of £35. Things did not turn out as hoped, Norman's rudimentary education standing in the way of his obtaining a job. Those that he did get, such as a trainee draughtsman, quickly fell through and so after only four weeks it was back to the army, this time with the 8th Hussars - later he transferred to the 10th Hussars - and a four-and-a-half year stint in India. Here the technical steps towards comedy stardom were even more pronounced - he set himself to improving his musical skills and learning more instruments: the clarinet, trumpet, saxophone, drums and the bugle; and he also learnt how to fall! 'Best of all I was taught how to fall from a galloping horse.

First I used to fall into a heap of straw, then they took the straw away. I wish they had told me first. All that was a great help for my later acts where I spent more time rolling about on my back than standing on my feet.' (*TV Times*.) He took up boxing seriously, rising to regimental flyweight and bantamweight champion, for the first time able to wallow in the glory of being top of the tree. Now dividing his time between the music, the outdoor sports and boxing, Norman's future as an entertainer got a huge boost when he taught himself to play 'Snowflakes' on the xylophone - an instrument no one else in the regiment could play - and thus Norman became a soloist. Other disciplines were added - singing sea shanties, a bit of tap dancing, and then he was spotted by some colleagues doing his shadow-boxing and they laughed. Once again, Norman sensed the difference between this laughter and the laughter his diminutive frame often aroused - and he liked it!

By now, Norman was doing the occasional concert party, and on one memorable date while playing at an officers' mess, he was enraged by the laughter caused by the sight of him doing his tap dancing in military boots, so he embroidered a mistake into a conscious comic turn, adding a couple of pratfalls for good measure. This went down well, and Norman's future as a comedian was even closer. In Spring 1939, the 10th Hussars sailed back to England and the 24-year-old Norman Wisdom left the army which had given him some schooling and many useful skills.

Once more, he took to the streets in an effort to find himself a civilian job. He attended L.C.C. evening classes while working for Triplex Safety Glass - in which a fast-rising executive was future radio comedy star Kenneth Horne. Wisdom soon passed the requisite civil service examinations to allow him to become a night operator in the Post Office Telecommunications department, supplementing his earnings with a daytime driving job with a car-hire firm. With the outbreak of war a few weeks later, he tried to rejoin the 10th Hussars but his post office work at the Willesden switchboard was a restricted occupation and he failed. 'It was when the blitz started that I realized what suicide seats we night operators occupied. We were on the top floor of the exchange, with a glass roof over our heads, and the Luftwaffe in the sky directly above. It was an uncomfortable role, though when we put on the headphones we were too busy to worry a great deal.' (*John Bull.*)

Wisdom was still not happy with his post. Annoyed that his army training was being wasted he persisted in his efforts to sign up. At last, his newly acquired skills admitted him to the Royal Corps of Signals, though in the end he never served overseas during the war. Instead he found himself posted to Cheltenham where he joined the regiment's band. Here his entertaining abilities got him noticed once more. Getting slightly tipsy at a dance, Wisdom stepped down from the orchestra rostrum and did his old shadow-boxing routine. The impromptu performance drew great applause, so he added a few falls, duck-waddled and pulled faces, unwittingly impressing the Entertainments Officer who happened to be amongst the audience. Immediately, Wisdom was drafted into the concert party and found himself performing at camp shows and local hospitals. Gradually, he took more care in his preparation, setting sketches to music and writing some scripts. The high point of his amateur career came at a Sunday concert at Cheltenham Town Hall and, with a review in the *Gloucestershire Echo*, Signalman Wisdom began to amass his pressbook. 'The highlight of the evening was provided by the screamingly funny comedian, Dizzy-Wizzy (Signalman N. Wisdom, RCS), whose shadow-boxing with an invisible opponent and other pranks made the company rock with laughter.'

There were other encouraging reviews collected from the local newspapers: 'Sig Wisdom . . . had everyone in fits of laughter as soon as he appeared. His knock-about fooling was perfect, and he showed the utmost originality.' 'The second artist 'Dizzie-Wizzie' (Sig. N. Wisdom) with his side-splitting antics, interspersed with jokes, caused roars of mirth and he finished with an expert demonstration of tap-dancing.'

There was now no doubt that his future lay in the entertainment industry. Wisdom had had an often hard and loveless life which would add conviction to his brand of pathos; he had the musical skills around which to base a good comic act; and he had the physical stamina and control which was to be the basis for his strongly visual and physical performance. The first tentative steps towards stardom were made soon after he was demobilised in 1945.

Wisdom was now one of many potential comedians on the lookout for work. He continued to perfect his act, living on the £83 he had saved from his gratuity, before beginning the dispiriting trek around agents and theatre managers. Having heard that many artists had started out at Collins Music Hall, Islington, he decided on the direct approach, and went there to see the manager, Lew Lake. Lake was not over-impressed by his visitor or by his cuttings, and it was only through sheer persistence that Wisdom got on the bill on the condition that he stopped his pestering if he flopped and settled for £5 for the week if he survived. Down to his last £3 and billed as a 'The Successful Failure' Norman Wisdom trod the boards as a professional entertainer for the first time on December 17th 1945. Dressed in a striped football jersey, cut-off trousers and a bowler, he did some tap-dancing and pratfalls, overrunning his eight-minute slot by six minutes in his enthusiastic search for audience approval. The act improved over the week, and on Christmas Eve an agent came backstage and offered Wisdom a few dates in the new year. Spots at the Basingstoke Grand, Portsmouth Coliseum and

1. Norman made manager Lew Lake's life a misery in order to pester his way on to the bill of the Collins Music Hall and make his first appearance. [programme + bill]

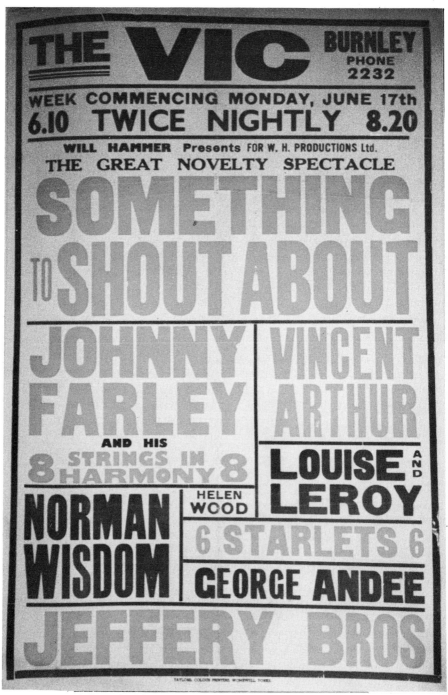

2. Poster for SOMETHING TO SHOUT ABOUT, Norman's 1946 tour.

the Hastings DeLuxe were followed by a touring revue, Will Hammer's *New Names Make News/Something To Shout About*, which helped to keep the wolf from the door. In this show, in which he did two spots and had a part in a sketch, Wisdom played the number two and three theatres before being paid-off to enter the realms of the unemployed once more. For one show, at the Blackburn Grand, Norman had the rather discouraging experience of being told to change his act by the manager because it was going down badly. 'As I rummaged through my suitcases, I came across two pieces of music. Frank Sinatra numbers . . . I was running downstairs as soon as the idea hit me. What was wrong with singing?' (*John Bull.*) Despite the trepidation of the manager, Wisdom's singing went down well, and by the end of the week he was actually receiving audience requests.

The end of the tour led into a 5-month spell of unemployment during which his search for work took him to an audition at the celebrated Windmill Theatre. Wisdom failed but another man, trying out his shaving routine on owner Vivian Van Damm that day was hired, Harry Secombe. In his book *Goon For Lunch*, Secombe recalls Wisdom's brief audition wearing an American-type college sweater, playing a few notes on his clarinet and doing a couple of falls. Another discouraging period came to an end, however, when a Brighton manager remembered Norman from an earlier date and took him on at £25 per week to play the Mate in *Robinson Crusoe* with Renée Houston and Donald Stewart as leads. 'Every Pantomime needs a really good comedian, and *Robinson Crusoe* . . . is lucky to have such a mirthmaker as Norman Wisdom, whose versatile antics stole the show.' (*Brighton Gazette.*)

Norman Wisdom's luck was now beginning to change. From Brighton he was signed by impresario Bert Montague and put into another touring revue, *Let's Make Hey*. Once more, Wisdom picked up the plaudits of the local press. The security of a 15-week stretch at £45 per week encouraged Norman to splash out on his first car, a scarlet 1937 Morgan, the beginning of a life-long passion with cars. During the show Wisdom met his future wife, Freda Simpson, who was doubling as a chorus girl and as an assistant to another comedian, Charlie Cameron, who shared a dressing room with him. While the rehearsals of *Let's Make Hey* were still in progress, Wisdom got an urgent request from producer Hastings Mann to take the place of a comic who had developed laryngitis in a Water Rats Sunday Charity Show at the Victoria Palace. Jumping at the chance of a West End date, Wisdom arrived at the theatre to find he was in the staggering company of Laurel & Hardy, Will Fyffe, Vera Lynn, Harry Tate Jr., Clarkson Rose and Nat Jackley. Since he was such a late replacement, Wisdom was not even on the programme. He was occupying a bad spot, warming up the audience soon after the interval for Vera Lynn who followed. 'I stood in the wings waiting

13

for the girls to come off . . . waiting to go on and face my first London audience. Then I heard a voice in my ear. It was Vera Lynn. She asked if we could change places, said she had a train to catch. So Vera went on before me. Then it was my turn. It was the most exciting night of my life. That applause . . . I'll never forget it. I gagged, fell flat, threw myself around the stage as though my life depended on it. Half way through the act I looked off the side of the stage and saw Vera Lynn applauding like mad! She didn't have a train to catch at all. She knew I was in a tough spot - so she volunteered to take my place and warm them up for me. That was one of the nicest gestures I've ever known in my theatrical life.' (*Daily Sketch.*)

His success at the Victoria Palace in front of a part-pro audience was an enormous boost to Norman Wisdom's confidence. The tour as warm-up comic with *Let's Make Hey* was a personal success - though he had problems with a jealous fellow-comic who tried to put Norman off his act and who got flattened for his troubles by the budding star at the tour's last date at the Edgware Metropolitan. The romance with Freda flourished during the tour and Norman Wisdom proposed once the end was in sight. After a brief separation while he fulfilled an engagement at a Skegness holiday camp, they were married at the Methodist Church in Shirley near Croydon in October 1947.

Norman and Freda took a room with the use of a kitchen at a house in Willesden for £3 10s a week, and the familiar pattern of rehearsing, perfecting and tramping round agents resumed. The next big opportunity came when he was offered the job of principal comedian at £50 per week in a show called *Piccadilly Nights* which was intended to tour Belgium. Freda also auditioned successfully and the couple travelled to Brussels to open with the show at the Alhambra Theatre. Wisdom learnt mechanically the spoken part of his act in French for the occasion. The programme following *Piccadilly Nights* was Laurel & Hardy who remembered Wisdom from the charity show the previous year. Stan Laurel, a fellow Englishman, was very enthusiastic about Wisdom's act, and was free with good advice to the up-and-coming comedian. Indeed, he offered to don a disguise and work as Wisdom's feed in a sketch, but management baulked at the idea and would not allow it. Sadly, *Piccadilly Nights* flopped and folded after only two weeks, and the whole company had to borrow and beg their way back to England. Once at home, the newly married couple had to make severe economies to survive, the car being one of the first casualties of this austere phase. Financial disaster was averted with a £15 fee earned by Wisdom for his first appearance on television, on November 22nd, 1947. Not much can be said about this auspicious occasion since this programme, like all Wisdom's work on television before 1961, seems to have been lost - miracles unforthcoming. The bare facts are that on that Saturday at 3.0, the

BBC broadcast a show from the Alexandra Palace called *Variety* with Gwen Catley (soprano), Frank Raymond (comedian), Dennis Forbes (conjuror), Norman Wisdom (comedian), and the Southern Singers (Negro Choir) introduced by Joy Nichols and produced by Eric Fawcett.

This was a lean period, and there were even thoughts of leaving the profession. Then Wisdom found himself a new agent in Billy Marsh from the Bernard Delfont Agency, to begin an association which would help make Marsh such a towering figure in postwar entertainment. After sorting out matters with Wisdom's contracted agent, Bert Montague, Marsh got Wisdom a booking at the Blackpool Palace theatre which led to yet another 'rave' review, this time from the *Blackpool Mail*: 'Last night a young comedian literally flung himself on to the stage and left a dent - marking himself for early stardom.' Derek Salberg, the eminent Midlands impresario, saw the act and booked him for three years of pantomimes; then Wisdom was given an immediate booking at the Brighton Hippodrome substituting for the indisposed A.J. Powers and thus made his first appearance at a Moss Empire. Despite going on without a band rehearsal, Norman had enormous success and Val Parnell of the London Palladium journeyed to see what the fuss was about. As soon as Bernard Delfont heard that Parnell was sounding out Wisdom for the Palladium, he booked his client for his own rival to the Palladium, the London Casino. Thus, in roughly two years, Wisdom had reached a proper spot on a West End stage. All was not well, though, because Delfont had decided to restrict the new-boy to only six minutes on an overcrowded bill topped by American singer Allan Jones. Wisdom took the law into his own hands and, pretending that he was going to drop most of the dialogue from his fourteen-minute turn, rehearsed all the music with the musical director Harold Collins. Knowing he had nothing to lose, Norman, billed as 'The New British Comedian', went on stage on Monday April 5th, 1948, and performed his entire fourteen minutes. After an announcement introducing Britain's gift to opera, the curtain went up to reveal a bizarre figure eating an enormous sandwich. He was dressed in a misfit evening suit with the trousers cut off short, everything too big, his hair parted down the centre and with a string tie to complete the outfit. The budding opera star, having abandoned all hope of digesting the sandwich, turns to the piano. He then performed his piano sketch with his hand getting lost in his voluminous trousers. The act stormed the audience, eclipsing the reception of Allan Jones, and Delfont allowed Wisdom to continue doing the complete turn throughout the show's run. It was an astonishing success and the next day Wisdom received the press plaudits, particularly from the *Daily Mail*, which proclaimed that he had 'joined the star comics'. Wisdom's success was such that when Allan Jones rested before going on tour, Wisdom was promoted to top of the bill for the rest of the run, maintaining the applause until the end despite contracting pleurisy!

PROGRAMME

Monday, APRIL 5th to MAY 1st 1948

BERNARD DELFONT presents INTERNATIONAL VARIETY

HAROLD COLLINS
and the
1. **CASINO ORCHESTRA**

FREDDIE CARPENTER'S
2. **CASINO GIRLS**

3. **THE SIX ELWARDOS**
HAND SPRINGING ACROBATS

4. **BENNETT & WILLIAMS**
THE B.B.C. COMEDIANS

The Boogie-Woogie
Pianist-Dancer

5. **MAURICE ROCCO**
" ROCKIN' RHYTHM "

6. **NORMAN WISDOM**
THE NEW BRITISH COMEDIAN

7. **HARRISON & FISHER**
AMERICA'S GREATEST DANCE STYLISTS

— *INTERMISSION* —

HAROLD COLLINS and the
CASINO ORCHESTRA
IN A SELECTION OF " BING CROSBY HITS "

8. **THE CASINO GIRLS**

9. **THE NEWMAN TWINS**
WONDER CONTORTIONISTS

10. **GEORGE DOONAN**
"THE LIFE AND SOUL OF THE PARTY "

11. **WILSON, KEPPEL & BETTY**
"CLEOPATRA'S NIGHTMARE"

THE SINGING STAR OF STAGE, SCREEN AND RADIO
12. **ALLAN JONES**
&
IRENE HERVEY
At the Piano
LEN EDWARDS

13. **MARIE WILSON**
TRICK CYCLIST

---

3. Norman steals the show on the first night at the London Casino, April 5th 1948. The *Daily Express* welcomes the new star who sensibly fulfils his pledge to gain more experience in the provinces before returning to the West End stage. [programme/review]

Wisdom's the name ..

HE WOKE TO FIND HE HAD JOINED THE STAR COMICS

His face is mobile, can be twisted into any shape. He tumbles on the stage, shadow-boxes, tries to play the piano, pulls out a clarinet, tires of it and turns his attention to . . .

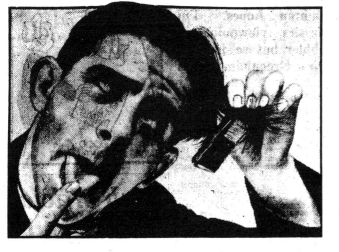

. . . a vast sandwich. Then he pleads with his audience to follow him in an Eastern song—in gibberish.

His props?

PORTRAIT of a comedian, Norman Wisdom, who woke yesterday, after a first-night appearance at the London Casino, and found himself named as a new star.

"I don't believe it," he said. "I've still a lot to learn."

After his month in the West End he goes back to the provinces to play in a concert party at Scarborough. There (writes David Lewin) he will learn about audiences; find out the best ways of getting laughs; see how to build up his act.

Wisdom, aged 27, married, living at Willesden Green, London, began entertaining when he was in the Army. He found he could get laughs by clowning; had no need to tell jokes.

A stringy tie, an old shirt, and a baggy evening suit, several sizes too large.

The West End gave this ex-shop assistant his big break. "I hope I shall come back later," he said last night, "and show I deserved it."

From the Casino triumph, Wisdom went straight to the top of the bill at the Golders Green Hippodrome at £100 per week, with higher offers being delivered in every post. However, Billy Marsh decided that Wisdom needed provincial dates to gain more experience, incorporate new ideas into the act and generally to learn the trade the only way it can be done - on the boards. His next date therefore came with a drop in salary to £35 in the *Out of the Blue* concert party summer season at the Spa theatre, Scarborough, then in its third edition. '*Out of the Blue* taught me so much about the business. It proved valuable training, and I looked upon the season as a cramming course in showbusiness. I learned how to act with other people, how to deliver dialogue, how to dance, put over a song, how to play in sketches, timing . . . As I progressed in the business, exploring new channels, I was able to call upon this grounding to keep me in good stead.' (*Stage.*) The show was to prove a landmark for Wisdom for another reason, for it was here that he invented his now familiar comic persona which he refers to as the Gump: 'In this show you had to do a different routine each week. So I was doing an act and sketches, singing and dancing - the lot - week after week. It was hard work by the time you get to the fourth week. By the fifth especially when you've only been in the business for a couple of years is tough going, but I found it, loads of it, loads of it. There was a conjuror on the bill and he said he was having trouble finding stuff for his fourth week and asked me if I'd come on as a volunteer from the audience to do tricks for him. I said alright and went out and got myself a 30 shilling suit - a real misfit - and a shilling cap. I went on with him and it was smashing.

'The conjuror, David Nixon, had a disappearing cabinet in which he was supposed to make me vanish. I got into it, only to dart clear again as if afraid of the darkness when he closed the curtains. He then explained once again what I was supposed to do, and climbed in himself to demonstrate. I fired the pistol and he disappeared. It was a simple idea, but it went over surprisingly well, and soon David was helping me to get laughs instead of vice-versa. In this "Gump" role, I felt the audience was more sorry for me than audiences had been in the past. I began to play it up, laying on the pathos to see how far it would stretch. Sometimes I overdid it, getting laughs where I had not intended them; yet a character was emerging that was more clear-cut than any other I had attempted.' (*John Bull.*)

The show was such a success that Nixon and Wisdom were booked in as a double act at the London Casino with Nixon acting as Wisdom's straight man. This did not go over as well as expected and anyway, neither Wisdom nor Nixon wanted to go into a double act. Nixon, a graduate of ENSA and the Fol-de-Rols, went on to fame and fortune on stage and television, and they remained close friends until Nixon's death.

A short tour followed, often accompanied by David Nixon, with Wisdom

16

adding material he had developed during *Out of the Blue* including a bout of shadow-boxing and impersonations of radio commentators. But the next major date was David Salberg's pantomime and Wisdom had more success in the 12-week Birmingham run of *Robinson Crusoe*, receiving good earnings of £90 per week. In his role as the tattered Billy Crusoe, Wisdom continued to develop and perfect his comedy pathos: 'He is the exemplar of the eternal and universal gamin, the solitary human boy in whom there is for ever welling the desire to shine and to please and in whom the tear and the smile are for ever chasing one another. "Laughter soft as tears, and tears that turned to laughter." This quaint and highly original comedian sets his signature on this part, endears it to us and makes it peculiarly his own.' (*Birmingham Mail*.) With the booking the following year at Wolverhampton and a summer show booked for 1949 in Blackpool, Norman and Freda decided that the most convenient way to live was in a caravan, neither of them liking digs or hotels. So a caravan and an old second-hand Vauxhall were purchased and once they had mastered the life it proved a very satisfactory way for the itinerants to exist.

Other events in 1948 made it a memorable year for Wisdom. He appeared in his first film, fully six years before *Trouble in Store*. This was, of course, no starring role. The film, *A Date with a Dream*, marked Terry-Thomas' big film break and was directed by Dicky Leeman, later familiar as a BBC producer of *What's My Line?* The story was a fairly unambitious, putting-on-a-show story. Comedians Bill and Len Lowe are demobbed and intend to build on their army concert party experience and become stars. Their C.O., Terry-Thomas, suggests a reunion in a year's time to see how the concert party members are getting on. Predictably, the anniversary reveals that none of the troupe have made an impact so they decide to put on their own show, inviting a heavyweight producer down to watch the rehearsals. Through various machinations, the magnate is impressed and all the leads get contracts including Terry-Thomas who was forced to improvise a stage-act to fill in for the late arrival of the Vic Lewis Orchestra. Wisdom's brief appearance is as one of the variety acts which the producer glimpses at the rehearsal, along with Elton Hayes, the Cox Brothers and Eddie Leroy. The earliest surviving recording of Wisdom in performance in any media is this thirteen-and-a-half second excerpt of his shadow-boxing skit, filmed at his initial stamping ground of the Collins Music Hall, and has him dressed in his misfit evening suit. The 56-minute film did little for anyone except Terry-Thomas who was already becoming known for his broadcasts and from his stint as second comedian to Sid Field in *Piccadilly Hayride*.

October 1948 also saw Wisdom's first headlining television appearance in a variety show, *Wit and Wisdom*, where his guests included Billy Reid

17

and Dorothy Squires. The *Radio Times* of October 15th introduced Wisdom to the tiny television audience: 'NEW COMEDIAN: Norman Wisdom, who tops the bill in *Wit And Wisdom*, is the newest English star of the music hall. He has broken the long run of American successes in the West End over the past year . . . Collins of Islington gave him his first chance and then, last April, he jumped into the limelight at the Casino. His "props" consist of no more than a comic baggy dress suit, an old shirt and stringy tie, and his clarinet.' So, though no Gump in his first starring television show, it marked the end of a fine year: television, film and West End stardom had all been broached.

1949 saw Wisdom again on television in an intriguing show called *Cuckoo College*, a comedy about an unsuccessful college trying to gain a government grant and having to con the official inspectors as to its proficiency. Directed by Richard Afton, Wisdom appeared as a janitor and was tipped by scriptwriter Ted Kavanagh - the creator of radio's *ITMA* - as 'one of the best bets in television today'. That year's summer season was *Buttons and Bows*, Wisdom's first in Blackpool. He was not the star of the show, that was Donald Peers - later replaced by George Formby - but it introduced him to presenter Henry Hall who was keen to get him on to the radio. Wanting to see the scope of Wisdom's work widened, Hall encouraged him to practise different voices and perfect dialogue delivery at his little private recording studio. 'I was pleased to be asked, but really I did not feel my style of comedy was suitable for radio, as I depended then on visual situations and was not a "talking" comedian.' But though Wisdom would never really make an impact on the radio, *Buttons and Bows* did give him the chance to introduce the straight instrument playing into the act. Back to the Midlands for another Salberg panto, *Robinson Crusoe*, this time in Wolverhampton, Wisdom was reunited with Eddie Leslie, who had also been the dame in the Birmingham production the previous year. They became firm friends, and he worked with Norman as feed and co-writer until his death.

1950 brought Wisdom his first major professional failure, when he made an abortive debut in a West End revue, *Sauce Piquant*. Norman had been anxious to do a show like this to help pave the way to films, to extend himself beyond the role of a variety artist. In this prestigious Cecil Landau revue at the Cambridge theatre, Wisdom did some singing and dancing, played instruments, performed a couple of sketches and undertook three solo sketches: 'The Boxer', 'The Singing Lesson', and 'Soho Soliloquy'. A great cast was gathered: Douglas Byng, Moira Lister, Tommy Cooper, Bob Monkhouse and, getting noticed in the chorus, a young Audrey Hepburn. Wisdom was not permitted to use his Gump costume, instead donning a 50-guinea dress-suit and shiny shoes for a three-minute slapstick routine.

18

His part was slightly cut during rehearsals and the show collapsed after ten weeks, despite the cast taking voluntary wage cuts - Wisdom's slipping from £100 to £15.

He was still doing the occasional television work with great success, including another *Wit and Wisdom* in August: 'Television has discovered, in Norman Wisdom, a clown so prodigally endowed with talent that he might become another Grock if someone will take him in hand.' (*Sunday Observer.*) Another small-screen triumph was his appearance in *Music Hall* which compelled the *Daily Herald* to state 'there has never been a better comedian on television'. However, these were the days before a living could be made out of television and Wisdom decided to throw caution to the winds. In November, wanting to try his luck in the States, he gathered up his savings and flew to New York. 'I didn't know any agents, I just went off to America, I must have been nuts. All the agents in New York said: "Go away, son, we've never heard of you." I even did a talent competition in Brooklyn, but nothing came of it.' Wisdom, now getting a bit hungry, did impromptu acts in bars, but no one seemed to notice. While drinking coffee he caught a show on television called *Ed Sullivan's Toast Of the Town* and he decided there and then that it was the show for him. Phone calls to Sullivan's agent yielded no result, so Wisdom went to visit Sullivan at his Park Avenue quarters in the Delmonico Hotel. 'I found his room number, knocked on his door one morning and his secretary showed me in after I told him I had an appointment. Ed Sullivan came out in his dressing-gown and I confessed to him that I was gate-crashing. He sat in a chair in this small hall and said: "Show me what you can do". So I did the falls and the jokes and the singing and after about four or five minutes he said: "I admire your initiative but I don't use that sort of thing on my show."' Wisdom respected Sullivan for not just having him thrown out, and this would prove to be by no means the last time they would meet. So, the American experience not proving a success, Norman flew back despondently after five weeks to his third Salberg panto, as Buttons in *Cinderella* at Birmingham, travelling to London each Sunday to appear in Frankie Howerd's radio series, *Fine Goings On*.

If 1948 had been Wisdom's breakthrough year, then 1951 was to prove to be the year he reached the top of his profession. While playing Buttons at Birmingham, his old ally Henry Hall, accompanied by impresario Claude Langdon, came to see him. Langdon was famous for his ice-show presentations at the Empress Hall in Earls Court, and wanted Wisdom for his 1951 summer show *London Melody*. Norman gave them assurances that he was an expert skater, and as soon as they were out of the way began his lessons! Between the pantomime and the summer season, Wisdom did indeed master ice-skating. He also appeared in his first television series, the fortnightly *Vic's Grill*, a café-set programme with regular acts: Wisdom; his friend from the Midlands pantomimes, Eddie Leslie; Beryl Reid and John Hanson, all introduced by 'proprietor' Vic Wise. The show caused the final adjustment to the Gump costume. Wisdom was on set when the director asked him to remove his cap because it was casting a shadow across his face. Wisdom refused, arguing that he was beginning to be known by the costume, and the compromise was for the peak of the cap to be turned up. By the end of the series, Wisdom was already rehearsing *London Melody* which starred Belita, an English girl who had been to Hollywood with some success before returning in 1947 to become a top ice-show attraction. *London Melody*, in which she did a celebrated aerial ballet on wires, was a big success for her, but it was Wisdom who stole the show. The BBC televised both the rehearsals and excerpts from the final production in which Wisdom, not in Gump costume but in his evening dress misfit and in a Spiv outfit, played a cockney waiter in a fanciful tale of feuds and loves set around rival hotels across the Franco-Swiss alpine border. One of the highlights of the show was Wisdom's rendering of his first composition 'Beware', which later became a minor hit. Two memorable events occurred during the tremendously successful seven-month run. Firstly Gracie Fields came to the show and, as Langdon recalled in his autobiography: 'I spied her sitting in a box and asked her to come into the arena and welcome the artistes. The microphone was switched on and, not caring two hoots, Gracie threw her arms around the little comic of the show . . . Gracie was enraptured with his style, hugged him and said, "In two or three years, lad, tha'll be the biggest comedian in Britain." The whole audience rose and cheered her, and they were right, for today [1953] Norman Wisdom is right on top.' Secondly, Ed Sullivan came over to see Belita, and sitting next to Bernard Delfont, pointed at Wisdom, not recognising him from their previous encounter, and said: 'I want him!'

So, barely a year after Wisdom's surreptitious audition for Sullivan in New York, here he was being offered £500 for a ten-minute slot on his show. Wisdom's appearance was a triumph, one critic moved to write: 'This guy looks like being the greatest international clown of his day.' It was only after the show that Wisdom reminded Sullivan of their previous encounter and they became friends, Wisdom guesting a number of times on Sullivan's programmes in future years. A minor deluge of film offers resulted from the spot, the most persistent being from Paramount Pictures with a project entitled *Pleasure Island*. Wisdom and agent Billy Marsh went to Hollywood to discuss the film but turned it down when it was apparent that only a small part was on offer. 'We went back to New York into a photographer's shop and got a very tall girl with big boobs and took a load of photos of her and me as if we were in a film studio. We sent them to the

British press with a story: "Everything's big in Hollywood - Norman Wisdom turns down film". The publicity was so enormous that I came straight back to Bernie Delfont and after doing the usual provincial pantomime walked into *Paris to Piccadilly*.'

In fact, Wisdom also did some television in the interval, including *Christmas Party* which was to prove important as we shall see, and *The Norman Wisdom Show* for director Bill Lyon-Shaw. He also signed up for a commercial radio series, singing four songs in each accompanied by Harry Parry and his Octet. But it was the new Folies Bergère revue presented by Val Parnell and Bernard Delfont at the Prince Of Wales theatre which proved to be Wisdom's greatest triumph of the year. *Paris to Piccadilly* opened on 12th April 1952 and was Norman's first West End solo star billing. However, it was something else which remained in his memory. 'I was installed in the dressing room used by the great Sid Field when he caused a West End sensation after years of struggle around the music halls. As I opened the greetings telegrams I came across one which read: "IF ANYBODY CAN TAKE HIS PLACE IT IS YOU, GOOD LUCK, THE SID FIELD FAMILY." It was such a touching gesture that I couldn't face anyone: I locked the door. I have never opened any telegrams before a first-night since.' (*John Bull*.)

The show proved a runaway success lasting sixteen-and-a-half months with a 12-week break at Christmas for Wisdom and his partner Eddie Leslie to fulfil their panto engagement, the show struggling on with replacements Archie Robbins, Leslie Randall, David Hughes and Patterson & Jackson. The Coventry panto was *Jack And The Beanstalk*, and had an 18-year-old Julie Andrews making an impression in the cast. However, it was the brilliantly staged *Paris to Piccadilly* (by Dick Hurran) which picked up the critical plaudits: 'In the first half Wisdom has to rely mainly on falling about on the stage, but after the interval he is seen as a wistful litter collector in the park and finally in a well arranged musical turn which really captured the house. As a spectacle *Paris to Piccadilly* eclipsed all the previous Folies Bergère shows seen in London.' (*Daily Telegraph*.)

During the tremendous Prince Of Wales run, Wisdom was honoured with an invitation to appear in the Royal Variety Performance at the London Palladium on 3rd November 1952, before the Queen and the Duke of Edinburgh. The fine cast included fellow comedians Tony Hancock, Vic Oliver, the Crazy Gang, Gracie Fields, Terry-Thomas, Ted Ray, Jimmy Edwards, Arthur Askey and Jewel & Warriss! 'The stage being littered with the globular debris of this pleasant affray, the curtain rose on four startled scarecrows in the persons of Norman Wisdom, and Jo, Jac and Joni (sans usual make-up), busily sweeping the stage. The last-named took fright and hurriedly decamped, leaving Norman capped and tousled to

21

work out his own salvation, he getting his first big laugh when he caught his hand in the piano. From that point he went on to his superb wrestling with a sousaphone and then with a harp, and having performed noble knocka-bouts with both, drifted into a straight rendition of one of his own com-positions, "Don't Laugh at Me", his pleasant tenor striking a marked contrast to his early buffoonery.' (*Performer.*)

However, another event had taken place which was to be of more lasting importance. Norman Wisdom, in addition to gaining a five-year recording contract with Columbia, had signed a film contract with the Rank Organisation.

3. The Rank Contract.

Norman Wisdom's success in the theatre and on television had not gone unnoticed by the film companies, but there were worries about whether his style could be adequately transferred to the big screen. The two dominant forces in the industry, the Rank Organisation and ABC, were both pondering on Wisdom's future, and the matter was brought to a head with his appearance on television in the 1951 *Christmas Party*. This was the first of three successive Christmas Party programmes he did for the BBC and in 1951 one of the hosts was Jerry Desmonde. Despite strong competition from the other principal guests, Terry-Thomas, Jewel & Warriss, Vic Oliver and Petula Clark, Wisdom stole the show, and one of the viewers that night was Earl St. John, the Rank Organisation's Senior Executive Producer. St. John decided that Wisdom must be signed to Rank and went about the business of persuading his colleagues to agree. By the time he got to negotiations with Billy Marsh, Wisdom was in the midst of the triumphant run of *Paris To Piccadilly*. By now, nobody could ignore him, and ABC, too, were actively in the hunt for his signature. With the pace hotting up, Rank signed Wisdom to a seven-year contract without the formality of a screen-test. Renewable on the Rank side only, the contract guaranteed Wisdom three films in the first two years for a total of £15,000.

So what was this organisation which had signed Norman Wisdom? Rank was the largest and most powerful British company in the film industry, though only recently recovering from one of the worst periods in its history. The crisis stemmed from a decision by the British Government back in August 1947 to levy a 75% tax on all foreign films coming into Britain. There had been great concern about the substantial amount of money leaving the country through the distribution profits of the American companies, and it is possible that the Government expected them to panic into making voluntary concessions - such as channelling back some of their profits into the British industry - in order to forestall the tax's imposition. The response was predictably more forthright, the Americans simply placed an embargo on export of all their films to Britain, in turn obstructing the distribution of British films in the States. All British producers were urged by the Government to take advantage of the boycott and make films to fill the gap, and Rank responded by announcing a production slate of 47 films at a cost of £9 million. The following year, realising that the tax was failing to have the desired effect, the British Government initiated talks which culminated in the lifting of both the ban and the embargo. As a result, all the films that had been produced in Hollywood in the intervening eight months were now available to British distributors: the cream of Hollywood was pitched against the films emerging from Rank's overambitious programme. Already, Rank's finances were strained by the production costs and the films themselves were, in general, of a lower than average quality because limited resources had been spread somewhat thinly. Rank faced a dilemma: if they shelved the bulk of their own films in order to show those from America in their cinemas, it would be tantamount to writing off most of the £9 million. Alternatively, if they showed their own films in preference to the imports they seriously threatened exhibition profits. It was a dangerous situation, reflected in the company's financial position which, in October 1948, showed overdrafts amounting to over £13.5 million.

To pull out of this situation the Rank Organisation savagely cut their costs. These cuts took place under the control of John Davis, a ruthlessly efficient administrator and accountant. Top executives took a 10% drop in salary, many contracts in all areas were not renewed and many personnel left for more congenial climes. Studios at Islington, Denham and Shepherd's Bush were closed and remaining production was concentrated at Pinewood under Earl St. John. All experimental work was stopped, as was much subsidiary activity. Davis's actions yielded his desired result. The overdraft fell, and by January 1951 Davis was able to announce that Rank was no longer losing money. By May 1952 debts were down to £9 million and 22 films were in production - still the biggest programme of any British company. Thus the Rank to which Norman Wisdom was contracted remained the dominant force in the industry, but its power was diminished and its production ambitions severely limited.

The worries about signing Wisdom can now be seen in their contemporary context, and are even more understandable when linked to the still fresh memories of Sid Field. Rank tried to launch Field in the cinema with a lavish £1 million musical comedy in 1946, *London Town*. It was an entirely ill-advised project which still looks an appalling disaster even when viewed in the recently restored, full-length technicolor print. The film flopped at the box-office, as did the scandalously ill-served Field's follow-up, *The Cardboard Cavalier*. Norman Wisdom came from the same kind of music hall tradition as Field, and the press were quick to point out the similar problems Rank faced in finding him a suitable debut project. In public at least, Earl St. John exuded confidence: 'We have the most exciting screen comedian since Chaplin - his art is essentially visual and he possesses the vital quality of being able to make people cry as well as to laugh.' It was at this point that they decided to give Wisdom a screen test. 'Ronald Neame, who was slated to do the first, directed. I hadn't read the proposed script,

24

but in the film test, which I did with a little girl called Petula Clark, they gave me lines to say like: "Your eyes are as light as gossamer" - this was for me, a comic!' The test was a disaster, and Rank got even more worried about their investment. Wisdom was paid off as per contract for the first film, which was never made, but efforts to buy him out failed as Wisdom was determined to fulfil his ambition to become a screen comic. The press were aware of the problems: for instance, as early as August 1952 *Picturegoer* carried a story: 'It's been three months since the perky little clown with the clever line in poignant comedy signed his first film contract. Now decision time is at hand. After months of worrying about the Wisdom debut, the Rank studio chiefs have reduced the field to three or four possible scripts . . . Now this question of choice of subject is a vital one for Wisdom, who, in just over six years has made a special kind of niche for himself in TV, radio, and revue. For let's be blunt, the odds are dead against him in his new venture.'

The second year arrived with no real project in hand. Getting slightly desperate at the increasing trade ridicule and the thought of once more paying Wisdom for doing nothing spurred Rank into action. Jill Craigie had been asked to write a script specially tailored to Wisdom's talents, and this was the project which Ronald Neame had been slated to direct with John Bryan as producer. 'Norman was thrilled with the script at the time. It was a satire on a big store in rather a Chaplinesque vein, with plenty of scope for slapstick. During the film tests, Ronald Neame lost faith in Norman as did John Bryan, though I personally thought him very funny. As a result they abandoned the project' (Jill Craigie). The outline remained the best Rank had. In 1953 Wisdom took a guest role in *Meet Mr. Lucifer*, directed by the usually reliable Anthony Pellisier and based on a play by Arnold Ridley, author of *The Ghost Train*, who later achieved renewed fame as an actor playing Pte. Godfrey in BBC TV's *Dad's Army*. *Meet Mr. Lucifer* was made at Ealing Studios, which were by this time financed by Rank, but Wisdom's part was deliberately cut from the final version and does not appear in any print I have seen. Actually, the fact that the film cannot justifiably be listed in Wisdom's filmography is no real loss. Despite a wonderful cast - Stanley Holloway, Peggy Cummins, Kay Kendall, Ian Carmichael, Barbara Murray - the story of a fading pantomime artist's dreams about the fates of those foolish enough to watch television instead of attending live theatre is a pretty poor attempt at satire. Wisdom was slated as one of the four guests from the world of television - the others being Gilbert Harding, MacDonald Hobley and Philip Harben - but though Wisdom filmed his role (with Eddie Leslie as feed), all that now remains is a scene where a family gather round the television set to watch their 'favourite television comedian' but nothing is seen.

Meanwhile, Craigie's script had been put into the hands of producer Maurice Cowan, who was experienced both on the production and scripting sides of the business. The story was reworked by Ted Willis, Cowan and the newly-selected director John Paddy Carstairs. It was completely overhauled: 'When I saw the final version, it bore no resemblance to anything which I had written and though obviously commercial I saw no point in claiming any credit for the final version' (Craigie).

John Paddy Carstairs, co-writer of the film now titled *Trouble In Store*, was a good choice to direct, and indeed the success of the film ensured that the next five Wisdom vehicles would be entrusted to him. Carstairs was by this time already something of a veteran of the British film industry, *Trouble in Store* being his twenty-first film. Born in 1910, he was the son of comic Nelson Keys, changing his surname by deed poll to that of his mother to avoid allegations that he was cashing in on his father's reputation. He managed to direct his first amateur feature while still at Repton public school, and this led to a job with Herbert Wilcox as assistant on the film *Dawn* in 1927. Carstairs learnt his trade by undertaking nearly every job the industry had to offer both here and in Hollywood before directing his first professional feature in 1934, *Paris Plane* with John Loder and Molly Lamont. He remains best remembered for his comedies, working with, amongst others, Ian Carmichael, the Crazy Gang, Charlie Drake, Jimmy Edwards, George Formby, Leslie Henson, Frankie Howerd, Lupino Lane and A.E. Matthews in either a scripting or directorial capacity. He also had a penchant for shooting fine atmospheric thrillers like *The Saint in London, Dancing with Crime* and *Sleeping Car to Trieste*. Carstairs' talents did not run just to filmmaking: he was an accomplished painter regularly exhibited in London and Paris, and a prolific author with a number of humorous thrillers, novels, autobiographies and film-scripts to his name, as well as completing a biography of his father. His vast experience in directing low-budget comedies was coupled with a reputation for good handling of personalties new to the screen. Wisdom found him a joy to work with - they were both short and shared a similar sense of humour, to start with! A good example of Carstairs' consideration occurred when he noticed that Wisdom was ill-at-ease during the first days on the set of *Trouble in Store*, though he was putting a brave face on it. 'We did three days work and I began to feel a little better, the old nerves were wearing off. Then on the fourth day John Paddy Carstairs said to me: "Norman, we know you're a hard worker and we're all chums, but I want to tell you something. I've spent the last three days filming nothing!" It was a shock. Actually, they had film in the camera, but it was being used for test purposes. We'd wasted three days' work. But actually Paddy had done it for psychological reasons, to help me. I was so inexperienced working in front of camera I just didn't know what I was doing.

Paddy pretended to film scenes, but instead was using the time to rehearse me. When we eventually came to do those scenes in the following twelve weeks I knew what to do.'

Trouble in Store was a Two Cities film and shot at Pinewood studios. Rank's doubts about their prodigy were allayed by the simple expedient of hiring an experienced supporting cast: Moira Lister, Derek Bond, Joan Sims and Megs Jenkins alongside Jerry Desmonde, Margaret Rutherford and Lana Morris.

Jerry Desmonde was the prince of the straightmen. Born in 1908, he had been on stage from the age of 11 with his family act. He then teamed up with his brother, Jack, as the Desmonde Brothers in a song-and-dance routine with 'guitar playing a speciality'. His first effort as a feed was with cockney comedian Gus Elton, and later with one of his favourite comics, Scotsman Dave Willis. He reached the West End in a double act with his wife, and achieved prominence during the Second World War when he was teamed with the great Sid Field in *Strike a New Note, Strike it Again* and *Piccadilly Hayride* (1943-46). With Field, whom Desmonde once described as 'the greatest natural comedian of them all', he made his first two films - *London Town* (1946) and the *Cardboard Cavalier* (1947). The latter's director, pioneer silent comedian Walter Forde, called Desmonde 'one of the greatest stooges in the English theatre'. With the untimely death of Field in 1950, Desmonde went on to partner most of the leading comedians: Bob Hope, Nat Jackley, Arthur Askey. Nevertheless, he is best remembered for his extensive collaborations with Norman Wisdom, with whom he worked in six films and in numerous stage and television shows. During the 'fifties he was also popular on television in his own right as a game-show host on programmes such as the *64,000 Question*, and as a regular panellist on *What's My Line?*, before tragically taking his own life in 1967.

Margaret Rutherford was brought into the cast as box office insurance, in case Wisdom's name proved not to be a draw to cinema-goers. This remarkable actress, already 61 years old when the film was made, had been on stage since 1925, making her first film in 1936. Specialising in charming fussy eccentrics, she graced many fine films before her outstanding performance as Madame Arcati in Noel Coward's *Blithe Spirit*, directed by David Lean. She graduated to starring roles in such popular films as *The Happiest Days of Your Life, Curtain's Up, The Importance of being Ernest* and *Miss Robin Hood* before being drafted into *Trouble in Store*. Her role as a rather unusual shoplifter is a highlight of the film, climaxed by her removal of a model railway engine, complete with carriages in tow, by having it drive up and disappear into her voluminous coat sleeve. After this, she made one other film with Wisdom, *Just My Luck*, before completing a series based on Agatha Christie's Miss Marple books with husband Stringer Davis. She died in 1972.

Lana Morris was the final choice for the part of Norman's sweetheart. Petula Clark was originally selected for the part, but turned it down because she did not want to be typecast as 'sweet and ineffectual', in the words of her father and manager Leslie Clark - an image she had gained from the 'Huggett Family' films. Lana Morris was born in 1930 and had entered films in 1946. She never really achieved star billing, acting in a string of second features both before and after *Trouble in Store*. She had been a Rank contract player until 1951, though 1953 proved to be a prolific year for her with the completion of a further four films. Her well-received performance in *Trouble in Store* led to speculation that she would be cast in the follow-up, but Carstairs rejected the suggestion as he did not want the public to perceive Wisdom's second starring feature as a sequel. She worked just once more with Wisdom on *Man of the Moment*.

With the cast settled, *Trouble in Store* went into production in the summer of 1953. Despite the problems caused by a stand-ins strike which lasted several days, it was generally a happy shoot. With so much depending on the star, the director and producer were happy to find Wisdom a perfectionist anxious to learn film technique. Cowan remarked: 'Norman was wonderful, as a person and as a performer. His behaviour - as a schoolmaster might say - was exemplary.' (*Picturegoer*.) And if it wasn't, Carstairs had a novel way of dealing with it as Lana Morris recalled to a BBC interviewer: 'On the Indian set we had a little hut made out of wood, nothing in it except a bench. If we got too giggly or out-of-hand he used to make us go and sit in the hut for five minutes in solitary confinement.' Wisdom was quick to implant his personality on the film, as was pointed out in *Picturegoer Annual 1954/5*: 'Working out the comedy sequences on the picture was largely a joint effort. You can put so much into a script, after that it depends on the director's ingenuity and the comic's imagination. It didn't take Wisdom long to appreciate this. He would button-hole director Carstairs and producer Cowan at every available opportunity to work out new gimmicks.' Wisdom himself told *John Bull*: 'It was a new, fantastic and rather startling world with a mystique all its own. I was alternately overawed and baffled. With my inexperience in the film-business, I just did as I was told until one day I saw the "rushes" of a scene in which I was trampled by eager shoppers in the store where I was employed. The extras doing the trampling must have worried about hurting me, for their delicate tread was like a ballet company's. I asked the director . . . to persuade them to tread on me good and hard - and in a retake, they did.'

Despite the tight schedule, Carstairs and Wisdom were not above playing jokes on each other. 'Norman had his moments of triumph. When they were shooting the outdoor scene where Norman has to wade into a pond fully clothed Paddy Carstairs called for repeated "takes", each separated by a visit to the mobile dressing room for Norman to change his wet clothes. Eventually it dawned on Norman that the camera was not turning film. Whereupon he picked up his director, little taller than his own 5' 4" and walked into the pond with him.' (*Evening News.*)

Wisdom was, in fact, working to a gruelling schedule whilst making the film. Every evening he had to rush off to the theatre to give twice nightly performances in *Paris to Piccadilly*, snatching five hours' sleep a night before being called on-set to film. These demands on his energy eventually landed him in hospital where he was found to be suffering from mild malnutrition: 'I had been working so much, I hadn't been eating. Stupid! I resolved I would never again attempt to do so much at once . . . We started to plan a holiday, the first genuine holiday I'd ever had . . . As so often happens when one puts too much store by something, the holiday was a disappointment . . . we found the sun, but I soon got bored with lying on a beach. It still worries me that I have lost the habit of relaxing: at any rate, I found holidaymaking an over-rated pastime.' (*John Bull.*)

If Wisdom found it hard to relax, so did the executives at Rank. Their nerves were not soothed even when they viewed completed scenes from the film, and they took the unusual step of showing some of these to the press to gauge critical reaction, even while the film was still being shot. 'Producer Maurice Cowan has just shown me privately two scenes from *Trouble in Store* . . . I laughed, I roared. I say that this 5' 4" clown with the sad eyes and whipped-dog look will rocket into position as Britain's No. 1 screen comedian. The film is slickly tailored to exploit all the Wisdom talents . . . All this is vintage Chaplin, with this difference - Wisdom is not afraid to laugh at his own lunacy.' (*Daily Mirror.*) But the Rank unease prevailed and the completed film was received with some trepidation. To test audience reaction, they gave the film a sneak preview on 25th November at the Camden Town Gaumont with a nervous Norman Wisdom in attendance, nursing his hand which had been injured in a fall during rehearsals for his Empress Hall ice show *Sinbad the Sailor on Ice*. The unsuspecting moviegoers were informed that Bernard Braden's *Love in Pawn* had been pulled and they were going to see *Trouble in Store*. Cowan was understandably shaky: 'If they think he's funny, I get £500,000 immediately from the Rank Organisation to make two more films with Norman. A flop - and I go back to producing weepies.' It proved to be a devastating success, with spontaneous applause at the end giving way to an ovation when Wisdom was spotted in the auditorium. At last, the executives who were present, including Earl St. John, knew there was no point in holding up release any longer and the film slipped out. The result is well-known, as David Robinson wrote in *Sight & Sound*: 'Its distributors denied it a West End release, yet in its first six days in London - Christmas week - it did 25% above normal business. After a quiet start, there was an explosion of praise and publicity. Records were broken and cinemas filled throughout the country.' Indeed, the film created box office records in 51 out of the 67 London cinemas in which it played, and Wisdom's future as a film comic was assured.

4. *Trouble in Store* and the Gump.

The antics of *Trouble in Store* revolve around a very simple plot. The department store in question, Bur-ridges, bears a remarkable similarity to Oxford Street's Selfridges, and it is here that Norman works in a stockroom. He has two ambitions in life: to become a window-dresser and to marry Sally (Lana Morris), who works in the record department. Norman has quite a tempestuous relationship with the store's new Chief, Mr. Freeman (Jerry Desmonde), which leads inevitably to Norman's dismissal. Soon after, Norman overhears plans to rob the store of its daily take, but is unable to convince Sally of the fact and cannot inform Freeman because he has been banished from the store. On the day of the robbery, Sally has second thoughts, but unfortunately shares her worries with one of the insiders of the gang and is tied up for her efforts. Norman finally manages to drill his way into the store, rescue Sally, and thwart the robbery. As a reward, Freeman gives Norman some money - enough to allow him to buy an engagement ring and propose to Sally. Norman's restoration to the staff is short-lived however, since he inadvertently ushers Freeman down an empty lift-shaft and is given his cards once more.

We are introduced to Mr. Freeman and Norman simultaneously. The setting is London's Oxford Street in the rush hour and Freeman is seated in his gleaming chauffeur-driven Rolls Royce. Norman is apparently sitting next to him. In contrast to the immaculately dressed Freeman, Norman is relatively unkempt - his jacket is ruffled, his cloth cap to one side and pointed upwards at a ridiculous angle. They seem unlikely travelling companions, and then the limousine pulls away from the traffic lights to reveal that Norman is actually on a bicycle. In full view, Norman's jacket is seen to be too small, tightly stretched where it is held together by a single button. His trousers are slightly too short, the collar of his shirt is rumpled. In other words, this is the now familiar Gump costume: aspirations to neatness, with each element letting him down in some form. This famous costume stays with Norman throughout the film except for one sequence where he 'borrows' an evening suit for a staff social - he is not the kind of character who would own a large wardrobe! The strong initial visual gag - Norman revealed to be on a bicycle - is capped by his using Freeman's Rolls as a resting place at the next set of traffic lights. Jerry Desmonde was one of the best straightmen in the business and the perfect rapport and timing of this opening whets the appetite for the coming film. Peeved at Norman leaning on his open car, Freeman swipes at his hand with his own, gloved hand. Norman moves to avoid the blow without even looking down. This is repeated, and each time Norman avoids the glove. Freeman is too proud to complain out loud, but is shocked at the audacity of this scruffy worker defiling his property. Norman is enjoying the exchange as a game, impervious to the class authority oozed by Freeman and is only annoyed when Freeman breaks the 'rules' by driving off and leaving him prostrate in the road. Freeman feels his status has been undermined by Norman's action; though, crucially, this was not Norman's intention, the whole conception of status being outside his experience.

Norman's second meeting with Freeman comes after the new boss decides to start his reign by meeting the store's lowliest member of staff - inevitably Norman. Norman's childlike status is re-emphasised when he enters Freeman's office. Rather than adjusting his jacket and tie before knocking on the door, he does so in full view of the boss, but it is of no concern to Norman, who does not realise who Freeman is, and neither do they recognise each other from their earlier confrontation. The laughs in this sequence arise from Norman's ignorance and Freeman's nonverbal attempts to assert his authority - he wants Norman to recognise and they pay appropriate respect to his position. Norman, of course, does no such thing. As far as he is concerned, the boss is out and he and this stranger can enjoy themselves in his absence. The action is unwittingly precipitated by Freeman who, trying to impress Norman with his rank, takes one of the cigars from the case on his desk. Norman copies Freeman and fills his pockets with cigars, an innocent gesture since the audience knows that Norman cannot possibly smoke. From here the situation becomes more frenetic as Norman begins to enjoy himself to such an extent that he is eventually left crawling under the desk, convulsed with hysterical laughter. Only then does the outraged boss call in his personnel officer Peggy (Moira Lister) to inform Norman of his rank. Norman, sacked, attempts attrition by restoring the office to its former condition, drenching Freeman with the contents of a soda syphon in the process, but even now he is only downcast, not humiliated.

This routine is a remarkably assured example of the most characteristic Wisdom set-piece which he will develop more fully in his later films, and gets the laughs splendidly while extending our knowledge of the characters. The playing of the scene, with its gentle escalation into frenzy, makes the situation seem plausible. Wisdom's expertise at logically building on a gag had already been displayed in a scene just before this second meeting between him and Freeman. Norman arrives at work on his bicycle, colliding with the security officer, Willy Dawson (Michael Brennan), as he enters the staff entrance. He is putting his bicycle into the bicycle-shed when he notices Sally arriving. Realising that the shed is very crowded, Norman considerately removes his bicycle, laying it on the roadway to make space for Sally's. Sally is unaware of Norman's kindness or indeed of his presence and walks off. Norman now has to rearrange the bicycles in order to put his own back in, so he takes out Sally's and places it in the road alongside the shed. Immediately a huge delivery lorry rumbles over it, writing it off. Norman, upset and furious, rushes out and takes the licence number. As he gesticulates agitatedly in the direction the lorry had gone, another destroys his own bicycle behind him. Norman notes that number as well, but the effort of holding so much information in his head at once proves too much and in his confusion he forgets them both. The sequence not only provides laughs but economically advances the plot. We now know that the security officer is a buffoon, that Norman is in love with Sally and that she is oblivious to his existence. The destruction of both bicycles leads logically to the later scene when Sally and Norman meet properly as a result of their encounter in a bus queue and it is when Sally receives a replacement bicycle from Norman that she is convinced of his sincerity towards her, confirming that Norman's story about the planned robbery is true.

The next set-piece in the film is a wonderful sequence where Norman - again through misunderstanding - gets the chance to try his hand at window-dressing. Norman finds a basket of crockery outside the empty window and takes it in. Placing the basket to one side, he picks out an empty stand and places it centre stage. He then selects a teapot from the basket and places it on the stand. Walking round, he tries to gauge the effectiveness of his display so far. But this proves too difficult and after a slight adjustment he rushes full speed out of the window through the shop to look at the teapot from the outside, from the public's point-of-view. Storming back, he makes another slight change before taking a plate and cup from the basket and pondering their arrangement. He places the plate under the teapot and delicately hangs the cup from the spout. Dissatisfied, he tries the cup on the teapot's handle. At this point he notices a couple looking at him through the window. Norman coyly obscures their view of his work, but a crowd begins to grow and will not be shooed away. Norman gawps at them, and they laugh. He is now enjoying the attention and treats his audience to a few dance steps. Strolling out of the window to check the coast is clear before continuing this impromptu entertainment, he bumps into the official window-dresser Wilbur (Michael Ward). Wilbur is slightly taken aback when Norman introduces himself as the new dresser. Then he, too, notices the crowd but takes it in his stride and, with a professional air, starts on his display, only distracted when he notices Norman on the other side of the window copying his every move. The two are now rivals for the biggest and best display, and this takes the form of precariously stacking the stands higher and higher. The film cuts to Freeman's office at this point where the Chief is informed that a crowd has gathered at the crockery window and is causing a nuisance. Meanwhile, Norman accepts the applause as he finishes his half of the display. Wilbur is not so happy and expresses his disdain by taking a cup off Norman's rather eccentric layout and flinging it to the ground. This is, of course, the signal for mayhem. Norman responds in kind and follows up the smashing of his teapot by demolishing two of Wilbur's cups. Norman escalates the destruction by picking up a hammer, swapping it for a much larger one when a member of the crowd looks on disappointedly. Soon there is only one tall display stand left untouched, and Norman dramatically and delicately fingers it to oblivion - all over Mr. Freeman as he enters the window.

Interestingly, Wisdom clashed with his director John Paddy Carstairs over this routine: 'In the window-dressing scene where I do the cup on the teapot spout and the jug on the handle, Paddy Carstairs said: "No, don't do that, Norman - you're a window-dresser, that's funny in itself, play it straight." I said: "No, this bloke is a fool, he wants to dress the window the way he thinks a window should be dressed and he would hang . . ." Now Paddy always used to wear these different hats, and after we had argued for a bit, he took off his hat, flung it on the floor, kicked it away and stormed out! You can imagine the state I was in - this was my first film and we had only been doing it for four or five days. But I stuck to my guns and when he came back about ten minutes later and demanded to know whether I was going to do it his way or not, I said: "Yes, on the condition that you do it my way as well. At least give me the privilege of looking at them both with you in rushes and then you can choose the one you like best." He agreed and of course this story went round the studio and the following day at rushes the place was packed. His came on first and there was amusement as I put the crockery in straight and looked at the crowd gathering at the window to watch me. But in mine, with the cup on the spout and pulling a face at the crowd - they fell about in the cinema. Paddy Carstairs just took my hand and said: "You bastard!"'

Indeed, it is the Wisdom touches which make this classic slapstick situation so memorable, touches grounded in the character of the Gump. Norman's only ambition is to be a window-dresser, yet it is obvious straight away that he has no aptitude for the job. He is such a fool that he has to dash outside for a customer point of view after placing a single object on display. When he does start building up, half the plates are facing the wrong way. Norman's pleasure comes more from being the centre of attention

34

than from the job, and he soon responds to the public gaze by performing. One of the characteristics of the Gump is that he has a need to be loved and accepted. He always tries to do the correct thing, but more often than not fails except by a last minute fluke. His desire to be accepted by the audience outside the window outweighs the need to get on with the work and in the lovely moment when he exchanges the small hammer for a larger one at the behest of a strange looking man in pebble glasses, it becomes obvious that he gains more enjoyment from the destruction than the construction.

Though Norman has maintained his dignity in the sequences so far - at the expense of Freeman's - he does half expect people to mock and make fun. At one point he sings a duet with Sally who is demonstrating the store's 'Make your own Record' service. As they sing, Norman constantly looks around, expecting the gathering crowd to laugh at him. When they don't, Norman's confidence flows back and he slips contentedly into the role of entertainer, only amusing the audience at the end when he shyly hands Sally a flower.

Embarrassment in a large group due to social shortcomings is a characteristic of Wisdom's humour. *Trouble in Store* provides a nice example of this at the staff ball. Norman has no decent suit to wear, so he 'borrows' one off a stand. Not familiar with social niceties, he mistakenly picks a full evening suit. While the rest of the partygoers snigger, he is only stopped from leaving by the motherly Miss Gibson (Megs Jenkins) who tells him that Sally has arrived. The band strikes up the 'Paul Jones' and Norman struggles to get a dance with her. This gives Wisdom a fine opportunity to display his physical skills as Norman is helplessly led into a series of dances with uncomplimentary partners. The highlight has Norman with a female Charleston expert. He attempts to follow her steps until, with some panache, he catches the tempo. His enjoyment is shattered when she flings him from left to right and he never recovers his balance, ending up flat on his back. By the time Norman gets to dance with Sally, the music has come to a close with Freeman's arrival, but they, oblivious to their surroundings, continue to dance under the Chief's angry eyes, much to the amusement of the other guests.

Later, the assembled staff are sitting at their meals as Freeman prepares to make his self-congratulatory speech. Norman is seated next to Miss Denby (Joan Ingram) and opposite Sally. As he goes to eat his ice-cream, he manages to lob a dollop directly down Miss Denby's cleavage, a delicate situation which he only exacerbates by trying to scoop it out with his spoon. But worse is to come when Norman attempts to light Miss Denby's cigarette with a faulty lighter. Inevitably for the Gump, he manages to engulf himself in flames. His fellow staff seem callously unconcerned and Norman is merely thrown out and, when a bucket of water is thrown over him, the only sympathetic faces in the hall belong to Sally and Miss Gibson. This disruption of Freeman's speech is an interesting attempt at generating pathos through the Gump's humiliation in a crowd. While it is not too well handled in this film - there is an unsure touch about the special effects - it certainly points to the type of routine which Wisdom was to perfect later.

The pleasure of all the sequences featuring Wisdom and Desmonde is the expertise and timing of their playing. Though Wisdom has no need of a regular partner, his work excels in the presence of a good straightman or stooge. He has worked with some of the finest: Eddie Leslie, Edward Chapman and latterly the schoolmasterly Tony Fayne. However, there was none better than Jerry Desmonde with his convincingly aristocratic demeanour and bombastic pomposity. Where Edward Chapman complemented Wisdom as the working-class or lower middle-class snob who needed the Gump's practical assistance, the Desmonde characters look rather put-out at having to be in the same room as Norman, constantly needled by his unpretentious directness.

Another neat comic routine in *Trouble in Store* is done with Eddie Leslie who plays Bill, the gangster who is ordered to tie Norman up when the little man discovers the plot to rob the store. Leslie was often Wisdom's straightman, notably in the *Norman Wisdom Shows* on television between 1952 and 1956, after first teaming up in the Midlands pantomimes. As well as working together as performers, they also collaborated regularly as writers on many of Wisdom's films. The routine here is a traditional one - Bill wants to send Norman to sleep with the help of a pill. This unlikely solution to the problem caused by Norman's knowledge is put to the test when Bill places the pill on Norman's outstretched tongue and tells him to swallow it. But Norman does not oblige, despite forcing down a few gulps of water and demolishing a ham sandwich. Bill then takes the fateful decision to blow the pill down Norman's throat with the help of a glass tube. Of course, Norman blows back - and wins. With Bill asleep in his place, Norman is able to tie him up, enter the store and frustrate the robbery in a parody Western finale. This is the kind of sketch which would work better if done in a single shot (or on stage) so that some skill was proven in the retention of the pill despite the eating and drinking. In a recent pantomime, Wisdom took a mouthful of water and spat it out periodically throughout a sketch. Many of the laughs came because the audience were astonished at how long and how much water he retained in his mouth until, well after everyone thought it was over - including his fellow actor in the scene - the last spurt reduced the audience to hysterics. Clearly this scene would not have been as effective in the cinema since we would assume that the water supply had been replenished between takes.

Trouble in Store is a remarkably assured debut and fully outlines the

BILLY MERSON

▲ Billy Merson. Pioneer of the transfer from music hall to the screen who tried to improve the lot of music hall comedians in the cinema by joining with others to form Homeland Films. ". . . not only very funny, but he was fast on his feet as well and had a good baritone voice. . . . this man had everything" (Maurice Chevalier).

▲ Walter Forde. Britain's most successful silent film comedian, though his inspiration derived more from the American screen comics than from his own unimpressive music hall background. Later became a prolific director.

▲ Gracie Fields. Britain's best-loved film comedienne whose success took her to Hollywood as the world's highest paid film star. She received the DBE in 1979.

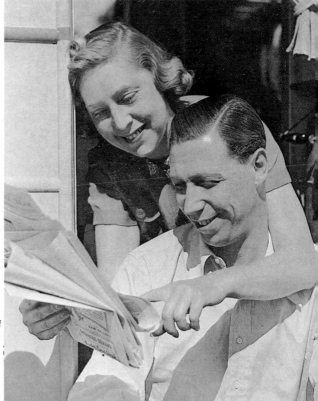

► George Formby with his wife Beryl. Britain's top-grossing star from 1935–41. His skilfully constructed films developed one of the most successful and consistent comic characters in the cinema. Beryl [Ingham], formerly a champion clog-dancer as one half of 'The Two Violets', forcefully nurtured and promoted her husband's career.

▲ Lucan & McShane. Arthur Lucan entered films as OLD MOTHER RILEY at the age of 49, going on to complete 16 features before his death in 1954. His stormy relationship with his wife and stage partner Kitty McShane has latterly attracted as much attention as his career; and his pre-eminent position as the screen's greatest dame has yet to receive its due acclaim.

▲ Leslie Fuller. Fuller was able to complete 26 features between 1930 and 1945 despite entering the industry at the late age of 41. This prolific and popular comedian, who owned his own studio at Elstree, has now been largely forgotten partly due to the vagaries of film preservation. Here he is seen in the 1935 film THE STOKER.

▲ Max Miller. The one and only 'Cheeky Chappie', probably variety's finest comedian, who took his 'white book' to the cinema with more success than his screen reputation would suggest.

◄ Will Hay. Here seen in his most famous role as the bogus schoolmaster in charge of the Fourth Form of St. Michael's. Hay, too, was in his mid-forties before beginning his popular and critically acclaimed series of films.

▲ The Crazy Gang. An anarchic combination of three double-acts: [Bud] Flanagan & [Chesney] Allen, [Jimmy] Nervo & [Teddy] Knox, [Charlie] Naughton & [Jimmy] Gold. At their best on stage, the Gang's sometimes bizarre films nevertheless provide many moments of delight. Flanagan & Allen's lilting songs have stood the test of time and they stand alongside Morecambe & Wise as the best-loved double act in the music-hall tradition.

◀ Frank Randle. Wigan-born comedian whose transfer to the big screen is one of the most triumphant in the music-hall tradition. His films broke all records in the North, but he has still to receive the general recognition he deserves.

▶ Sid Field. Field's premature death robbed the stage as well as the cinema of one of the greats. Sadly, Field never appeared at his best on film, though at least LONDON TOWN has the priceless virtue of preserving some of his most celebrated sketches for posterity.

▲ Tony Hancock. Hancock was launched into film after mastering the radio and becoming one of television's greatest comedians. He entered film in 1954 playing a bandmaster to provide many of the scarce laughs in ORDERS ARE ORDERS. His two starring film vehicles are far better than most critics allow.

▲ Henry Hall (left) and Ted Ray. Hall, a wildly popular band leader and later radio host of GUEST NIGHT, tried to encourage Norman Wisdom to use the radio more effectively and hosted the comedian's radio debut. As an impresario, Hall produced some of Norman's early stage hits. Ted Ray was at his best on the radio, especially in the aptly titled RAY'S A LAUGH.

▲ Ernie Wise (left) and Eric Morecambe. Television's greatest duo seen here in THE INTELLIGENCE MEN, their first feature film. Their work in the cinema sadly never came close to displaying their abilities adequately.

▲ Early publicity handout (1946/7) which shows Norman in pre-Gump costume with hair parted down the middle.

▲ The Queen, Princess Margaret and Prince Philip congratulate the 1954 Royal Performance line-up. Norman Wisdom and Gillian Moran wait their turn between David Whitfield and Frankie Laine.

▲ Norman's first performance at the London Palladium is also his first Royal Variety Performance. The 1952 line-up includes a veritable Who's Who of comedians.

▲ Wife Freda and children Nicholas and
Jacqueline visit the star on the set of
A STITCH IN TIME.

► John Paddy Carstairs. A prolific stage, film and television director:
painter and author. Carstairs helped to guide Norman through his first
six starring vehicles.

▲ Norman dons his famous Gump suit in an early publicity shot.

◀ Norman sings a song in his 1960/61 panto at the London Palladium —TURN AGAIN WHITTINGTON.

▲ A chat with Vivien Leigh.

▼ Norman is hailed by the fans after a performance of PAINTING THE TOWN at the London Palladium in 1955.

character who will appear in the remainder of the Rank films. Whether he was dressed in the Gump suit or in uniform (police, army, navy), the basic personality shows only slight variations. The little man who wants to fit in but whose childlike trust in people, coupled with his need of love and acceptance, make him easy prey for the less than honest, the unkind, or the unthinking. The Gump often tries to gain acceptance through providing entertainment or sharing laughter, but as often as not he provides both of these in a totally inappropriate situation which backfires on him, making him an object of ridicule and humiliation. However, he can only be pushed so far before he fights back and then he displays an inner resilience and strength.

Women in his films tend to feel sorry for him and want to look after him, responding sympathetically to his genuine gentleness and kindness. The Gump exudes a knowing bashfulness and is surprisingly confident in women's company. Not much humour is extracted from his romances which are all fairly straightforward and unexciting. In *Trouble in Store*, for example, Norman rushes after Sally to return her handbag which she left with him in the bus queue. Finding her alone in the park feeding the ducks, he sits down, accepting her offer of bread which she intended for the ducks but which he proceeds to eat himself. In this simple meeting full of typical Gump misunderstandings, with Norman wading into the pond to ensure the smallest bird gets its share of food, the seduction is complete, even before he sings his great theme song 'Don't Laugh At Me' over a cup of tea. That there is no sharp edge to the romance is a weakness of the film and remains a fault with most of the Rank comedies. This is no criticism of Lana Morris' engaging performance: 'In comedy, even as broad and as unreal as this, you've got to be inside as real as you can, more real than in drama really. I looked at him singing this song ["Don't Laugh At Me"] and I was so in love with him, with this poor little man who couldn't do anything right, I started to cry. And the director said: "Cut, God, if you're not laughing, you're crying. Can't you just get it right in the middle because it's not Chekov." But it was a very moving little moment.' (BBC TV.)

The problem seems to be in the timidity of the writing of the female role. There could almost be an embryonic self-criticism of this in the film itself, with the recurring image of the mannequin. Our first glimpse of Norman in the stockroom has him fondling a mannequin which he has made up to look just like Sally. Later, in the only 'fantasy' shot in the film, Norman recoils in horror when the dummies used to display wedding costumes take on the features of Sally and his supposed rival, Gerald (Derek Bond), with himself as the living best man. When Norman breaks into Burridges to thwart the robbery, the first item he comes across is what he takes to be his 'Sally' mannequin tied up. Only when he starts to free it does he realise that it is flesh and blood. Finally and ironically, the climax has both Sally and Norman evading detection by pretending to be dummies themselves. If the last provides a lovely opportunity for Wisdom to demonstrate his mime - one of the crooks throws balls at the dummies and Wisdom has to sway as if he were an inanimate object on being struck - the persistent strand of the mannequin might nevertheless also be construed as an authorial admission of the unreality of the central romance.

5. The films with John Paddy Carstairs: the Wisdom comic style.

Norman Wisdom completed another six starring feature films to fulfil his contract with Rank: *One Good Turn* (1954), *Man of the Moment* (1955), *Up in the World* (1956), *Just My Luck* (1957), *The Square Peg* (1958), and *Follow a Star* (1959). This chapter looks at the first five of these which were all directed by *Trouble in Store*'s John Paddy Carstairs and, like Wisdom's debut film, minted money at the box office. The fact that these comedies provided Rank's production arm with a solid and highly profitable financial return made the company a little timid about any plans to tamper with the personality of the Gump, around which all these films are built. The last chapter outlined the general characteristics of the Gump and some of the comic routines which his personality generated. Here, we trace through the variations that were made and look at some of the subterfuges undertaken in order to allow Wisdom to extend his range beyond the increasingly constricting demands of the original screen persona.

The Gump appears in full costume in the first four of these films, but immediately Wisdom softens the outlines of this simpleton's character, making him less gormless and idiotic. If the effect of this went little beyond an ability to comb his hair in *One Good Turn*, the changes did allow more subtle and less physical routines to be mixed with the overt slapstick with which the Gump was associated. *Man of the Moment* soon has Norman out of the Gump costume and into neater garb more becoming to his unexpected diplomatic status. Of course, this provides a convenient excuse to put Norman into his misfit evening suit, a costume Wisdom returns to in his films more than is generally realised. *The Square Peg* puts Norman into uniform and provides Wisdom with a second role as a Nazi general to increase further the range of comic possibilities. *One Good Turn* uses the excuse of having Norman behave under the influence of a hypnotic trance to present routines which might otherwise seem inappropriate for the Gump.

Not all these changes went unresisted. Carstairs was far from happy with Wisdom taking the part of General Schreiber in *The Square Peg*, uncertain that the star's audience would accept the mixing of the two types of humour. 'It was Jack Davies', the writer, and my idea that I should play the German general which is a straight part. Paddy Carstairs said: "No! No, you can't do that." The producer, however, approved so Paddy said: "Well you can direct the bloody thing yourself then!" He eventually agreed that he would direct the film, but he wouldn't direct the parts where I was the general. When it came to the part where I hit Eddie Chapman around the face - I played it dead straight. Paddy was watching and came over and kissed and hugged me and we never had another cross word over anything I wanted to do.' The film actually proved to be Carstairs' last with Wisdom and ironically it is the scenes with General Schreiber - especially when singing a duet with Hattie Jacques' Wagnerian opera singer - that provide *The Square Peg* with its highlights.

Overall, however, the character of Norman - as he is called in all the Rank films - remains remarkably consistent. One of Wisdom's wishes was to introduce more pathos into his films. Right after *Trouble In Store* he was asked by *Picturegoer* whether the pathos in that film was overworked, and he replied: 'If anything, I think it was underworked. I'd like to get more in. But this is the sort of thing we hammer out in our conferences. To continue the purely personal viewpoint, though, I'd like to have more situational pathos. Say, for example, that I'm keen on a girl and save up to buy her some flowers - then, by the time I've found her, they are dead. See the kind of situation I mean?' Wisdom got his way, but the increase in pathos was sometimes handled clumsily, especially in the second film, *One Good Turn*, when Norman is placed in the far too sympathetic environment of an orphanage and spends the film trying to buy a car for one of its young inmates. The easy squeezing of sentiment out of this situation with shots of wide-eyed tearful little children becomes maudlin and false. Carstairs was clearly not happy with pathos and Wisdom's successes in this area only start with *Follow a Star* under the direction of Robert Asher.

One of the most familiar comic sights of the 'fifties was Norman Wisdom falling over, his enormously expressive body being buffeted and bruised in all manner of ways, on stage, screen and television. Whether sliding off the top of a grand piano or collapsing down a flight of stairs, Wisdom delighted his fans (and exasperated his critics) with his acrobatic abilities. He excelled at traditional slapstick knockabout and utilised a number of recurring situations from which to generate these laughs. The most common of these arise from Norman's obliviousness to the signifiers of class. In these situations, the laughs come as he acts in an entirely inappropriate manner, often intending to entertain and please his captive audience, but merely achieving self-humiliation. In *One Good Turn*, he insists on engaging the occupants of a first-class railway carriage in conversation. Not recognising their attempts to freeze him out, he only leaves when a bee flies up his trouser leg! Wisdom's musical attributes are sometimes brought into these sequences. In the same film, Norman finds himself mistaken for an orchestra conductor and once placed on the rostrum his uncontrollable urge to entertain takes over. The actor's real ability to conduct enhances and underlies the brilliant comedy generated through Norman's attempts to rid himself of a tacky candy-floss stick which the orchestra misread as an eccentric conducting style. Surprisingly, *Up in the World* is the only film in which Wisdom demonstrates his prowess on a musical instrument - and even so it is on the drums rather than one of his favoured wind instruments. It occurs in a scene which exemplifies the comedy of humiliation when Norman demonstrates the Jive to members of an aristocratic bridge party and follows this up with an excellent, though equally inappropriate, drum solo in the belief that he is entertaining fellow staff. The sight of Norman slinking away from one of these situations when truth dawns is a familiar one - the contrast between the eagerly amiable Norman and the hostile onlookers enhancing the pathos.

Wisdom relies almost entirely on our being completely sympathetic to the Gump for these routines to work, and the concordant emphasis on pathos requires that the comedy and gags are meticulously grounded in a reality which we can accept. Wisdom keeps all the action in character and the individual gags are not allowed to take precedence. To destroy this basis would be to risk losing audience empathy which is essential to Wisdom's comedy and if it is not created his antics are likely to leave one unaffected.

Luckily, Norman has another trait; he is extremely resilient, always picking himself up from a fall or a defeat unhurt and undeterred to bounce back and achieve his limited aims. Occasionally, when Norman succumbs to his urge to entertain, the audience applaud his efforts - however inappropriate they may be - and though his downfall is assured, he is not humiliated. One of the finest examples of this is the window dressing scene in *Trouble in Store* and another, equally brilliant, occurs in *Up in the World*, a film which contains many fine sequences of pure physical slapstick. Norman finds himself at a nightclub watching a performance by the magician; DeMilo (Edwin Styles). In a manner which recalls the birth of the Gump, Norman is called up on stage to assist the conjuror in his act. Reluctantly, he goes centre stage and allows his prized watch to be used for a disappearing trick. With his watch miraculously returned, Norman cannot resist the impulse to perform himself, parodying DeMilo's antics. Norman blames DeMilo for the eventual and inevitable destruction of his watch when the trick goes awry and, in front of a delighted crowd, brings the magician's act to a chaotic close by inadvertently setting loose the entire gamut of DeMilo's props.

Another of Wisdom's favourite routines has Norman trying to follow a set of commands which are either not intended for him or which he misunderstands, leading him to carry out a series of absurd and ridiculous actions. To bring the best out of these sketches Wisdom worked with some of the finest stooges available, in particular Jerry Desmonde, and they complete a splendid example in *Man of the Moment*. Norman is the reluctant tea-boy to a conference being briefed by Desmonde on the geographic and geological particularities of the Tawakian Islands. Norman is more concerned with getting details of how Desmonde wants his tea, information he somehow gleans from the discussions, and a very strange tasting brew results! However, the best example comes once more from *Up in the World* in a beautiful routine with Lionel Jeffries. Norman is being vetted for security purposes before taking up a post at Banderville Park. The whole sketch revolves around Norman confusing 'forefinger' with 'four fingers' while having his fingerprints taken. The situation methodically proceeds to its climax with an ink-stained Lionel Jeffries left a nervous wreck without even a set of prints to show for his efforts, the humour enhanced by the slow pacing and deliberate playing of the intentionally obvious, enacted in near silence. One related sketch in *The Square Peg* has Norman acting correctly to badly given commands. The Medical Officer, Eddie Leslie, is listening to Norman's chest through a stethoscope and telling Norman when to breathe. Unfortunately, he keeps repeating 'breathe out' until Norman collapses in a deflated heap on the floor. It is a favourite sketch which Wisdom has performed in his live act throughout most of his career. In these routines, Norman himself seldom says a word, just reacts to others. Only in one film, *Man of the Moment*, was there a concerted attempt to bolster the script with spoken gags and one-liners, and the result was disappointing. It is his obvious physical dexterity and acrobatic bodily control which are the cornerstones for much of Wisdom's humour.

In *One Good Turn*, Wisdom even manages to do a couple of rounds of boxing and show off his skills learnt in the army. Norman's expertise in the noble art are passed off as being the result of hypnosis, and Wisdom shares a savage battle with a bruiser in a fairground booth in his efforts to raise money. Only in the third round, when the hypnotist removes the confidence-boosting suggestion, does the bout take on a comic tone when Norman tries unsuccessfully to keep out of trouble. Wisdom is a first-rate mime artist and relishes any opportunity to take on silent sequences. In *Up in the World*, Norman displays a virtuoso piece of mime as the alert goalkeeper waiting for something to happen - anticipating attacks from all sides, alternating between total absorption and relaxation. A goalkeeper mime every bit as good as that by the masterly Jacques Tati ends with Norman going to rest against the goal-post - but he misses and plunges straight downwards. This meticulous and perfectly executed climax, only possible on film with its distortion of depth and its single point of view, has Norman seemingly leaning on the post for a mini-second before he falls.

Another trademark of Wisdom's comedy is his laughter which, like his miming skills, is more fully used with a live audience than on film. When he laughs it is total, taking over his whole body until he collapses in hear hysteria. Wisdom was well aware of the contagious effect of laughter and used it in many sketches. Its best known outing is perhaps that preserved on a record he made with Joyce Grenfell, 'Narcissus' ['The Laughing Record']. In *Man of the Moment*, there is a nice filmic version of the idea with Norman going to have a passport photograph taken. In the studio, Norman tries to put on a sober face to fit the official requirements, but the more he tries, the more he laughs and the only way the picture can be snapped is when Norman has been conveniently knocked out by a falling prop.

It has often been remarked, usually by way of criticism, that some of Wisdom's film routines have been lifted from the work of a wide range of classic comedians. While this is true, especially of the first film, *Trouble in Store*, it is an irrelevant and pointless task to trace their heritage. As John Fisher pointed out in *Funny Way to be a Hero*: 'One must not lose sight of the fact that even the comedians of the silent screen had a reserve of traditional comedy material inherited from the Music Hall and Vaudeville and regarded as common property.' Wisdom and his collaborators borrowed for the best, and managed to integrate the routines thoroughly with original ideas, the whole growing naturally out of the personality of the Gump.

When writing a slapstick comedy, there is always a problem of incorporating knockabout routines into a plot. Too involved a storyline can get in the way of comedy, diverting attention away from the characters and the humour - a problem which plagues *Just My Luck*. If the plotting is too loose, the entire proceedings can take on an air of pointlessness, lacking in motivation. One solution is to make the plot advance and provide information about the characters through the comic routines themselves, as in *Up in the World*.

To get his films off to a good start, Wisdom always insisted on a strong opening, recognising the importance of the first laugh to focus the attention of the audience. *Just My Luck* starts weakly, so it is no surprise this film turns out to be the least happy of the Carstairs films. Its attempts to blend a more restrained Norman into a vehicle which perhaps demands a more extrovert knockabout response are not entirely successful. *Up in the World*, Carstairs's finest film with Wisdom, has a splendid gag which sets the film off nicely. Norman tries his hand at poster-hanging and stands back to admire his handiwork in putting up a particularly large poster. Immediately, windows are opened through the bill - Norman has pasted it over a row of terraced houses!

One of the surprises to the makers of *Trouble in Store* was the enormous success of the songs. In *Picturegoer*, Carstairs talked about the next film and stated: 'Norman will certainly sing. You know, we've had an enormous number of letters form picturegoers about the tunes in *Trouble in Store*: . . . many people enjoyed his singing more than the comedy!' In fact one of the songs, 'Don't Laugh At Me', later to become Wisdom's signature-song, was a Top 20 hit reaching a peak of No. 2 during its 15 weeks in the charts. The uncertainty of the handling of this song in the film, with frequent and irrelevant comic cutaways, reflected a lack of confidence in the audience accepting Wisdom's singing. From the second film onwards there were no such worries and the songs are filmed with much greater confidence. The presentation of Wisdom's own composition 'Please Opportunity' in *One Good Turn* is especially effective. Norman, battered and bruised after the boxing match, wanders around the fairground. The beautifully lit nighttime set with carousels and stalls closing down at the end of the evening while the last stragglers and lovers go home to bed, makes a superb background to the song.

A traditional climax of slapstick is the chase, but for someone so adept at physical comedy, Wisdom uses the device surprisingly sparingly, preferring his characters to be silently frozen out of situations rather than chased. *One Good Turn* does have Norman hastily pursued from the rostrum by the theatre staff on the arrival of the genuine conductor and the resulting furore disrupts the orchestra's playing of the 'William Tell Overture' to hilarious effect. The most interesting chase in the early films occurs in *Man of the Moment*, though not so much for the star's antics as for its setting. The chase takes place at the BBC's Lime Grove Studios, with Norman, dressed in the full regalia befitting the eminent diplomat he has become, hotly pursuing the kidnappers of his fiancée. The chase takes him through many early BBC television productions: Philip Harben's kitchen, a dramatic Parisienne red-light ballet, the Grove Family, Fabian of the Yard and a Greek tragedy, which endows the sequence with an enhancing nostalgic glow.

The problems with the plotting of the central romance remain unsolved in the early films; it is as if the way the Gump would react to the opposite sex has not been entirely worked out. In *One Good Turn* the problem is exacerbated by the inability to incorporate Shirley Abicair adequately. The Australian singer and zither player was popular on television at the time and plays Mary who is set up as Norman's final love in place of the woman he prefers. When Norman walks off with her at the end as second best, it seems arbitrarily insulting! Even in the magnificent *Up in the World* which has a fairly uncomplicated and straightforward romance there seems to have been an attempt at one stage of the script's life to provide a disrupting influence in the person of Jill Dixon, but this subplot lies forgotten about halfway through. The best film in these terms in perhaps *The Square Peg*, simply because the officer, played by Honor Blackman, though touched by Norman's interest does not reciprocate and they remain apart at the end.

Norman Wisdom made one further film with Rank to fulfil his seven-year contract. This was *Follow a Star*, with Robert Asher taking over from Carstairs as director, and his work with Wisdom is the subject of the next chapter. Meanwhile, Rank's attitude towards Wisdom is neatly summed up in a report on a celebratory luncheon at the Dorchester at which it was announced that the star would stay with Rank in some form. 'Mr. Davis, the Rank director, looked at Mr. Wisdom with the sort of expression that Uncle Sam must have in his eyes when he looks at Fort Knox. Norman Wisdom's films have all made money, Mr. Davis said. After the Christmas pudding and affectionate oratory, Mr. R.M.D. Odgers, the general manager of Rank Overseas Film Distributors, said that Norman Wisdom is beloved not only in this country but also abroad, especially in Holland and Denmark, where exhibitors always try to show his latest film during the Christmas season, and in Persia, India, Singapore, and Hong Kong.' Norman Wisdom had indeed become one of Rank's most important assets!

6. The films with Robert Asher: consolidation of the Gump.

After *Follow a Star* (1959) and the completion of his contract, Norman Wisdom stayed with Rank on a film-by-film basis, starting with *The Bulldog Breed* in 1960. It is with these films, all directed by Robert Asher, that the development of the Gump continues: *Follow a Star, The Bulldog Breed, On the Beat* (1962), *A Stitch in Time* (1963), *The Early Bird* (1965) and *Press for Time* (1966). Leaving to one side Wisdom's cameo in Robert Hartford-Davis's *The Sandwich Man* (1966), which does not add appreciatively to our knowledge of the Wisdom screen persona, there remain the films which are considerable departures from the usual Wisdom screen incarnations. These include three British films, the two made for Knightsbridge Films: *There was a Crooked Man* (1960) and *The Girl on the Boat* (1962) and Wisdom's last feature to date, *What's Good for the Goose* (1969) made for Tigon, all of which will be discussed in the next chapter. Finally there is Wisdom's sole American venture, *The Night they Raided Minsky's* (1968) which will be covered in Chapter 9.

Robert Asher had been working in the film industry since 1934 when he started out as a 14-year-old call boy. He graduated to third assistant director after the war and slowly worked himself up the ladder to the role of first assistant on two Anthony Pelissier/John Mills films in 1949 - *The History of Mr. Polly* and *The Rocking Horse Winner*. Over the next few years he earned a reputation as one of the best first assistants in the business and it was in this capacity that he worked on two Wisdom films, *One Good Turn* and *Man of the Moment*. His good understanding of the Wisdom screen persona made him a natural choice to succeed John Paddy Carstairs, and he was trusted with *Follow a Star* for his directorial debut.

Follow a Star proved to be not only one of the best of Wisdom's films, but also one of the most demanding on the star's resources. Despite this, Asher's following five films with Wisdom show only minor changes in the Gump's development. This is not to imply that the films were unsuccessful: *On the Beat* and *A Stitch in Time* certainly rank with Wisdom's finest. Unfortunately, Asher and Wisdom were constantly under the added pressure of having to submit to the public's expectations of a Wisdom film to compensate for the relative financial setbacks of other ventures. After the two films with Knightsbridge, all the parties were anxious that the next film at Rank - *On the Beat* - should return Wisdom to his usual high flying box office figures. At the time Wisdom was quoted as saying: 'I think we've got the sort of comedy they like, and although I want to do more varied roles, I must give the public what they want.' In the same interview with journalist William Hall, Wisdom stated: 'I've been criticised by the Press for my comedy because I fell over so much. So I went the other way - in one pantomime I think I only fell over once. Now I've found the happy medium, a few falls but none of the bang-bang-bang.' Similarly, after the phenomenal success of *A Stitch in Time* at the box office, Wisdom had a public break with Rank which led to his stating: 'I want to do this film for them and I'm still willing to work for them. But I feel they ought to let me have more say in production. It was my idea for the story [*Turn Again Wisdom*] - a modern Dick Whittington. But instead of ending as Lord Mayor of London, I finish as a ticket tout at Wembley. They don't seem to realise that I have grown up and can get laughs without falling downstairs.' (*Evening News.*) In the light of this it is perhaps surprising that when Wisdom does go back to Rank he begins the film - *The Early Bird* - with a string of falls down flights of stairs, but again, it is to recapture his position as top film comedian by giving his fans what they wanted after a period away from the studios. During the making of *Press for Time*, the last of the films in Gump territory and made by Titan for Rank distribution, there was much talk of a new image; nevertheless, the final film came out much as expected. Arthur McGill, the author of the book *Yea, Yea, Yea* on which the film is based, wrote the following in the *Evening News*: 'With this film . . . Norman would be launched as an international star. Money would be no object, he would be surrounded by the top names . . . The first script was rejected because it was too far out. Now Mr. Wisdom's was rejected because it was too far in . . . A fourth script had been written and more or less approved.' When McGill got down to the locations in Teignmouth to see how shooting was progressing, Robert Asher confirmed that: 'This is to be a formula Wizzy film, he wants to get away from the formula but they don't want him to. You can see their point actually. They shove a Wizzy picture out at Christmas and the money pours in. The Little Man is just like the Pied Piper. The kids follow him wherever he goes. Showing a Wizzy film is like owning a bank.' When Robert Hartford-Davis, the producer, was asked by McGill about the plans to turn Wisdom into an international star, he replied: 'We've tried baby, believe me. I want it, Norman wants it, but They don't. They want the Norman everybody knows. If you had been paid what the rewrites cost you could have retired. This is purely a Wisdom comedy now.'

Of course, there are no major reversals, none of these films resurrects the complete Gump outfit, but there is not the same consistency about the

Gump's development as had been apparent in the earlier films. Though certain hard and fast rules are followed to maintain the character's basic innocence, the little man and his background have already been generalized enough to ensure that plenty of screen stories could be formulated to accommodate him.

Follow a Star has Norman donning a fairly traditional Gump costume for much of the film, but the Asher films continue to utilise uniforms to provide variation. He is in the navy for *The Bulldog Breed*, often in misfit police uniform in *On the Beat*: *The Early Bird* sees Norman as a milkman, and he dons a variety of uniforms in *A Stitch in Time* - including a nurse's. Only in *Press for Time* does Norman wear just an ordinary suit. The strategy of a hypnotic trance is used to devastating effect in *Follow a Star* to expand the character's possibilities, and Wisdom takes a double role in *On the Beat* and, rather unimpressively, multiple roles in *Press for Time.*

The growing intelligence of the character makes some of the routines used in the earlier films redundant. The urge to entertain when in front of a crowd, the source of so many great moments, has disappeared, as has the embarrassment engendered by his inability to recognise the signifiers of class. There are still scenes based on a similar idea, where he misunderstands the actions of his superiors, but the climax is now more likely to have the little fellow fighting back determinedly. The need to entertain crowds is replaced by the wish to please individuals, and such scenes become far more intimate: the lovely play with the matches and the handkerchief, when Norman does little tricks and seemingly brings the handkerchief to life to amuse and entrance a girl in the pub in *The Bulldog Breed*, and the whole action of *A Stitch in Time* is generated through his wish to bring happiness into a sick little girl's life. Norman is more often consciously and forcefully assumed to be in the right: the forthright speech about charity at the climax of *A Stitch in Time*, and Norman's tirade against petty party politics near the end of *Press for Time*. Other familiar Gump routines are all but discarded: the infectiousness of laughter, misunderstanding of commands (except for a brief exchange with the doctor in *On the Beat*).

The problems in handling 'love interest' remain in these later films, though more often than not the Asher films dispense with romance. *Follow a Star* gives Norman a girlfriend before the film has started, and is the most successful in this area. Norman's relationship with the crippled Judy does not come over as a formula necessity but as a genuine affection between the two characters and is well integrated into the proceedings, with Norman's inadequacies explained rather than assumed. Norman's marriage in *On the Beat* is peripheral - he even abandons his bride on the church steps to rejoin his police colleagues. It is only with *Press for Time* that he is given a girl to pursue as an integral part of the plot and the film falls into the old trap:

Norman in love with one girl and settling for a second, Liz, by way of compensation. Actually, this largely dispiriting film exacerbates the problem with a scene where he organises a beauty contest and puts the self-consciously plain Liz on the throne instead of the chosen winner. Norman seems to be trying to justify his involvement by proving that his girlfriend is pretty and succeeds only in humiliating her.

One of the characteristics of Asher's films is the disorientating opening to demand the audience's attention. *Follow a Star* has a particularly effective pre-credit sequence. It starts with a close-up shot of pressure gauges before widening to reveal the tense and sweaty features of Norman and his co-worker Fred. The atmosphere builds to breaking point as the gauges show dangerously high readings, the men seeming to work feverishly against time in this threatening environment. This dramatic opening is at odds with expectations of a Norman Wisdom film! It seems as if this is some wartime submarine movie of the sort so popular at that time. But no, minds are put at rest when the setting is revealed to be a steam laundry and Norman and Fred are pressing a particularly recalcitrant suit. This opening leaves the audience in a frame of mind of being ready-for-anything, and in fact introduces Wisdom's most ambitious film so far with its wide ranging set of gags and routines. *On the Beat* begins with a fast tracking shot behind a police car, siren blazing, which transports us into the world of Scotland Yard thrillers with the fearless Inspector Pitkin (Wisdom) disarming an armed gunman, Trigger O'Flynn. After the credits, the scene is revealed to have been a dream of the more familiar Norman character. Similarly, though less well achieved, *A Stitch in Time* opens with what appears to be Norman as a surgeon performing a delicate operation.

One of Asher's less successful innovations is the use of gags dependent on special effects. In *The Bulldog Breed*, Norman is encased in a deep-sea diving suit and as soon as he gets in the water the air control goes wrong and the suit blows up like a balloon. The officer in charge agitatedly orders the airline to be chopped and, with a blast of escaping air, Norman skids across the water into the distance. In *The Early Bird*, Wisdom's first film in colour if we discount his guest spot at the climax of Jack Buchanan's 1955 film *As Long as they're Happy*, Norman gets dragged by a rampant lawnmower through the immaculately landscaped garden owned by Mr. Hunter (Jerry Desmonde), the boss of the rival diary. Nothing is safe from the machine's rapacious appetite, and it ploughs through flower-beds and hedgerows before spectacularly demolishing an entire greenhouse. The mower only comes to rest after an underwater dip through a pond when, with an agitated Mr. Hunter holding precariously to Norman's ankles, it strikes a tree, which in turn collapses under the impact, neatly splitting Hunter's Bentley in two. Though these two scenes are reasonably successful, on the whole the reliance on the mechanical and on special effects detracts from a belief in the characters and fails to utilise Wisdom's great strengths as a visual comic. After all, anyone could have been in the diving suit. Also, these routines are sometimes done with effects of variable quality; especially in the mountaineering sequence in *The Bulldog Breed* which climaxes in the unlikely sight of Norman's fellow climbers, trussed in their sleeping bags, plunging over the side of a cliff to be left hanging on a pine tree like Christmas decorations.

Producer Hugh Stewart received many complaints from the public over the lack of songs in *The Square Peg* and this was one of the factors in choosing the story for *Follow a Star* which made Norman a budding singer and giving him five numbers to perform. This proved to be overkill and Wisdom did not sing again in a film until his 1968 American debut, *The Night they Raided Minsky's*. One of the songs in *Follow a Star*, 'You Deserve a Medal for That', illustrates how far Wisdom and Asher were initially prepared to stray from the path set for them by the Gump. This sophisticated revue-style number, performed by Wisdom backed up with a full all-male chorus, allows him to demonstrate a series of comic walks, a bit of table-top mock ice skating and some cleverly choreographed routines developed by Eleanor Fazon. Though Norman's sophistication is explained through his being under hypnosis, no excuse is offered for the chorus-line to materialise from Norman's fellow diners, and the semi-fantasy number is a totally welcome departure for Wisdom on film, allowing his cinemagoing public to experience branches of Wisdom's talents generally kept under wraps by the conservative Rank regime.

A routine which has sharp affinities with 'You Deserve a Medal for That' occurs in *On the Beat*. Here Wisdom is in his second role of Giulio Napolitani, a ruthless gangster who maintains a high-class hairdressing salon as his front. Double roles are notoriously difficult to pull off, not least because it is obvious that the plot will call for one of the characters to impersonate or be mistaken for the other, and the knowledge that they are both played by the same person tends to undermine credibility and suspense. Here, Wisdom creates one of the most successful doubles ever. His Napolitani owes little to make-up - a few extra curls and a moustache - and everything to Wisdom's movement, which is in sharp contrast to his embodiment of Norman. Napolitani is given a rounded burlesque personality, fussy and fluttery, prancing around the salon voicing his mastery of his job in his broad Italian accent. Though no song is involved, Napolitani dealing with his customers is essentially a musical number. As he flits from woman to woman, putting the final touches to their hair, Wisdom gracefully displays a variety of funny walks, eccentric dance steps and flamboyant gestures with an elegance unbeknown to the lumbering Norman. Though Wisdom goes 'over the top', his actions never strike one as being ridiculous and become even more convincing when we see the boss behind the scenes, shedding all his extrovert showman affectations. He then becomes the ruthless gangland boss who uses his salon to record his rich clientele's conversations in order to plan his robberies. A tribute to Wisdom's playing of Napolitani is a later sequence when Norman is being trained to impersonate the gangster, and it is totally convincing when Norman has trouble getting to grips with Napolitani's mannerisms which he copies from a film.

It is only with the Asher films that Wisdom is successful in pulling off that difficult blend of pathos and comedy. A wonderful sequence in *Follow a Star* illustrates this well. Drawing on his years of stage experience, Wisdom knows the value of gently undermining over-sentimentality through careful presentation and unexpected climaxes, taking his audience through extremes of emotion. In *Follow a Star* Norman goes to a florist to buy flowers for his girlfriend, Judy. The camera remains static outside, watching the action through the shop window. Norman is seen to be unable to afford his chosen bouquet and has to settle for a single bloom in its place. Wisdom and Asher pile on the sentiment in this silent scene by having the shop-assistant spot Norman's disappointment and make a point of giftwrapping the flower. Once Norman gets to Judy's flat, however, the package is empty - the flower has dropped out unnoticed en route. With *The Bulldog Breed*, Norman is placed in a harsh and unfriendly environment even by the standards of the earlier films - indeed worse as he cannot claim any friends whatsoever. Great emphasis is placed on this isolation, demanding audience sympathy. In *A Stitch in Time*, there are some worries when a recently orphaned child is used as a springboard for the film's pathos. Nevertheless, as in the case of *Follow a Star* which raises similar concerns when we discover Judy is a cripple, Wisdom gets away with it because his performance carries an unmistakeable sincerity which transforms the potentially maudlin into the effectively touching. There is a lovely moment in *A Stitch in Time* when Norman kisses the little girl goodbye and leaves. The nurse who has been watching him has noticed how he has managed to get the girl to smile and says: 'You must have a gift', to which Norman replies: 'Oh no, I don't want anything', one of the actor's favourite lines in his films and which works because it is delivered with patent honesty.

The finest additional attribute of these later films is the carefully planned, essentially silent, single situation routines. Unlike the earlier versions where the routine would generally climax in hysteria or violence, these remain restrained and deadpan, moving splendidly from one absurdity to the next with a brilliant logical momentum. In *A Stitch in Time* it takes Norman and the ambulanceman (Glyn Houston) nearly five minutes to get the unfortunate Edward Chapman on to a stretcher and into an ambulance in a marvellously thought out sequence which milks all the laughs possible through variations of what can go wrong with such a seemingly simple task. The opening of *The Early Bird* lasts a full ten-and-a-half minutes before a line of dialogue is spoken and is a masterly piece of cinematic as well as comic timing. All that is involved is the fumblings of the early rising dairy workers, with Norman and Edward Chapman's Mr. Grimsdale stumbling about half asleep, and includes Norman falling down flights of stairs no fewer than six times! This beautifully judged routine gains much of its fun precisely from the inevitability of each stage in the unrolling saga of a morning at Grimsdale's, humorously enhanced by the expertise of the mute playing and captured well by Asher's sympathetic direction. Perhaps the best example of all occurs in *Press for Time*, a film otherwise bereft of great routines. Norman, now a budding journalist, has cycled to the house of the Mayoress to apologise for a previous indiscretion. He has been followed by some obnoxious children who have designs on his bicycle. To frustrate their attempts, Norman brings it into the house with him after the maid answers the door, carefully propping it up against the fireplace. Greeted by this strange sight, the Mayor, Mrs. Corcoran (Noel Dyson) - a pretty dotty lady herself - suggests that Norman place it in the kitchen. Norman tries to wheel the bicycle round the furniture, but is unable to find a clear route through. The obvious solution is to lift it over the obstructing settee but this plan misfires when the bicycle gets inextricably caught in an overhanging cluster of lights. Norman surveys the scene, climbing on the back of the settee for a closer view - but it overturns. After clearing the area, Norman selects a small side table as a firmer base to stand on. Mrs. Corcoran removes the table cloth and a vase of flowers in the nick of time, and indicates to Norman that he must take off his shoes in deference to the polished surface. Standing on the table, Norman tries to free the bicycle, managing only to overbalance, kicking away his support to leave himself hanging on to the bicycle and swaying gently in mid-air. Mrs. Corcoran replaces the table and Norman finally manages to disentangle the bicycle, only to catch his sleeve on the light-fitting in its place. Again he loses his balance and now he is attached to the light by the sleeve of his left arm, holding on to the bicycle with his right. Mrs. Corcoran takes the bicycle from his and it is to this bizarre sight that her daughter, Liz (Frances White), enters. With a great deal of misplaced aplomb, Mrs. Corcoran politely introduces her daughter to the suspended Norman before a rather puzzled Liz suggests they let him down. The table is brought into action once more, and Liz steps up to free Norman. After one false attempt, which leaves them both momentarily suspended, she succeeds and they get down safely. This masterly sequence, almost free of dialogue until Liz's entry, is very carefully worked out. Wisdom manages to take an absurd and hilarious climax - Norman plus bicycle hanging from the light-fitting - and builds to it relentlessly and logically so that at no point does the progression of disaster stretch credibility. This brilliantly executed routine, perfectly in character for the accident-prone Norman, rates with the best of cinema Wisdom.

Asher could certainly deliver great moments, but he is less consistent than John Paddy Carstairs and must take some of the responsibility for the dreadfully misjudged golf course sequence in *The Early Bird* where Norman fools Mr. Hunter with his disguise as a priest in a sketch which leaves both Norman and Hunter perched in a tree. The scene breaks one of Wisdom's own cardinal rules, that any developing insanity should be grounded in the believable - the gags here seem to have been grafted somewhat uncertainly on to the situation. To make the scene work we have at least to believe that Hunter would be fooled by Norman's disguise, which is not the case. The sad failure of *Press for Time* to raise many laughs - excepting its one masterful routine - is also largely due to Asher's surprisingly flat direction and a story which gives little space for Wisdom to display his clowning skills.

To compensate, Asher and Wisdom do experiment with various ideas. The welcome blackness of *The Bulldog Breed*, with Norman attempting suicide at the beginning; the lunacy of the doctor's inspection in *On the Beat*, with Norman trying to satisfy the police height requirements by donning stilts; the oddly sadistic dental routines in *A Stitch in Time*. Asher also seems at ease with traditional slapstick stand-bys which display Wisdom's expertise well. For example, the lovely hosepipe sketch in *On the Beat* - in which Wisdom is aided and abetted by the splendid Raymond Huntley - has Norman misunderstanding the Police Commissioner's actions as a game, leading to a mutual drenching. Wisdom dons drag in a number of films, but never as effectively as in *A Stitch in Time* where much more consideration has been given to his disguise, with especially convincing make-up by George Blackler. Though Wisdom burlesques woman's movements, it is not so overdone as to render the Jerry Desmonde character's interest in 'her' ridiculous. *On the Beat* contains the best chase in any Wisdom film as a growing band of bobbies pursues Norman, unaware that their quarry is running alongside them. When they finally realise who they are trying to arrest, the hunt turns into a human Grand National complete with fences, hedges and water jumps as the chase continues through the back gardens of a row of terraced houses. Shot with verve and imagination, the sequence gives Wisdom many opportunities to display individual 'pieces of business' which are often as unexpected as they are amusing - such as his glorious launch into a sprint by curling one leg around the other as if to wind himself up. The chase comes to a climax with a spectacular high long-shot of Norman being inexorably encircled by a mass of policemen. The camera returns to eye-level, following the Superintendent through the crowd until Norman is glimpsed, still trying to find a way out, dashing in each direction in turn like some demented mouse.

Follow a Star has the incalculable bonus of staging its finale at the London Palladium and presenting a part of his stage act on film. The essential gag is that Wisdom doggedly remains in front of the audience to sing his song despite all that the manager does to get him off the stage. All of the resources of that magnificent theatre are brought into use - Norman nearly disappears through a trap-door, is almost whisked out of view by the rotating stage, clambers through a set of falling curtains, and even has to survive the dousing of the house lights. The sequence begins with a brilliant fall. Norman is alone on stage dressed in his misfit evening suit and is looking for somewhere to put his false shirtfront which is not behaving itself. He places it in the body of a grand piano standing behind him, only for the lid to drop on his hand with a sickening crunch. Angered by the audience's laughter at his discomfort, Norman steps forward to remonstrate with them, but his hand is well and truly trapped and he is dragged backwards, falling spectacularly on his back.

Press for Time proved not only to be Norman Wisdom's last film with Robert Asher but also with the Rank Organisation. This highly profitable relationship had been Rank's mainstay on the production front for many years. The series of twelve starring vehicles produced one of the most distinguished and sustained comic incarnations in the history of British cinema, and with *Trouble in Store, Up in the World, Follow a Star* and *On the Beat* some of our finest individual comedies. Nevertheless, Wisdom always had a strong desire to attempt other styles of comedy on film, and to complete our survey of his British film work, we move on to those films which fall outside the development of the Gump.

7. The Big Screen continued: other directions.

Since the remaining three films, *There was a Crooked Man* (1960), *The Girl on the Boat* (1962) and *What's Good for the Goose* (1969), totally dispense with the Gump, they have been left to last in this survey of Wisdom's British film work to date. Sadly, the first two of these, made with Knightsbridge for first-time directors, are seldom aired, having been out of copyright for some years, and *What's Good for the Goose* is usually screened in a butchered version. For these films represent Wisdom's most insistent experiment with different forms of screen comedy and, in the case of *There was a Crooked Man*, the result is one of his very finest films.

What unites these works is that Norman Wisdom adapts himself to the roles, rather than taking a part especially tailored to both his talents and his familiar screen persona. An indication of this is that his screen name in each of these films is not Norman but, in chronological order, Davy Cooper, Samuel Marlowe and Timothy Bartlett. The plots thus take on a greater importance, the themes stemming primarily from the narrative rather than through the clown persona of the star. In order to discuss their characteristics it is therefore essential to give plot synopses, especially as these films are rarely screened.

There was a Crooked Man tells the story of Davy Cooper (Norman Wisdom), the driving force behind the new town development of Sleath. In flashback, we find Davy wandering the streets of Soho, jobless and nearly destitute. By chance, he bumps into an old army colleague Flash Dan (Timothy Bateson) who recognises Davy and recalls his expertise with explosives. Flash Dan is a member of a gang of robbers led by Adolf Carter (Alfred Marks) who are desperately in need of Davy's talents. After some persuasion, he is recruited into the gang. With Davy's invaluable help as a safe-breaker, the thieves thrive until a major break-in at a bank goes awry. Davy is captured by the police and sentenced to a prison term of seven years. Life at Coldhaven Prison suits him well and he is most unhappy to be released from this secure existence with two years' remission. The friendly prison chaplain finds Davy a job in the northern town of Sleath-on-Sea at the knitting mills owned by the town's premier citizen and Mayor, McKillup (Andrew Cruickshank). McKillup, a crook, has set up the Sleath Redevelopment Corporation, ostensibly to invest in the future of the town, but in reality a fraudulent scheme to raise money from the townspeople through a share issue. Davy unwittingly aids him at a public meeting with an impassioned speech which helps overcome the scepticism of the audience. On learning the truth, and after escaping a trap set for him by McKillup, Davy contacts his old gang and they go into operation to thwart the swindle. Disguised as high ranking American army officers, they drive into town and let McKillup think that they wish to purchase the land from him should he manage to acquire it. McKillup buys back all the shares, to the profit of the townspeople, and Davy goes ahead with his plan to demolish the entire town. Only then does he inform McKillup that the site is not suitable for his purposes. In Washington, an American General at the Pentagon admits to having unwittingly aided Davy in his plans, and the Government offers to recompense the British by building an entire new town. Davy is thus perceived as Sleath's benefactor. With a return to the opening scene at the unveiling of Davy's statue during the town's first anniversary celebration, the hero receives his plaudits before being led off to his beloved gaol once more.

The Girl on the Boat, the second film for Knightsbridge, takes Wisdom into the world of P.G. Wodehouse and has him playing an upper-class layabout, Sam Marlowe. The story is taken from a fairly representative Wodehouse work. The year is 1920, and the film begins with Sam Marlowe trying to persuade his Aunt Adeline (Athene Seyler) to rent out her English country home, Windles, to two clients of his father. She refuses, and then is upset by the news brought to her by another visitor, Bream Mortimer (Philip Locke), that her son Eustace Hignett (Richard Briers) is planning to get married that day to Billie (Millicent Martin) with whom Bream himself is in love. Adeline successfully puts a stop to the nuptials and packs Eustace off to England with Sam via the luxury liner S.S. *Atlantic*. Unfortunately both Bream and Billie are making the same crossing. Romantic complications multiply as Billie veers from Bream to Sam and back to Bream again in the search for her Sir Galahad. Meanwhile, Eustace finds happiness in the arms of Billie's cabin-mate, Jane (Sheila Hancock), a strong-willed big-game hunter. On returning to England, Sam cleverly gets his clients - the respective fathers of Billie and Bream - into Windles in the hope of being able to rekindle Billie's affections. The whole entourage takes up residence at the country house, but Sam's pretence of being a protective hero is exposed and the impulsive Billie decides to elope with Bream as revenge. The same night, Sam attempts to kidnap his beloved's pekinese in another devious scheme to win her favours. Mistaken for a burglar, Sam is forced to hide in a suit of armour to escape the attentions of the gun-toting Jane. The huntress still roots him out, at which point his Aunt Adeline arrives to find out what is going on. Her investigations are cut short when Billie's father reads a note revealing his daughter's elopement. Sam hurries off in pursuit, complete with horse and armour. At last Billie has found her shining knight and she and Sam join Eustace and Jane in a double marriage.

What's Good for the Goose is the film over which Wisdom had most control, being its associate producer and scriptwriter as well as star. Unfortunately the unsubtle directorial 'style' of Menahem Golan is also to the fore, and the film is certainly the most vilified critically of all Wisdom's films. The reviewers were horrified by his latest change of image and his delving into light sex comedy. In an interview with Peter Oakes the star said: 'This new film isn't filthy - it's got plenty of funny sequences - but it's a good sex film. It's not the sort you'd expect your maiden aunt in Eastbourne to see. I am sure it will appeal to the teenagers however.' In response to the critical onslaught Wisdom told Godfrey Winn: 'You've got to experiment or stand still . . . There's nothing that I could do that would ever please the critics at home. They used to sneer at me for doing slapstick comedy and when I try something else, they sneer at me all over again.' It is not difficult to understand the critical reaction to the film. Wisdom, hardly the reviewers' favourite film personality, had made far too bold a break with his image - it was made, after all, seven years after the Knightsbridge films - and they could not even sneer 'more of the same'. The reviewers were also horrified by the nude scenes, although they are all very discreet - Sally Geeson is exposed topless only in the continental version! Nevertheless, the idea that the film was 'dirty' stuck and, with its initial 'A' certificate, audience figures were down on that expected for a Wisdom film, though it moved effortlessly into profit and scored well in some European territories. To regain the family audience, 19 minutes were hacked out to produce a 'U' certificate release version, but this made no noticeable improvement on its performance at the box office.

The film is perhaps the one which most insistently plays on contemporary fashions and attitudes. Wisdom plays Timothy Bartlett, an assistant bank manager working in Central London, who lives in resigned security with his wife Margaret (Sally Bazely), three children and assorted goldfish. An unexpected career opportunity opens up for him when he attends a bankers' conference in Southport. On the drive there, he picks up two teenage hitchhikers, Nikki (Sally Geeson) and Meg (Sarah Atkinson). Nikki intrigues him and he embarks on an affair with her, slowly getting drawn into her young, swinging lifestyle. Near the end of the week's conference the affair comes to an end when Timothy discovers Nikki in bed with one of her entourage, Peter (Karl Lanchbury). Timothy calls his wife to the resort in an attempt to relive his recent adventures with her, but not all goes as well as Timothy intended. The following day the couple cut short their weekend and drive back to London. However, the tensions between them have been exposed and there is a high probability that they have been brought closer together by the experience.

Davy Cooper has the closest relationship to the Gump; he is somewhat naïf with a childlike trust in people. He joins Adolf's gang because the leader convinces him that without crime there would be mass unemployment. It takes him a long time to work out McKillup's involvement with the fraud, not realising that people in authority can be crooked too. Like the Gump, he can only be pushed so far before he fights back. He also has an ability to make himself absurd - the ridiculous way he stuffs his ears with cotton wool before detonating the explosives, a habit which leads to his downfall. Unlike the Gump, he has practical, indeed expert, skills in which he can take pride. When he turns his mind to things he does them well, whether it be blowing safes, tending flowers in the prison governor's garden or impersonating an American General. Further, when Davy does go for his revenge, it is planned and executed with precision and intelligence - not instinctive recklessness - and he is happy to do it in co-operation with others. Davy is rather shy with women, quite content to leave the admiring Ellen (Susannah York) behind to return to the solitude and peace of the gaol cell. Finally, Davy is the only Wisdom character in these three films who one assumes has a working class background. In stark contrast *The Girl on the Boat*'s Sam Marlowe is from the idle rich. The 'twenties setting separates the film immediately from the standard Wisdom vehicle, and the star has great fun attacking the untypical role with gusto - as he had done in *There was a Crooked Man* in the scenes where Davy impersonates the American General. Sam is studiedly inconsequential in typical Wodehouse style. Life is just one carefree succession of pleasurable pursuits, inane conversations and flights from boredom. On the other hand *What's Good for the Goose*'s Timothy Bartlett is a middle class suburbanite who is already constrained by the routine and monotony of his safe and secure lifestyle. Timothy is a man who has done all the right things, but thinks real life has passed him by as he approaches middle age.

The three films are directed with different levels of competence. Stuart Burge proves the most sympathetic director with *There was a Crooked Man*, giving the film a sharp pace, good atmospheric lighting, and handling the faster slapstick sequences with skill and imagination. *The Girl on the Boat* is a fine film, but the pacing by director Henry Kaplan is often too slow and obvious, and there is a sense that the film could have turned out much better with a more experienced director in charge; and it probably suffers from Kaplan's refusal to take advice from his star. The film does have a nice period sense, but the direction allows little space for any of the cast to add much to the script, and the intentionally silly plot is given too much weight.

In complete contrast, Menahem Golan has no time for subtlety, and any sensitivity *What's Good for the Goose* is trying to display gets lost under the weight of his direction. The film allows no room for observing emotional development and the bane of the physical clown, speeded-up motion, is used dispiritingly for the long opening sequence. A typical example of Golan's blunderbuss approach to film-making occurs when Timothy is awaiting the return of Nikki to his bedroom for their first night of passion. In ecstatic anticipation he bounces up and down on the bed, a reaction which seems absurd given Bartlett's sexual apprehensiveness; and indeed it was shot against the actor's wishes.

The Knightsbridge films offer splendid supporting casts, and they are used well. Alfred Marks, Susannah York and Andrew Cruickshank shine in *There was a Crooked Man*, and *The Girl on the Boat* is packed full of actors expert in the art of genteel dialogue comedy: Richard Briers, Millicent Martin and Athene Seyler. On the other hand *What's Good for the Goose* gives most of the cast, other than the two leads, little to do, and though there are many familiar names in support including Derek Francis, Terence Alexander, Paul Whitsun-Jones and David Lodge, none are given scenes of any consequence.

The depiction of the circle of friends around Nikki and Meg in *What's Good for the Goose* probably worked against a good reception from a young audience. The members of the group are depicted as happy-go-lucky free young things living life for kicks. Commercial cinema usually has trouble depicting teenage lifestyles convincingly, and the swinging 'sixties/flower-power 'in-scene' was no exception. The depiction of the Screaming Apple Discotheque where Timothy meets Nikki and her entourage on his first evening in Southport is unintentionally amusing with its brightly coloured surroundings enclosing a cleaned-up Pretty Things in concert, their fans dazedly drinking cokes and swaying, colour supplement style, in suspended car-tyres. The characterisation of the circle of friends around Nikki and Meg almost defies description. It seems as if the director and scriptwriter are not quite sure what to make of their own inconsequential creations. Naïve, innocent, yet fun-loving hedonists, presumably into peace and love, they merely provide a somewhat unconvincing background to the affair which is about to begin. What must then have struck its target audience as ludicrous, now strangely takes on a nostalgic glow at a time when the media representation of the 'sixties is of as much interest as the events themselves.

One of the problems which all these projects have to confront is how to utilise Wisdom's special talents. *There was a Crooked Man* is exemplary in the manner in which it allows Wisdom space to include 'bits of business' as well as providing him with fine extended sequences of visual slapstick. At the opening of his story, Davy is shown wandering the rain-sodden streets of Soho, capable only of clawing at a restaurant window in hunger as he watches a well-rounded customer tucking into a plateful of spaghetti. Davy then hears the cry of a woman shouting for a taxi, and he gallantly goes to her aid, opening the door for her. His aim was not monetary gain, and he is surprised when she hands him a tip of a 3d piece. He looks down at the coin in his hand - but realises when he spots a poster that it is not enough to purchase a four square meal. A man behind him hails a taxi and Davy tries his luck once more. However, the ruse misfires and the gentleman insists that Davy take the cab and almost pushes him inside - much to Davy's subsequent financial embarrassment. The same film incorporates excellent silent sequences such as the well-observed parody of the famous robbery sequence from Jules Dassin's classic French thriller, Rififi. Here the gang have to drill their way into the bank vaults from the neighbouring hospital, and thus they pretend they are a team of surgeons performing an emergency operation. The parallels between the two activities are effectively understated - the building blueprint on the X-ray machine, the 'nurse' handing Davy the drill bits - and Burge is able to spice it with quick sight gags: the 'body' at one point seems to have its feet on the wrong way round. When the robbers are interrupted by a nurse, the 'body', quickly reconstituted from its toolbox components, lacks a torso: the feet coming straight out of the head. The most ambitious of the set routines in this film is where Davy hides in the shower to escape the attentions of McKillup's assistant, Ashton (Brian Oulton). Unfortunately for Davy, Ashton decides to take a shower. He strips off and enters without noticing Davy. The water is turned on, and Davy has to take a drenching silently, looking a sorry mess over Ashton's shoulder. Somehow Davy manages to keep out of sight. Ashton rubs himself down, surprised that he feels nothing - since he is in fact only making contact with Davy. Shrugging this off, Ashton takes the soap out of the holder and lathers the back-brush and begins to scrub himself clean. Again, and more disturbingly, he feels no sensation as it is Davy's suit which is receiving the unwanted scrubbing. Davy realises that discovery is at hand unless he thinks fast. Suppressing his giggles when the brush tickles him, Davy spies a nail brush and uses it on Ashton's back, simulating Ashton's motions. Ashton is reassured by the sensation and remains innocent of Davy's presence. Another crisis arises when Ashton tries to replace the bar of soap in the holder, and Davy has to take the tablet in his mouth to forestall Ashton from turning round. Of course, he has the misfortune to swallow it as well! On his final rinse, the flabbergasted Ashton finally spots Davy. Davy's lame assurance that he did not look does not placate Ashton, who is in fact more concerned that his conversation revealing the share fraud has been overheard.

There are no such extended comedy routines in either of the other two films. *The Girl on the Boat* all but dispenses with Wisdom's strengths as a visual comedian in a vehicle which could well have made use of them. The star's best moments are all brief touches. When Aunt Adeline whips Sam's trousers away to thwart Eustace's marriage, Sam is sent spinning like a top; Sam's infectious laughter when Eustace heads for his cabin on the cross-Atlantic cruise, suffering from seasickness even before the boat has left harbour; the smoothly caught hoopla which he sends back on its way whilst striding across a deck game; the practice golf swing to impress Billie, the club slipping from his hand and curling gently into the sea; the imitation of various voices as he pretends to be calling his father's clients from America; and the splendid walk down the stairs at Windles when encased in the weighty armour. These are the moments which stick in the mind, but there should have been more. For the most part, one has to settle for the gentle and unassuming charms which the inconsequential plot yields. Of course, these are many. When Sam rather unfairly gleans knowledge of Billie's likes from the unsuspecting Eustace, he assumes her preference as part of his character. She likes golf, so Sam appears on deck with a golf bag, she admires men who break up dog fights - and he tells her how much he likes to undertake the task. But his real success stems from his knowledge of her adoration of Tennyson. Walking with her on deck, Sam deviously drops a book of the poet's collected works and love begins to blossom. Sam takes to reading aloud her favourite poem, 'Idylls of the King', and she begins to fall in love with her suitor, despite the disconcerting lapse when Sam turns over too many pages and merges the poem with 'Charge of the Light Brigade'! To top it all, when Sam finally gauges the moment to propose, a surfeit of Tennyson renders him incapable of speaking in anything but rhyming couplets.

There was a Crooked Man is sparing in its verbal gags, though it does contain a nice line which echoes Wisdom's favourite from *A Stitch in Time*. Davy is now serving his time in gaol and has settled down well, making himself quite at home. While tending to his duties in the Governor's garden, the padre has to inform Davy that his release is imminent. He approaches the diligent gardener who indicates the flowers and says: 'Aren't they lovely?' The padre responds: 'Yes Davy, God's works are wonderful.' Norman immediately takes issue: 'I beg your pardon, Sir, I did these!'

What's Good for the Goose is intended to work in a different way - Wisdom moves away from physical comedy and attempts a comedy of manners and attitudes. In the entire film there are no stand-out routines, though Wisdom makes nice use of facial expressions when pretending that he is enjoying the exertions of the carousels at the amusement park. Overall, there is just a gently amusing undercurrent to the reawakening of Bartlett's sexuality through his meeting with Nikki. Indeed the film actually stands up reasonably well as an attempt, within a comic framework, to deal with middle-aged *angst*. Its main failings are the extreme caricatures of both bankers and youths - which add nothing to the comic effect - and the problem it has resolving the issues, with the rather distasteful summoning of Margaret to Southport. However, Wisdom's central character is well thought out with his urge to roll away the years and prove to himself that he is still young and sexy, and the film generates successfully an underlying melancholia as he takes advantage of the flighty nymphet to achieve his aims. The film needed to be more critical of Timothy's actions since, as it stands, Nikki is denied the ability to reflect and have feelings.

These three films were certainly brave departures for the star, discarding the safe and proven formulae of the Gump. It is sad and curious how resistant the British public were to this wholesale change of image, the moderate commercial showing of the two Knightsbridge films, especially of *There was a Crooked Man*, being particularly depressing. Only on stage and in America could the tenacious hold of the Gump be broken with critical and commercial success.

What's Good for the Goose proved to be the last starring feature film Norman Wisdom has made to date. The reception of the picture, coupled with the general decline of the industry, led to Wisdom being offered only low-budget films which he rejected, preferring to concentrate on cabaret, other live shows and television. As he said in 1976 to *Photoplay*: 'Well, unfortunately, the films I get asked to do are the cheap, economy films they expect to do in three weeks instead of the usual ten or twelve. I know I've got a good reputation from the 19 films I made, so I'm not going to risk spoiling that reputation by doing one silly, cheap film.'

8. The Film Years: other work 1953-1966.

While the moguls at Rank were pontificating over Norman Wisdom's film career, he himself was not idle. 1952 had been taken up with *Paris to Piccadilly* which finally ended its run on 22nd August 1953, and just over three months later, on 23rd December, Wisdom was back in the limelight starring in *Sinbad the Sailor on Ice* at the Empress Hall. While *Trouble in Store* was packing in the customers at cinemas throughout the country, Wisdom was breaking records at the Empress Hall, attracting 6,000 people a night to his first, and Claude Langdon's fifth, ice pantomime. Langdon's pantos had a reputation of keeping to the traditional stories, and in this one Wisdom played the Keeper of the Slaves with Andra McLaughlin co-starring as Sinbad in a production complete with the requisite flying carpet and a spectacular set for the Caliph of Bagdad's Palace. 'Everything is cut to the size of arena entertainment. Norman Wisdom, the principal comedian, has exactly the right effects to traverse the vast spaces between him and his present audience, and indeed his pursuit, at full speed up and down the whole length of the rink, of an evasive beam from a spotlight is a stroke of visual humour scarcely to be brought off in circumstances less spacious.' (*The Times.*) In February 1954, Wisdom marginally increased his *Sinbad* earnings of £1,200 a week by appearing in over an hour's excerpts on television which featured such highlights as Wisdom being chased around the auditorium by a gorilla (Ronald Privett) and the finale, set amongst 18 scale models of battleships and aircraft-carriers. The entire show, which was highly successful in transferring Wisdom's stage antics on to ice - complete with Gump suit in some scenes - was also given the accolade of a special charity performance before Princess Margaret.

Another happy event of 1953 was the birth of a son, Nicholas, to Freda and Norman, an event which prompted the Wisdoms to give up the caravan life they had been leading and purchase their first home, near South Mimms in Hertfordshire. Wisdom's television appearances, though always notable, were becoming increasingly rare, but later the same year he was involved in a particularly memorable broadcast. It was called *For Your Pleasure* and it marked the first time the newly crowned Elizabeth II had visited a television studio as monarch, where she watched a show being filmed live. Wisdom had, by this time, developed many good television routines in partnership with Eddie Leslie while working on BBC TV's *Vic's Grill*, and they had adapted a number of these for the stage, but when the prestigious Royal appearance arrived, Eddie Leslie was touring with a production of *South Pacific* and could not make it to Lime Grove studios. Instead, Wisdom teamed with Bill Fraser, later famous as Snudge in the hit television series *The Army Game*. Wisdom chose as his sketch one about a raw chump trying to break into showbusiness at the Agent's office - a routine he had tried out on television before, and which was based on his own experience. 'I remember arriving at a small agent's office. The agent was speaking on the 'phone, but I wasn't sure whether he was speaking to me or to the bloke on the telephone. I said: "I want to go on the stage." Agent: "I can fix you up." Me: "I don't mind anything you suggest." Agent: "Well all right, send me some photos and I'll get you into the show at . . ." When he put the 'phone down, he turned to me and said: "Well, what do you want?" I told him I was looking for work, and that show he'd just mentioned sounded fine: "Get out of here," he said. I would embroider that, I'd have him say, "Well OK, I can offer you £5 a week to start. You'll have to have a suit. You can repay me £1 a week. The accompanist will cost you another £1, and . . ." In the end the expenses would come to so much that I'd have to pay him 2/6. "Good," he'd say, "now I can eat!"' (*Stage*.) This routine, which Wisdom reworks in *Follow a Star* when he negotiates a wage with Jerry Desmonde, was very well received and had the Queen asking him why he did not appear more often on television. Sadly, the only bits of the show that have survived are Jimmy Edwards' turn and an interminable ten-minute sequence of the Queen shaking hands with the cast!

1954 brought the birth of a second child, a daughter, Jacqueline, and the first of a series of triumphs at the London Palladium. Val Parnell had taken over the Palladium on the death of George Black in 1946 and his main rival in the presentation of international variety in London was Bernard Delfont who controlled the London Casino, and to whose theatrical agency Wisdom was signed. In 1948, as we have seen, Parnell let it be known that he would like Wisdom on his Palladium bill, but Wisdom refused since it would have entailed changing his agent, and as a reward was given his chance at the Casino. The rivalry between Delfont and Parnell, which had been quite bitter at points, was patched up when they undertook joint presentations at the Hippodrome (later The Talk of the Town) which Parnell had run since 1947. Their first production was London's first Folies Bergère in 1949, and they continued to present these annual revues, changing locale in 1952 to the Prince of Wales for Wisdom's *Paris to Piccadilly*. Delfont had always wanted to present the biggest variety show in town, and for this he needed the Palladium. The Palladium now had to have Norman Wisdom since he was Britain's premier comedy attraction, and Delfont would only allow it if he could present the shows. Finally a deal was struck with Parnell which left Delfont presenting international variety at the Palladium for about twenty years.

Wisdom's first conquest of the 'Palace of Varieties' was simply entitled *The London Palladium Show*, and he was teamed with Jerry Desmonde in a number of sketches including one with Desmonde trying to hail a taxi and getting no help from Norman; 'A Lesson in Rhythm', a Wisdom favourite with a sadistic machine hammering out the rudiments of tempo; another with Wisdom as a football fan trying to get into a sold-out match. But the production's greatest innovation and triumph was a ballet sequence 'Romance in Town'. This beautiful routine, in which Wisdom was deftly partnered by Gillian Moran, was devised by Dick Hurran with choreography by Alan Carter and allowed Wisdom to display his superb skills as an acrobatic dancer in addition to those as a comic mime. The show, which opened in May, was one of the most successful ever staged at the Palladium, and at its scheduled closure, the demand for tickets was still so great that the production was transferred bodily to the Prince of Wales theatre, one of the few changes being the incorporation of 'Sporting Impressionists' Tony Fayne and David Evans as a replacement support act. *The Palladium Show* eventually ran for eleven months and the entire four-part ballet sequence was selected for the year's Royal Variety Performance. Wisdom also gave a private show for the Royal Family that year at Windsor along with Desmonde, Beryl Reid and Peter Brough. After this, Wisdom's triumphs at the Palladium surprised no one, and he gained a reputation as one of the few British acts who could fill this venue at a time when the policy was still to use top American attractions.

In 1955, box office records were again shattered by the seven-and-a-half month run of *Painting the Town*, in which he was partnered once again by Jerry Desmonde with principal guest Ruby Murray. 'With his urchin grin, gleaming eyes, and collapsing walk, Mr. Wisdom is one of those small men who are inwardly big enough to command a stage alone. His domination of the Palladium audience, so warmly appreciative last night, has its source in a sentimental complicity. In dress suit much too large for him, he is on top of the world by submitting with much cheerful readiness to its knocks. These worldly knocks are administered in the main by Mr. Desmonde . . . The number in which Mr. Desmonde gives the ineffectual little man a park bench lesson in how to approach the ladies is a joy of its kind; another called The Cold War, in which Mr. Wisdom, suffering from a fever, tries out different miraculous cures evincing immediately their different after-effects, is one of the most intricate pieces of knockabout seen on the London stage for some time. But how considerable Mr. Wisdom's resources in fact are is only really apparent in his long solo appearance at the end of the evening. The tumbledown walk and roguery with the orchestra, which at one point he conducts, lead now to interludes on the trumpet and saxophone, to wonder at the effect of the microphone on his voice, and to coy and impassioned songs. And throughout this triumph he manages cleverly to sustain the feeling that he is one of life's born losers.' (*The Times.*) Wisdom's remarkable stage presence was also noted: 'His control over his audience has grown with his greater self-control. It is fascinating to observe how, in the space of a few minutes, he can charm the audience into laughter; then next, abruptly break the spell of pathos by telling them what fools they were to be gulled by such sentimental tricks as his; and then as they laugh once more, embark on a lachrymose ditty that holds them silent once again.' (*The Times.*) 1956 brought with it Wisdom's first Palladium pantomime, usurping the principal boy's role of Aladdin in *The Wonderful Lamp.* Under Robert Nesbitt's expert direction, and with Sonnie Hale as Widow Twankey and Valentine Dyall as Abanazar, Christmas box-office records were rewritten. 'Mr. Wisdom is a perky street Arab. There is a happy smack of incongruity in the spectacle of the urchin daring to pay addresses to the lovely Princess Yasmin (Stephanie Voss) under the terrible eyes of the Emperor . . . Mr. Wisdom manages the comic pathos of this scene so well that we do not wonder that the little princess also should fall in love at first sight with the small Sam Weller . . . This is the most charmingly spectacular pantomime that London has seen for some year.' (*The Times.*)

Due to the pressure of other commitments, Wisdom was severely limiting his television appearances. But the importance of the medium could not be ignored, especially with commercial television digging its firm foundations. The comedian who had been declared the BBC's top comic since 1952 was eager to appear on ITV, and it looked as if there might be a series. *TV Times* on 4th November 1955 announced: 'NORMAN'S COMING BACK. Are you a Norman Wisdom fan? Does the little fellow double you up with laughter as he struggles to play a piano concerto; clowns his way, mouthful by mouthful, through an impossibly large sandwich; or surprisingly switches from the gaiety of his high jinks to the pathos of a plaintive little song. Then you will be pleased to hear that there is a Norman Wisdom series coming which will consist of shows lasting thirty minutes each. They will all have a story line but will be completely self-contained in themselves. You will see the shows live. Only later will they be filmed so that American viewers will have the chance to see one of Britain's favourite sons . . . Starting date for Norman's fun and frolics looks like being early in the New Year.' This confident statement probably emanated from Bernard Delfont, who had formed his own television production company to supply programmes to ITV, but, like a similar announcement made by the BBC in

1952, nothing more of the plan was heard. In fact, it would be another 25 years before Wisdom got a situation comedy series.

As it turned out, Wisdom's first significant television appearance for over one and a half years, and his first ever on the commercial channels, was in the third edition of *Sunday Night at the London Palladium* in 1955. This series, still unchallenged as British television's most celebrated and prestigious variety programme, was one of the few important productions to come out of ITV in its formative months. The commercial channels seemed dominated by American imports at the time, though these were actually restricted by a 14% quota. The first *Sunday Night at the London Palladium*, complete with the soon-to-be-obligatory 'Beat the Clock' session, was broadcast at 8pm on 25th September 1955 to an estimated audience of 387,000 with Gracie Fields and Guy Mitchell heading the bill. The series ran for 12 years, with summer breaks, ceasing as a regular broadcast in 1967, though there were intermittent attempts to bring it back. It came out under the auspices of Palladium boss Val Parnell, who was also managing director of the company which screened the series, ATV. For Wisdom's first appearance at the Palladium under television lights the host was, appropriately, his old stooge and partner Jerry Desmonde. The outing was very well received, and he was quickly back by popular demand in January 1956, again with feed Jerry Desmonde, though this time Tommy Trinder, the show's first regular host, was at the helm. However, Wisdom had by no means abandoned the BBC during this period, and he completed a number of shows in the *Saturday Comedy Hour* slot with director Ernest Maxin and old friend Eddie Leslie as stooge, taking the *Radio Times* cover for the 25th November-1st December edition.

Wisdom's next departure was into musical comedy with *Where's Charley?*, the musical version of Brandon Thomas' perennial favourite, *Charley's Aunt*. The music and lyrics are by Frank Loesser, the co-writer of *Guys And Dolls*, and the book is by the celebrated stage director George Abbott. This classic farce has Charley Wykeham, an Oxford University student, impersonating his aunt from Brazil (where the nuts come from!) in order to chaperone two eager young lovers. Complications arise when Charley falls in love with Amy Spettigue and Amy's father begins to pursue the 'Aunt'. Then, of course, the real aunt arrives . . . The title role was created on Broadway by Ray Bolger in 1948, and ran for three seasons before he filmed it in 1952. Wisdom had been slated to bring the show to London back in 1953 in a production to be presented by Henry Hall, and indeed had already recorded a couple of songs from the show, but the project fell through unexpectedly. Finally, in 1957, Wisdom opened it in Manchester, taking the show to Glasgow before its London première at the Palace theatre on 20th February 1958. Pip Hinton took the part of Amy, the wonderfully dapper Jerry Desmonde made a perfect Sir Francis Chesney, a rival for Charley's 'Aunt', and Felix Felton was Mr. Spettigue. This was Wisdom's first experience of 'legitimate' theatre, and with the exception of pantomime, where there is much more space for improvising comic business, his first sustained character acting on stage. As he said at the time: 'Of course, Charley Wykeham is an ideal part for me in every way, but you must remember that this is the first time I have acted a part in which the comedy comes chiefly from situations in which others are also intimately involved. I have never learned so many lines at one time in my life before, let alone "belonged" to a production from start to finish. It is quite another thing playing a spot, however big, in a variety bill, or going on a number of times in a revue.' (*Stage.*) He need not have worried; the show was another winner. Ray Bolger himself praised Wisdom's performance, labelling him 'the biggest Charley of them all!' The critics were enthusiastic both for Wisdom and for Loesser's fine score. 'The score is written with the wit and verve that later flowered into *Guys And Dolls* . . . the songs are airborne and the plot is secure . . . For the most part Mr. Wisdom was subtle and restrained, saucily genteel in the manner of Sid Field, and ebullient with a joyous, hand clapping zest that recalled the young Eddie Cantor. The show is well sung, brilliantly choreographed [Hanya Holm] and dashingly played.' (Kenneth Tynan.) Harold Hobson, no Norman Wisdom fan as he was the first to admit, and who had expressed mild outrage during rehearsals at the thought of Wisdom playing a university graduate, wrote: 'I was by no means alone in the madness of my delight at the meticulous timing of his jumps and falls, at his cheerful blast on the hunting horn, his engaging joy at being asked to give an encore for one of his songs and dances, and at his slick work at the tea-party with the piled-up cups and saucers. *Where's Charley?* is the best American musical since *Oklahoma!* And for once the London production, directed by William Chappell, is as good as New York's. In fact, I prefer Mr. Wisdom to Ray Bolger, who made a great success of the piece on the other side of the Atlantic. Mr. Bolger was a brilliant dancer, but he had not Mr. Wisdom's simplicity.' Caryl Brahms: 'The important thing is that the situations still hold; the tunes come sweeping out into the auditorium; and that Mr. Wisdom has forsaken all other media of entertainment to be hugely funny in our sort of way - the playgoing public's way - and thus increased his dominion . . . It takes great courage in an artist to leave catch-phrase and gag in the wings of his past successes and to come out to his audience shorn of all last resorts . . . For Norman Wisdom has for the post-war public what Bobby Howes had for the between-wars public - the heartbreaking gaiety of an orphan at play. He's perky and you want to befriend him. In addition Wisdom has some of the best comedy timing in the business. What more could Charley ask of his Aunt?' The show ran for 18 months, including a special Royal Performance in memory of Jack Buchanan who died in October 1957, and, in June 1958, an hour of excerpts was broadcast by ITV. During the run, the show was represented in the Royal Variety Performance, which, if we add the Royal Première granted to *The Square Peg*, made 1958 a right regal year for Wisdom.

Wisdom's television appearances were still limited, though he had been given the rather dubious Eamonn Andrews accolade of *This is your Life* in 1957. However, in 1959 and 1961, he made two celebrated appearances on *Sunday Night at the London Palladium*, both times doing the entire show without supporting acts, accompanied only by host Bruce Forsyth. Bruce Forsyth had been on stage since the age of 14, coming to a degree of prominence with a two-and-a-half year stint at the Windmill after the war. Stardom came when Billy Marsh brought him to the attention of Val Parnell and he was engaged as regular host for TV's *Sunday Night at the London Palladium*. Forsyth was the latest in a long line of hosts: Tommy Trinder, Dickie Henderson, Bob Monkhouse, Hughie Green and Robert Morley, and he made an immediate success of his extraordinary break. Unfortunately the strain of the weekly appearances took its toll, and between the two landmark Wisdom appearances, Forsyth took a break from the show due to ill-health, being replaced by Don Arrol. Back for the 1961 season, Forsyth alternated the spot with another newcomer, Norman Vaughan, and both were put at the top of their profession through their involvement with the show.

The first of Wisdom's solo guest spots was hailed by one critic as 'the funniest TV show ever', but sadly it seems not to have been preserved. Thankfully the second, already repeated in 1962, 1983 and 1987, is still available and may well constitute Wisdom's earliest surviving television appearance. Both these hour-long programmes were broadcast live, and the quality of the first is best gauged by the fact that though it took place over two years before the 1961 outing, a brief reference to it got a huge roar of delighted recognition from the Palladium audience. Wisdom, as always the perfectionist, insisted on a far longer rehearsal period than the usual two days, undertaking twelve 13-hour sessions with Forsyth. The resulting programme, which Wisdom devised, took full advantage of Forsyth's talents and the night, which Wisdom described as one of the most exciting highlights of his career, proved a total success.

The curtain opens on an empty stage, and then in waddles Norman Wisdom wearing an 'I'm in Charge' badge, mimicking the traditional Forsyth introduction. The conductor refuses to continue without Forsyth, so Wisdom seizes the opportunity to have a go with the baton. With the theme music replayed, in strides the unsuspecting host, gamely trying to sing to the weird accompaniment emanating from the orchestra pit. Forsyth recognises Wisdom and, outraged by his impertinence, chases him through the auditorium before a compromise is reached. Forsyth agrees to allow Wisdom to keep the smart compère's suit as long as he can complete a joke without laughing. This sketch, which has affinities with *Man of the Moment*'s photographer routine, leaves Wisdom collapsed in mirth without advancing more than a sentence into the joke - his infectious laughter taken up by the audience. A quick costume change leads into a solo act 'Me and my Imagination', with Wisdom displaying his incomparable skills as an athletic mime, becoming a tramp who dreams of attending a society ball. The music for the 'Paul Jones' is heard and Wisdom begins the fantasy. Parallels with the staff social in *Trouble in Store* occur as he finds himself dancing with a tall lady, then a fat one, though here the 'partners' are imaginary. Then Norman 'spies' the girl he loves, but their waltz is disturbed by an unsociable lout and Wisdom launches spectacularly into his immaculate shadow-boxing sketch - at one point appearing to be brutally punched headlong across the stage.

The next sequence, the highlight of this masterly show, is a silent wallpapering sketch with Forsyth as the foreman and Wisdom as the little worker, both dressed in overalls and caps. This brilliant routine demonstrates the benefits of so much rehearsal, the whole piece dependent on perfect timing. The superior foreman settles in a seat to watch his underling struggle to set up a trestle table. The poor man constantly finds himself trapped between the two planks which make up the pasting surface. Matters become even more complicated when the exasperated foreman comes over to help, leading into a beautifully choreographed lazy slapstick routine as the two men try to place the two planks in the correct position. Finally the table is constructed and they set to pasting the roll of wallpaper, but the roll stubbornly prefers to remain cylindrical rather than be stuck to the wall. At last, with Norman stretched out over the table holding the ends, the pasting is completed, and Norman strolls to the ladder in order to paper the wall. Holding the sheet in front of him, he treads on it as he mounts the steps, thus inadvertently wallpapering the ladder! With a second piece, Bruce shows how it should be done - by walking up the ladder backwards. All seems well until his underling somehow manages to get the boss stranded on his shoulders as he goes to replenish the bucket of paste. At last, the paper is brought into contact with the wall, but the bucket ends up over Norman's head showering him with glue to bring the sketch to a close. The pleasures of this routine are multiplied by the knowledge that it is executed live, its effect totally reliant on precision teamwork.

The next sketch - after a shortened and interrupted 'Beat the Clock' session - is a favourite which Wisdom retains in his cabaret act to this day. Norman enters in misfit evening dress complete with animated shirt front. He tries to sing 'While Irish Eyes are Smiling', but is interrupted when the 'phone on the grand piano starts to ring. It is for Bruce, and when he answers it, Norman tries to resume his song. Confusion reigns in typical Gump fashion when he sings louder, then softer, moves further then closer to Bruce in response to what he takes as orders, but are really just Bruce's half of the conversation on the 'phone. Realising that he is fighting a losing battle to complete his song, Norman sits at the piano and taps out a few notes, before Bruce slams the lid on his fingers. When Bruce is connected to his sweetheart and begins to smooch at the piano, Norman mischievously copies him - until his victim sits on top of the instrument. This is too high for the little man, each heroic effort to perch himself next to Bruce ends in failure as he slides delicately back off. Not to be beaten, Norman takes a run up, but this fanatical effort takes him clean over, tumbling spectacularly into the nether regions beyond. When the compère leaves, Norman perseveres with the song, but now the stagehands have had enough and come on to remove the props, dispensing Norman through a trapdoor. The climax is a welcome reprise of the Palladium section of *Follow a Star*: Norman is whisked away by the rotating stage, fights through descending curtains before being reduced to singing by the glow of his lighter when the house lights are doused. Forsyth reappears to take control and as Wisdom shuffles off pathetically, tells him that the problem is that he has no rhythm. Of course, this is the signal for Wisdom to show off his abilities on a variety of instruments. If some of the wind instruments cause problems - Wisdom is out-of-breath from the previous antics - his expertise on the clarinet is unaffected and he completes a nice duet with Forsyth playing the accordion. Following a brief drum solo from Wisdom, Forsyth tries to close the show, but the star protests that he want to sing. The audience rises to the bait and calls for 'Don't Laugh At Me' which he renders immaculately. The show ends with an extended comedy dance before they both collapse in exhaustion on to the rotating stage and are swept out of sight, the curtain falling on arguably the best-ever television variety show.

In 1960, between the two television Palladium spots, Wisdom made his fourth appearance in a Royal Variety Performance. With the show staged at the Victoria Palace, it was appropriate that Wisdom should team up with (amongst others) Diana Dors, Jimmy Edwards, Benny Hill, Frankie Howerd, Hattie Jacques and Bob Monkhouse to perform sketches 'Stolen from The Crazy Gang'. What made this, the 31st Royal Variety Performance, special was that it was the first to be televised.

Wisdom was back at the Palladium later the same year to take the record for the longest running and heaviest booked pantomime at that theatre with *Turn Again Whittington*. Wisdom again usurped the role of the principal boy, to the outrage of some purists, under the direction of Robert Nesbitt. Support came from Yana as the Alderman's Daughter, Eddie Leslie as Captain Barnacle and Billy Whittaker as the First Mate in this spectacularly set production. The previous year, 1959, had seen Wisdom destroying attendance records at the Manchester Palace with *Robinson Crusoe*, again with Billy Whittaker (Mrs. Crusoe) and Eddie Leslie (Captain Atkins) accompanied by Patricia Stark as Polly Perkins, Elizabeth Larner in the title role and Wisdom as brother Norman Crusoe. This memorable production, with occasional cast changes, went to the Bristol Hippodrome in 1961, the Birmingham Hippodrome in 1962, the Liverpool Empire in 1963 and, with Marion Grimaldi replacing Larner, to the BBC on Christmas Day 1964.

For the BBC production, Wisdom was given an unprecedented degree of freedom. He starred, wrote much of the script, supervised the editing and decided on the broadcast time. With a budget exceeding £50,000 it was one of the BBC's costliest productions up to that date and Wisdom negotiated a deal which included a cut of the overseas sales, standing to take home £15,000 to £20,000 for his efforts. The two-hour show took a fortnight to write (with Eddie Leslie and Len Lowe, based on a traditional book by Harry Bright), three weeks' rehearsal and four days to record from the stage of the Golders Green theatre. It was a traditional production, complete with a glamorous principal boy, a dame and lots of action. Wisdom set the atmosphere with an opening sequence showing people going into the theatre past a row of buskers singing 'Don't Laugh At Me'. The orchestra is seen tuning up, and Wisdom himself dashing into the dressing room. The broadcast reached a huge audience, estimated at 18.5 million, who thrilled to the gripping fights with a giant octopus and a crocodile and were suitably impressed by the spectacular storm and shipwreck staged in this glittering pantomime.

1964 also contained something now rare in Wisdom's career, a flop, with the failure of Anthony Newley and Leslie Bricusse's *The Roar of the Greasepaint - the Smell of the Crowd*. This was the same songwriting team who wrote *Stop the World - I Want to Get Off* which had triumphed in the West End and on Broadway in 1961. With *The Roar of the Greasepaint - the Smell of the Crowd* which they described as 'the story of the Game of Life, a sort of Laurel & Hardy set to music', Newley and Bricusse wanted to further some of the experiments they had made in the book of the earlier musical. The plot revolves around two characters: Sir (Willoughby Goddard), one of the 'haves'; and Cocky (Wisdom), one of the 'have-nots', and follows the various challenges to each other's position. The action is complicated by the appearance of The Girl (Dilys Watling) who gets stolen from Cocky by Sir, and The Negro (Cy Grant), who is even more downtrodden than Cocky. The score for the musical is entirely successful and characteristically jaunty, full of bouncy melodies and well-written lyrics, including

'The Joker' which Wisdom put on record with another song from the show, the plaintive 'Who Can I Turn to' often cited by the star as his favourite song written specially for him. The production, under Newley's direction, was tried out to mixed response in Nottingham, Liverpool and Manchester with the intention of bringing it to the Shaftesbury theatre in the West End. Troubles were immediately apparent with the World Première in Nottingham twice postponed, and it was soon clear that audiences were not accepting Wisdom in this unusual production - the experimental scripting which undermined identification with the characters was not found appealing. Bernard Delfont demanded changes which Newley refused, and the West End première was postponed indefinitely during the run at Liverpool's Royal Court. Soon after the beginning of the Manchester run, the West End transfer was cancelled. The lesson Wisdom learned from 'the greatest disappointment of my career' was never again to 'take complete direction, I must be allowed to put in a few ideas or, at least, talk them over with the director and try them out'. In fact, Wisdom was able to rework the show during the final playdates in Manchester with the full co-operation of the dispirited cast and at least the show finished on a higher note. Despite its failure in Britain, the musical made it to Broadway, where producer David Merrick insisted on Newley himself taking the role of Cocky - Wisdom being still relatively unknown in the States - and Cyril Ritchard was cast as Sir. Sadly the show flopped there as well despite last minute changes and came off after a short run, though happily, a cast album did result.

By now, Wisdom's dominion had extended rapidly with the worldwide success of his films which had caught on in South-East Asia, Europe, South America and Russia. In April 1965 he accompanied *A Stitch in Time* to the Argentine Film Festival at Mar del Plata and was awarded 'The Golden Flame' as the most popular visiting foreign star, before getting caught up in an earthquake while visiting Chile in a mini South American tour. Wisdom's enormous popularity in Russia resulted in offers as early as 1955 to appear on stage in Moscow, and when he visited the country during a cruising holiday in 1963 he was instantly recognised by the locals shouting for their 'Mr. Pitkin'. He was invited several times to attend the Moscow Film Festival with his films, and eventually made it in July 1965 after the organisers delayed playdates to make it possible. He found himself mobbed by fans wherever he went, his visual humour easily overcoming all language barriers in his personal appearances and television spots. *A Stitch in Time* was screened to 10,000 people at the Sports Palace after which Wisdom gave a spontaneous knockabout demonstration of his skills. As he waved in response to their applause, he caught the awesome sight of what appeared to be the entire audience moving towards him in welcome.

The only major territory remaining unconquered was the United States.

Trouble in Store had got a few playdates when released there under the Republic logo, but without success - indeed picking up a review from Bosley Crowther which made the attacks the British critics made on Wisdom's later films seem generous by comparison: 'He would be honoured to have the privilege of holding the third Ritz Brother's coat. To put him in a class with Lou Costello would be to flatter him recklessly. To mention his name with Red Skelton's would be to libel the latter . . . Perhaps his miserable showing in this picture is not all his fault . . . in a film which, by Hollywood standards, would not do credit to Poverty Row. Heaven help the British, if Mr. Wisdom is really their boy.' [! !]

But now came Wisdom's chance to show the Americans what he could really do, and from 1966 to 1970 he spent much of his time in the States, doing two Broadway shows, a major television musical and one film.

9. America.

In 1965, producers Cy Feuer and Ernest Martin were preparing a new musical, *Walking Happy*, for the Broadway stage. The musical was based on the classic British comedy, *Hobson's Choice*, by Harold Brighouse, which had opened as far back as November 1915 in New York. The play had been constantly revived on both sides of the Atlantic ever since, with a film version in 1954 which starred Charles Laughton, Brenda de Banzie and John Mills. The setting is Salford, Lancashire, in 1880 where Will Mossop, a highly skilled bootmaker, toils in the shop of Henry Hobson. Hobson, bullheaded and a crafty seeker of the good things in life, is astonished when his eldest daughter, Maggie, a spinster who runs his business, decides she is going to marry Will. Will, too, is rather taken aback by this development, but succumbs when ill-treated once too often by Hobson - not only agreeing to marry Maggie, but also to setting up his own business in direct rivalry to her father. The show finishes with Will and Maggie's wedding reception, when Hobson, stung by loss of trade, agrees to go into a business partnership with Will. Will is now happy, realising that he really is in love with his wife.

For the musical version of the play, the score was composed by Jimmy van Heusen with lyrics by Sammy Cahn; a good augury for the final result. Plans for the casting of *Walking Happy* did not go too smoothly, as Norman Wisdom related in an interview with the *New York Times* in December 1966: 'I had no idea I'd get star billing on Broadway. I'm still not known in America, I think they creep my films over here and don't tell anybody. This was originally supposed to be Mary Martin's show, but she chose *I Do! I Do!* Then they had a hard time finding the right man. I played *Where's Charley?* for 18 months in London for Cy Feuer, so he asked me if I'd come over and meet Sammy Cahn and Jimmy van Heusen. So I came last March and did a few songs, but I still didn't know I had the part until a week before rehearsals started. I learned the script on the ship and had a bit of rest and still arrived two days earlier than necessary.'

The show started its tryout at the Shubert theatre, Philadelphia, on 4th October 1966 to a fairly lukewarm response. Wisdom's own performance as Will Mossop underwent some changes before moving on to the Fisher theatre, Detroit, as its pre-Broadway run continued. 'They cut my big one-man band number where I played a scrub board and cymbals between my knees, but they put in my big dance number, so now I'm a dancer for the first time.' (*New York Times*.) In Detroit, the first enthusiastic reviews were recorded, and *Walking Happy* moved more confidently to its Broadway première at the Lunt-Fontanne theatre on 26th November. Even so, it is unlikely that the cast were really expecting the raves which were about to come their way. 'We opened on a Saturday, so we had to wait until Monday to find out what the critics said. The next day, a Sunday, we recorded the album for Capitol and in the middle of the recording session Sammy Cahn came into the studio and read an advance copy of Mr. Walter Kerr's review aloud and everyone applauded. I was among people I didn't know as well as I do in London, and I was embarrassed. I didn't realise what had happened till the violinists began tapping their fiddles with their bows. It was one of the best moments in my life.' (*New York Times*.)

New York Times, 28th November, Walter Kerr: '*Walking Happy* is an easygoing, unpretentious, minor-league musical that is neatly put together. Its principal asset, however, is a chap who knows how to take himself apart. That's really what he seems to be doing as the new show glides toward its final curtain. The clown's name is Norman Wisdom, he comes from the British music halls, and he's supposed to be undressing himself as the orchestra begins to whisper the finale. But that's not how it looks. As he slips out of his jacket, he seems to have shrugged off his shoulders. When he pops loose his collar he tends to loose support for his head. And when his shiny white cuffs come off, to be placed like napkin rings on a table, his wrists vanish too. He could be packaged for the night, stored on a shelf, and reassembled in the morning if anyone wished. He is a jack-in-a-box absolute, a forlorn Punch on a spring, and when an overloaded barrow he's tugging through Lancashire streets suddenly tilts backwards and lifts him high in the air - turning him into a dervish clinging to the handlebars for dear life - you're not the least bit surprised. It is his fate to be caught by the scruff of the neck and shaken out regularly, like a well-used duster, and each time he's pounced upon our pleasure grows greater ... Choreographer Danny Daniels has had the good sense to notice, and make use of, Mr. Wisdom's angular, knockabout, rag-doll shape. If the performer's knees knock together, for instance, all the rest of him does, too, leaving his elbows suspended in a most mysterious void, and an image of that sort can be parlayed - come dance-time - into broken-necked struts, stiff-legged leaps, and a seven-league stride that George Cohen might have envied. Actually, Mr. Wisdom looks rather more like Fred Astaire crossed with Stan Laurel - perhaps with a few shreds of Jimmy Savo thrown in - but he is, it must be said, his own man, a zany original with ruffled hair, rueful eyes and an altogether irresistible appeal ... there are ballads, both wistful and cheery, to tell us what two nonlovers are thinking of now. Mr. Wisdom and Miss Troy [Maggie] sing 'I Don't Think I'm in Love' most engagingly, and the former confides to a cobbler-friend, George Dilworth, that 'It Might as Well be Her' with a splendidly wry resignation. Mr. Cahn's lyrics are generally prosaic

. . . but the score doesn't press; and its easy sociability will do. All in all? A light, slight, attenuated but occasionally charming pastime, given its one genuine flash of distinction by Mr. Wisdom's gift for being indelibly present no matter what he is doing - leaning cross-legged against the proscenium, catching his foot in a cantankerous stool, stealing backward in a crouch from the striped night shirt he is expected to wear once he's married. He is a Harlequin come to life among the British lower classes, and it was nice getting to know him on Saturday night.'

Though several critics expressed reservations about the production, there were none about Wisdom. John Chapman in the *Daily News*: '. . . now that Wisdom has been brought over from England we should adopt him and never let him go . . . In Wisdom, we have found an entertainer of many accomplishments. He is a superb dancer, an extraordinary pantomimist, a most ingratiating comedian and a splendid singer. They hardly make entertainers like him anymore.' Norman Nadel in the *World Journal Tribune*: 'The one joy of *Walking Happy* is . . . Norman Wisdom. Wisdom is a superb comedian, and so fine an actor that his comedy seems ingrained in the man he portrays, rather than merely superimposed. His walk is eloquent of his gentle little man. With his suitcoat peaked out in the back, he looks like a timid bantam; he sits on a chair as if he expected to be electrocuted.' Radio reviewer Ted Hoffman said: 'It's Norman Wisdom I'm applauding. He's a cross between Stan Laurel and Marcel Marceau, a marvellously charming anthology of the best of British music hall, so let's be grateful for him.'

With reviews so important to the survival of a Broadway show, *Walking Happy* was off to a flying start, and it launched into a very successful run of 161 performances, closing 16th April 1967 to go on a tour reaching Michigan and Los Angeles. Wisdom received a couple of awards for his performance, but missed out to Robert Preston in *I Do! I Do!* as Best Actor in a Musical in the 1967 Tony Awards. The show received six nominations in all: Composer and Lyricist (Sammy Cahn and Jimmy van Heusen), Supporting Actor in a Musical (Gordon Dilworth), Choreography (Danny Daniels), Actress in a Musical (Louise Troy), Best Musical as well as that for Wisdom; but the year was dominated by *Cabaret*, and *Walking Happy* failed to pick up a trophy.

One evening during the run of *Walking Happy*, Wisdom was accosted by an unknown gentleman who was trying to interest him in some project. Wisdom was used to this kind of attention and was not taking him too seriously until the man revealed he was Richard Rodgers. Realising this was the legendary composer, famous for his collaborations with lyricist Lorenz Hart (*On Your Toes, Pal Joey*), and with Oscar Hammerstein (*Oklahoma!, South Pacific, The King and I, The Sound of Music*), Wisdom listened to him more intently. It turned out that Rodgers was suggesting that he take the part of Androcles in a television musical version of George Bernard Shaw's *Androcles and the Lion* which Rodgers had been working on since late 1966. Wisdom enthusiastically accepted the part, especially on hearing that the Roman Emperor was to be played by the legendary Noël Coward. The plot, a satirical reworking of an old Roman legend, has Androcles, a slave, remove a thorn from a lion's paw. Many years later, as a Christian, he is thrown into the arena with ravenous lions. To the chagrin of the watching Caesar, the lion is the very one relieved of its pain many years before and the slave emerges unscathed. For the musical, the script was prepared by Peter Stone, writer of such films as *Charade, Father Goose* and *Mirage*. It was at this stage that some insoluble problems emerged. Stone had to confer with the Shaw estate, who controlled the rights to the original play, and had the duty to ensure that the 'original work has been treated faithfully'.

'It goes like this,' explained Stone to the *New York Times*. 'You submit your finished manuscript to the estate committee. They send it back with every change crossed out - that's standard operating procedure - so you're right back where you began. Then you prepare a detailed argument for each change . . . then the horsetrading starts. In this case, we were lucky. About 300 of the 400 changes were granted us in the first hearing; many more than Alan Lerner got on *My Fair Lady*. Of course 18 or 20 disallowed ones were important.' Richard Rodgers, for only the second time - after *No Strings* - supplied his own lyrics, and was able to incorporate some of Stone's wishes into the introductions to the songs, which did not need approval, and the completed work was ready to go into rehearsal by late 1967. An impressive Anglo-American cast was assembled with leads Wisdom and Coward joined by Ed Ames, Brian Bedford, John Cullum, Patricia Routledge and Inga Swenson. Tony award-winning choreographer Joe Layton was slated to direct for NBC. Layton, who had directed *No Strings* for Rodgers, was best known to the public as the man responsible for staging the Barbra Streisand specials. The show was taped at NBC's Brooklyn studio over five days, under some pressure on the last day as they headed towards the midnight deadline of a technicians' strike, pulling through with 25 minutes to spare.

Wisdom recalls two amusing moments during shooting. At one point, when Noël Coward was about to give his big speech to the amassed throngs at the arena, he paused for a moment and said: 'Ladies and Gentlemen, the Master has forgotten his lines!' much to the amusement of the cast and crew - a wonderful out-take if anyone could find it. The other incident marked the moment when Coward and Wisdom became friends. To the consternation of the crew, Coward kept on walking away from his mark in one scene with Wisdom. In desperation Wisdom surreptitiously grabbed the back of Coward's costume and held on tight. Coward completed the scene and turned round to demand what Wisdom thought he was doing, only then realising that the restraint had kept him in position! Coward even suggested that they work together again, but any such plans were dashed by Coward's death soon after.

Androcles and the Lion was broadcast on 15th November 1967 in a blaze of publicity. Sadly it proved an anticlimax, though Wisdom and Coward escaped the critical flack. The *Variety* review was typical: '. . . a disappointing televersion of the Shaw play, abridged to accommodate songs as well as commercials, and insufficient in either music or conception to make it really work. There were some entertaining bits, to be sure, but their presence couldn't offset the general lack of presence of the Shavian spirit . . . Joe Layton's studio-bound staging appeared constricted and boxed in . . . The two male leads were the brightest assets. Noël Coward played Caesar with the blithest possible spirit . . . Norman Wisdom was a perfect choice for Androcles. His Stan Laurelesque movements, limpid eyes and timid mien were just right for the Clark Kentish tailor.' The *New York Post* found Wisdom 'endearingly gentle and funny', and the *New York Times* regretted that 'his gift for poignancy was not accorded fuller leeway'.

Wisdom's American period continued strongly when he was signed for a role in *The Night they Raided Minsky's*. He played Chick Williams, the 'top banana' at Minsky's burlesque where he is teamed with straightman Raymond Paine, played by Jason Robards. The film is a highly fanciful version of the birth of striptease at this famous New York Lower East Side theatre. The strong cast also included Bert Lahr, Forrest Tucker, Denholm Elliott, Elliott Gould, Joseph Wiseman, Harry Andrews and Britt Ekland. Producer and co-scriptwriter Norman Lear gave the job of direction to William Friedkin, only his second film after the Sonny & Cher vehicle *Good Times*, but a man with extensive experience in television and who would go on to make *The French Connection* in 1971. The score was by the writers of *Bye Bye Birdie*, Charles Strouse and Lee Adams, and the choreography was by *Walking Happy*'s Danny Daniels.

The film covers the last day of operation of the Minsky burlesque before being closed down by the Vice Squad. Rachel Schpitendavel (Britt Ekland), the daughter of a fundamentalist family from Pennsylvania, arrives in town yearning to become a dancer. Innocent of the goings-on in burlesque, she wants to perform her dances based on stories from the Bible on Minsky's stage. Minsky's is run by Bill Minsky (Gould), whose father Louis (Wiseman) is unhappy about the attentions being paid to the show by Vance Fowler (Elliott), head of the Society for the Suppression of Vice. Raymond Paine, the straightman of the show's popular comedy duo, comes up with an idea to get Fowler off their backs. He persuades Bill to put Rachel on stage to do her Bible dances, but to advertise her as the notorious French dancer Madame Fifi 'who drove 50 million Frenchmen wild' and thus provoke a raid which would humiliate Fowler. All seems to be going well, but Chick, who has fallen in love with Rachel, is unhappy about the attentions being paid to her by the more cynical Raymond. Rachel is also being pursued by local racketeer Trim Houlihan (Tucker) and her stern father (Andrews) who has come to rescue her from the sinful flesh-pots. By the time of the heavily publicised midnight performance of 'Madame Fifi', everyone, including a crowd of cops, has gathered at the theatre. The music strikes up and Rachel creeps dazedly on to the stage to be greeted by the large catcalling crowd. Instead of the Bible routine, she satisfies her audience by innocently executing a couple of 'bumps' and 'grinds' copied form the chorus girls she had watched earlier. Her outraged father tries to pull her off the stage, but only succeeds in tearing her dress, and Rachel resolutely continues the act, slipping her dress-straps off her shoulders. Then she notices that Raymond is leaving, realising he really cares for her, and in her effort to gesticulate at him to stay, lets her dress fall, to expose her breasts and thus give birth to striptease. The raid takes place and everyone is arrested except the ageing relic of true burlesque and Chick's predecessor as 'top banana', Professor Spats (Lahr), who despondently strolls across the stage knowing that what has just happened spells the end of burlesque as he knew it.

Friedkin's main achievement in the film is to recreate convincingly, if nostalgically, the atmosphere of the run-down burlesque show. The subject is well-suited to his rather flashy style, with its inserts of scenes of Lower East Side street life, changing from black & white to colour to help match authentic footage. His rapid cutting suits the presentation of excerpts from burlesque routines which are snappily staged by Danny Daniels. Wisdom is splendid throughout, managing to project the part of Chick Williams as a complete character, not just using it as a vehicle to show off his talents as a music hall entertainer to a new and receptive American audience. Wisdom has three major sequences in the film. The first has Raymond and Chick perform a song, 'Perfect Gentleman'. This comes just after Raymond has deduced from Chick's behaviour that he has fallen in love, informing his partner that he will have no success with women unless he acts like a bastard - Chick's sincerity will be his downfall. Raymond strides confidently on stage and calls for his partner. Chick, wearing the remains of a dress suit, shins his way down a rope which hangs from the theatre roof. Raymond launches into the song, in which he describes Chick - 'From Head to Toe You're a Gentleman' - telling him that things do not match up to his requirements as a member of the privileged classes. The payoff comes when one of the chorus girls bounces past and invites Chick to go with her. Raymond restrains him, hands him his cane, and flamboyantly kisses the girl and then declares that she is not good enough for Chick. Another woman wriggles past, stands on a spot and 'jiggles'. Raymond entices Chick to go up to her and grab one of her vibrating bosoms. Chick resists the temptation, only to take a quick grope once she has steadied herself, and in good burlesque fashion she knocks Chick spinning across the stage for his pleasure. Then Chick goes into a solo rendering of 'Perfect Gentleman', displaying immaculate comic dance steps and a precision routine which Wisdom executes effortlessly. The non-vaudevillian, Jason Robards, sensibly remains in the background, but, fine actor that he is, comes in to complete the dance before chasing Chick off stage.

The second sequence comes when Chick watches Rachel's dance, which is an embarrassment even given the purpose (unbeknown to her) to which it is being put. Chick decides to demonstrate what burlesque is all about, improvising with whatever props are scattered around the otherwise deserted stage. The scene, which is both touching and funny, gives Wisdom the chance to demonstrate the basics of knockabout slapstick with all his expected expertise, including a glorious fall down a flight of stairs. Interestingly enough, when they came to shoot this sequence, Wisdom was horrified to discover that a stuntman had been hired to take the plunge. It took some time for Wisdom to persuade the director that he was perfectly capable of executing the fall himself. Once he succeeded, Friedkin's main concern was to make the authenticity apparent to the viewer, so Wisdom casually asked the director and cameraman (Andrew Laszlo) on what step would they like him facing the camera on his way down!

The third sequence comes just after Chick has discovered that not only does the lecherous Raymond have designs on Rachel, but that he has got her ensconced in his hotel room. Rushing to save her from a fate worse than death, Chick knocks on the door pretending to be a messenger, arriving just as Raymond is manoeuvring the now willing Rachel towards his put-down bed. When Raymond opens the door, Chick drenches him, and his passions, with a fire hose. Raymond gets his revenge on stage. Coming to the theatre late after drying off, Raymond spots Chick already in front of the audience trying to do the drunk act on his own. The opening of the sketch has previously been acted out in the film, and has Raymond coming on and telling the drunken Chick to keep away from 'the Devil's brew'. Now, Chick is valiantly extending the opening drunk skit, struggling before an increasingly restless audience. On rushes the furious Raymond intent on executing his revenge, brutally hurtling Chick all over the stage in a savage mockery of the sketch. Wisdom has to convince the film viewer that these falls are not part of burlesque pretence, but are really hurting the character, whilst maintaining the illusion that the theatre audience would still take it all as part of the act - a difficult piece of double play which he brings off smartly.

The film, 'an absolutely brilliant re-creation of classic burlesque' (*The Times*), was a great personal success for Wisdom, picking up plaudits from the British as well as the American press. 'So easily does Wisdom dominate his many scenes, other cast members suffer by comparison' (*Variety*). 'Wisdom recalls Keaton in his split-second spills and deadpan pantomime' (*Time*). 'His pratfalls and expert knockabout pantomime, as the fall guy, is an absolute delight' (*Daily Sketch*). Though much of the British press was predictably patronising: 'Even Wisdom is a pleasant surprise (he really is a first-class music hall artist)' (*Guardian*). 'I am happy to say that Norman Wisdom, for once, gives a performance as [Robard's] fall-about colleague that is quite tolerable' (*Daily Express*). Informed sources consider that Wisdom's performance might well have won him the Supporting Actor Oscar had it not been for a sad event which disrupted the production. The great Bert Lahr, still best remembered as the Cowardly Lion in *The Wizard of Oz* and a genuine veteran of burlesque, died, aged 72, during the making of the film. One of the themes was to have been the Lahr character's handing on of the traditions of burlesque to his young success as 'top banana' played by Wisdom, thus making the entire piece more poignant. Crucial scenes had them working together, a few of which were actually shot and would have provided some of the film's highlights, but could not be incorporated into the final cut. Sadly, Lahr's role was finally reduced to little more than the opening and closing of the film.

Wisdom's last major American appearance was the least successful, the Ray Cooney/John Chapman farce *Not Now, Darling*, but Wisdom's own standing was unaffected. As the American poster for the play stated, the farce had been a worldwide smash hit, already earning its authors £250,000. Leslie Phillips starred as Mr. Bodley in the hugely successful 19-month London run as well as reprising the part in the subsequent film version. *Not Now, Darling* is a quick moving farce set in a high class London furriers called Bodley, Bodley and Crouch. The two Bodleys, husband and wife, were played by Rex Garner and Me'l Dowd in the American production, and Wisdom is the third partner, Arnold Crouch. The complicated plot basically consists of the male Bodley getting into trouble over a proposed gift of a mink coat to his mistress via the surreptitious route of allowing her husband to purchase it at a vast discount. But the husband recognises a bargain when it comes his way and decides he would prefer to give the coat to his secretary. Arnold Crouch then gets involved in helping his partner out, as complication piles upon complication. It is the kind of farce which goes down well in London, but even Ray Cooney, who went with Wisdom to direct the latest version (and would later take the part of

Arnold in the film), had little confidence in its survival in America. On leaving Britain, Wisdom expressed the odds as being 10 to 1 against success, and Cooney thought that even this was optimistic: 'American theatregoers are notoriously indifferent to English farce and this one is not being adapted in any way. Which means references to No. 9 buses and places in Chelsea are staying in the script. Norman and I both know that the show will either be on-and-off in five or six performances, or else enjoy a long run.' (Evening News.)

The out-of-town tryout was at the Fisher theatre, Detroit, where it opened on 16th September to a very mixed critical response. 'Touted as an hilarious British romp, the comedy consists of every cliché imaginable, jokes that are old, mistaken identities and a great deal of slapstick.' (Pontiac Press.) Even those who liked the fare were pessimistic about its chances of survival under the harsh lights of Broadway. But Wisdom himself picked up an excellent press: 'A chance to see our fabulous Wisdom again in America. Wisdom's movies, especially Trouble in Store, which is as good as anything the Marx Brothers ever did, never caught on over here and his only legitimate appearance has been in Walking Happy . . . His role in the American film The Night they Raided Minsky's was his first real introduction to Americans. He calls upon all his comic resources (and they are many) to make Not Now, Darling what is termed in the trade, a "Laff Riot" . . . Norman Wisdom is a continuous joy.' (Dearborn Press.) 'Wisdom stumbles, he jerks, he prances and he takes pratfalls. His timing is excellent and the audience loves him.' (Pontiac Press.)

The criticisms that the production as well as the humour was too English led Cooney to relinquish the director's chair for the preparation for the scheduled opening at the Brooks Atkinson theatre in New York. Chosen was the 80-year-old George Abbott, the writer of the book for Where's Charley? and a revered veteran of 113 previous Broadway shows. The pace was tightened for its 29th October opening, but though the audiences seemed to be loving it - and the reviewers admit as much - the notices proclaimed a blind spot for this type of farce and damned it. 'Not Now Darling is listed as "a romp" and some of the opening night spectators seemed to believe it. They laughed and applauded, while I sat numbly by.' (Newsday.) The New York Times's crucially influential Clive Barnes stated the case plainly: 'Not Now, Darling is a sex farce. I freely admit that a lot of people - many of them smarter than myself - get a great deal of pleasure out of this kind of play. So please read between my lines and remember that I despise this particular form of theatre. I would prefer to watch I Love Lucy on television - and there are few activities of which I could say as little . . . Mr. Abbott points Mr. Wisdom at the audience as if he were a shy and reluctant howitzer, and fires. In my case he missed, but I did feel the wind as the missiles passed my mind.' The unenthusiastic reviews killed off any hopes of a good run, but for the most part Wisdom was well-liked. 'Comic acting unrivalled since the late Bert Lahr' (*Evening News*); 'A masterful little comic, if you are breathing you will laugh' (*United Press*); 'Wisdom is the greatest comic artist you have seen in years' (*New York Post*); 'If there's anyone for hilarious, no-questions-asked farce with a devastatingly battered and triumphant comic genius, Norman Wisdom is your meat' (Radio WINS); 'He is the funniest man of his type since, maybe, the days of Mack Sennett' (*Daily News*). *Not Now, Darling* closed on 15th November 1970 after just 21 performances.

10. Career to date: mainly television.

Norman Wisdom spent most of the years 1966 to 1968 in America, his most public return visit being to perform in a special Royal Variety fund-raising show before the Queen on behalf of the British team competing in the Olympic Games. However, he finally came back, resisting the temptation of taking up residence in the States, to settle once more into the luxurious farmhouse which had been the Wisdom country home since 1957. Known as Laker's Farm, it was situated in Chiltington in Sussex, dated back to 1492, and was reputedly once the home of Anne of Cleves. The house was now complete with all modern gadgetry, and was set in beautifully land-scaped gardens which included a paddock, tennis court, a pavilion and two cottages. Another of Wisdom's passions, his cars, fitted neatly into the five-car garage, and he had improved the property over the years by installing a swimming-pool. Like every self-respecting house of its age, it had a ghost: 'Very friendly one, though I've never seen it . . . I don't know who the ghost is, but it's supposed to have this very sweet and peculiar aroma about it' (*Picturegoer*).

Everything seemed well with the family. While Wisdom was in America, his son had gained entry to Charterhouse and his daughter was attending the Royal Naval College for Girls. Their financial security was already assured by the late 'fifties, and a series of lucrative investments had provided extra insurance. Wisdom co-owned a brickworks and a transport company in Coventry and had become a director of his local football club, Brighton & Hove Albion, then in the fourth division, for whom he had recorded a club battle-chant to the obligatory tune of 'Sussex by the Sea'. His biggest investment was his Spanish-built yacht *Conquest* which he had purchased for £80,000 in 1963 and had left at Shoreham for extensive fitting-out to the highest modern standards. After three years of work refitting, repainting, trials and tests, and incorporating luxurious extras, the value of the 92' yacht had rocketed to over a quarter-of-a-million pounds before being made available for hire at around £6,000 a month.

For a London 'office' Wisdom maintained a three-bedroom flat in Kensington which he had turned into an elegant semblance of a Spanish town house with the help of a Pinewood studio craftsman. The interior was fitted with furniture, paintings and knick-knacks that he had gathered on his trips to Spain to give it a relaxing atmosphere. On the whole Wisdom's business ventures proved successful, though his entry into the brick-building concern was ill-timed and was sold off with the linked transport operation in 1972: 'The trouble was that though my partner knew about bricks, we were in the business at the wrong time: the only people who seemed to want bricks were agitators - for throwing at Embassies!' One of his financial transactions hit the headlines when he went to court to appeal against the Inland Revenue's claim of tax on £48,000 profit he made in a silver bullion deal. The claim that the silver was bought as a security against a drop in the pound's value and not as an adventure in trade was upheld in the Chancery Division but was overturned by the High Court in a celebrated case.

However, if Wisdom could take such minor financial setbacks in his stride ('I'd rather lose a few quid than tell a flat joke'), more serious news reached the outside world of upheavals in the family home when Norman Wisdom petitioned his wife for divorce in an uncontested case. The decree nisi came through in 1969, ending 22 years of marriage. In 1973 he reflected on this moment when asked by TV Times why he had no intention of marrying again: 'I cannot say anything about that, because it might seem to reflect on my ex-wife, and I don't mean it that way. I have custody of my two children . . . there must be pain, you can't live with anyone for many years and not think there is something wrong with yourself if it finally breaks up. But the danger is to start placing the blame. When you do that, you continue to hurt others. I have tried to learn my own lessons from that experience without taking sides. Anything like a broken marriage means that you reassess yourself. But it's a private matter, isn't it?'

Partly as a response to this difficult period for all the family, Wisdom threw himself into work, touring his cabaret act throughout the country. His partner at this time was Tony Fayne, a highly successful association which continues to this day. Fayne first came to the public's attention when, in partnership with fellow Bristol-born David Evans, he made his professional debut as an impressionist at the Bristol Empire in 1940, undertaking London dates the following year. The pair re-teamed after the war in 1949 in an act which specialised in sporting impressions and songs. They rose to prominence with appearances on radio's Starlight Hour and Variety Bandbox, and were on the bill of the Royal Variety Show in 1951. They supported another of the stars of that Royal Variety Show, Jimmy Edwards, in the revue Take It From Us, before capping a fine year by supporting Judy Garland for her British debut at the London Palladium. Fayne first appeared with Wisdom when, still in partnership with Evans, he was brought in as a speciality act for the transfer of The London Palladium Show to the Prince of Wales theatre in late 1954. Tony Fayne went solo in 1959, made a number of now sought-after comedy records and toured extensively. For three years he was a regular partner for the late Arthur Haynes.

Wisdom's cabaret act was not only sensationally successful, it proved to be a highly lucrative undertaking. This was the peak period for the clubs and earnings could be phenomenal - Morecambe & Wise used to refer to their club appearances as bank-raids. In the 'seventies, Wisdom made numerous cabaret appearances, played regular summer seasons and pantomimes, and toured extensively overseas: Iran, Canada, New Zealand, Tasmania, Rhodesia, Hong Kong, Malaysia and Australia included. However, the most important development in his career for the decade was a new commitment to television.

The first indication that Wisdom was turning emphatically to television was with his guest appearances in the ATV series *Music Hall* which started broadcasts in September 1969. Obviously intended as much for the American market as the British, *Music Hall* was hosted by Tony Sandler and Ralph Young, and Wisdom was a regular guest along with British-born, 'sock-it-to-me' star of *Rowan and Martin's Laugh-In*, Judy Carne. 'Music *Hall* offers Norman Wisdom more opportunity than ever before to exercise his many talents, whether it be dancing, singing, acting or merely making people laugh. The show is virtually taken over by his antics. And during this new series he will be making several return visits - a unique chance to see him in action. He plays several of his best character parts - his disguise often hiding his real self but revealing the true facets of his ability as an actor.' (*TV Times.*) The writers of the series were Sid Green and Dick Hills, best known for their scripts for Morecambe & Wise. No expense seemed to have been spared in the provision of top-flight guests: in the episodes featuring Wisdom in this series and its follow-up in 1970 there were such luminaries as Ella Fitzgerald, Lena Horne and Sid Caesar, the last of whom appeared regularly in the second series.

Between the two seasons of *Music Hall*, Wisdom starred in his first situation comedy, *Norman*, a series of six half-hour episodes made for ATV. 'The part I'm playing is based on my film characters. He's a music loving civil servant, an Inland Revenue man who can't stand taking people's money.' (*TV Times.*) The scripts were written by the authors of *Not Now, Darling*, Ray Cooney and John Chapman. Wisdom plays Norman Wilkins, a civil servant who yearns to be a freelance musician. The principal support was from Sally Bazely, the wife from *What's Good for the Goose*, and David Lodge, a prolific stage and film actor who had been in several of Wisdom's films. *Stage* said of the first episode: '. . . the new Norman is certainly a lot quieter, more subtle, and much less concerned with the belly-laugh . . . In fact, the script . . . was thoughtful and entertaining, and makes much more use of fantasy than one is accustomed to in this kind of programme.

This combined with the talents of Norman Wisdom, resulted in a strange mixture of comedy fantasy a la *Q* or *Monty Python*, and slapstick knockabout of the kind normally associated with Norman Wisdom films.' Wisdom was clearly trying to break the tenacious hold that his Gump character still maintained over the British public, but the series was only a partial success. It allowed Wisdom a lot of room for bits of business, but the pacing of the episodes was not right. Wisdom's residual popularity, nonetheless, kept the series high in the ratings.

Between *Norman* and his next series for ATV, *Nobody is Norman Wisdom* in 1973, Wisdom's television appearances were few and far between. It was a critical period for Wisdom with the failure of *What's Good for the Goose*, the Broadway flop of *Not Now, Darling*, and his prolonged absence from the film studios. Most of the time was spent touring abroad, though he did his four spots on *Music Hall* and guested regularly on *Stars on Sunday*, often in the same line-up as James Mason. *Nobody is Norman Wisdom* differed from most situation comedies of the time, and indeed from *Norman*, by dispensing entirely with canned laughter and with a studio audience, with Wisdom declaring he wanted the content of the show to do the work. It was a decision he later regretted: 'I'm beginning to wonder whether hearing others laugh does have an effect on viewers, even if it's only subconscious. Laughter is very catching after all.' (*Sun.*) In *Nobody is Norman Wisdom*, Wisdom plays an ineffectual little man who is completely under the thumb of his domineering mother (Nathalie Kent). Norman is in love with a woman called Grace (Priscilla Morgan), and deals with life's problems by flitting in and out of a fantasy world. 'The idea behind the series is a pleasing fairytale notion. Instead of a magic cloak, Norman needs the dress or a uniform of a profession to give him confidence and power. Dressed as a barrister, and assisted by the loyal and attractive Priscilla Morgan, he was able to conduct the successful defence of an elderly war hero accused of theft.' (*Daily Telegraph*.)

It was a fine idea for a Wisdom comedy series from the show's principal writer Watt Nicol, with Wisdom perfectly cast in the Walter Mittyish role. Sadly the show was let down by unimaginative direction and a general sentimentality which was not balanced by enough solid laughs, displeasing some of Wisdom's fans with its more sophisticated humour. The viewing figures dropped drastically after the first episode registered at No. 4 in the ratings. 'One of the reasons for Mr. Wisdom's low key approach may have been his wish to escape from the slapstick image. But a major factor for the failure of the programme to register was undoubtedly technical. Had it been produced as a film, with more scope for camera and editing technique, plus a judicious contribution from the special effects department the result would have been far more rewarding. The inclusion of a little 16mm filmed footage here and there is simply not a good enough substitute. Indeed the filmed inserts were so obviously filmed inserts that they detracted from the credibility of the piece . . . Had the production been fully geared to the cinema, Mr. Wisdom would have made a greater impact,' wrote James Towler in a perceptive review. Ironically, as the viewing figures dropped, so the show improved. One of the problems was the amount of time taken to establish the central character, but the later episodes were funny and affecting, giving full reign to Wisdom's brand of pathos. Indeed, *Variety* wrote of the final episode: 'This farce is fun - replete with traditional English slapstick staples . . . and moves along happily. Keyed to the well-known underdog personality of its star . . . everything is in broad sendup and thoroughly predictable but is sure to generate enough goodly helpings of chuckles. Show is lavishly mounted, well produced and cannily directed to lift it out of the potboiler mould.'

The same month that *Nobody is Norman Wisdom* was being screened, proof, if it were needed, of Wisdom's worldwide fame occurred when he was invited to present his hour-long comedy and musical act in Peking and other major cities in China. The invitation came at a time of cultural exchanges which had involved the London Philharmonic Orchestra and the People's Acrobat Company of Shanghai. It was due to these very acrobats informing Embassy officials of Wisdom's popularity in China that the invitation was eventually proffered. Had Wisdom performed there he would have been the first Western popular entertainer to have done so under Chairman Mao. Sadly, though Wisdom accepted the invitation and was prepared to make any necessary dates, the offer fell through in the lengthy diplomatic discussions which followed. Similar problems beset yet another approach from the Russians for a stage tour there, after a revival of *Man of the Moment* attracted huge audiences at a Moscow festival screening.

In October 1974, work began on another Wisdom house, to be built nearby to Laker's Farm. Wisdom's love of all things Spanish was taken to an extreme, with the house built to his own hacienda-style design, based on photographs he had taken of houses in Spain and France. To make the idea into a reality, Wisdom had to scour the country for almost a year to find a firm of specialised builders who could undertake the expert stone and wood work required. By mid-1976 it was completed, the culmination of a ten-year dream. His children moved in with him. Nicholas, who had been signed straight from school to play for the Sussex County Cricket Club Second XI, was now learning the sports retail trade, and Jackie, who had had a spell at drama school, was working as an air hostess.

Wisdom's next television series was *A Little Bit of Wisdom*, which ran in slightly different formats for three successive seasons on ATV. In these he reverted to a more familiar knockabout character, getting himself out of trouble in each of the episodes to excellent viewing figures. If again the show was undercut by variable direction, it offered Wisdom some imaginative routines with generally good scripts. His character, as ever called Norman, encounters various situations in the first series which had no connecting storyline through its seven episodes, the separate 'one-act comedies' penned by an assortment of top television writers. Roughly the same format was used for the second series, mainly scripted by Lew Schwarz and Jon Watkins. The third season did offer a consistent format with a connecting narrative. Norman works as a clerk in a builder's office and lives in a flat which he shares with the more extrovert and brawny Alec (Neil McCarthy). At work, Norman spends much of his time being pursued by the boss' daughter, Linda, played by Frances White from *Press for Time*, with unpredictable mayhem resulting.

By 1976, the year of the last series of *A Little Bit of Wisdom*, Wisdom also completed a one-off slot for the BBC, which he did on the understanding that it would lead to a series - the latter, however, never materialised. The show was made specially for the Knokke television festival, where it competed for the award for Best Comedy. To satisfy the rules of the competition, each of the nine competing European networks had three days to rehearse and produce a half-hour show. Wisdom's special - simply entitled *The Norman Wisdom Show* - was directed by Alan Boyd for ace television producer John Ammonds. The result was basically an adaptation of Wisdom's cabaret act, and is complete with feed Tony Fayne and guest Rod Hull with Emu. Wisdom and company taped the show in front of an invited international audience in July and it was submitted to the jury the following weekend, taking the first prize known as the Golden Seaswallow.

The show opens with the title *The Tony Fayne Show* and we glimpse Wisdom in the audience dressed in his Gump suit. Fayne walks on and starts to perform 'Singing in the Rain', until Norman joins in from the stalls, encouraging the audience to do likewise. Fayne is annoyed by this unwanted interruption, but his challenge to Norman to do better is accepted! The show then reprises many of Wisdom's familiar routines. He tries to sing but cannot find the correct pitch with the orchestra. He does a solo on the post-horn interspersed with a few gags with members of the orchestra before Fayne reappears. Fayne's constant attempts to throw Norman off the stage are rebutted by the audience who sympathise with the Gump. Fayne makes a very stern, almost violent straightman, flinging Wisdom about mercilessly, and seems genuinely unamused by the little man's antics. Audience sympathy for Norman is accordingly intensified by their antagonism towards someone who could treat the little man so cruelly. Fayne then settles down to sing, graciously allowing Norman to accompany him in a performance of 'Yellow Ribbon' while they sit next to each other in modern leather-bound chairs. But the little man's microphone is sucked into the stage, and when he manages to commandeer a change of places, his seat begins to lower and then rise. Fayne, unaware of Norman's misfortunes, completes the song leaving Norman perched in the air on his high-rise seat.

The next routine, with Rod Hull and his Emu attacking Norman, leads into the straight part of the act, with Wisdom's beautiful rendition of 'What Kind of Fool am I?', followed by a display of his skills on the clarinet and drums and a splendid piece of mock ice skating. Next is the masochistic 'A Lesson in Rhythm', a sketch which Wisdom had performed as long ago as the 1954 *London Palladium Show*. Tony Fayne tries to teach Norman the basics of rhythm with a contraption which bonks him on the head when he has to beat a bass drum, biffs him with a boxing glove on a stick when he has to stop, and pokes spikes in his backside through a hole in the seat when he must crash the cymbal. Norman passes the lesson, but not before being beaten senseless by this cruel instrument manipulated by the sadistically meticulous Fayne. Lastly, Fayne walks off in a huff, complaining that all he wanted to do was perform 'Singing in the Rain' leaving Norman alone to sing the lovely 'Who Can I Turn To' from *The Roar of the Greasepaint - the Smell of the Crowd*. The show comes to an end with Norman stretchered-off through the audience after another fight with Emu.

Despite its success at the Knokke festival, *The Norman Wisdom Show* lacks the magic of many of his television variety performances. The bullying of the character looks too harsh and Norman appears too insistent in begging for audience sympathy when caught in close-up on television. This over-emphatic appeal is sadly not leavened on this occasion by the sort of remark he made in his famous Palladium shows when he would turn to the audience subdued by his pathetic drifting off stage to shout at them hysterically: 'You ought to see your faces!' Here Wisdom is constantly thrown off the platform and each time calls for the audience to demand his return. Live in cabaret, this act is sensational, as he has confirmed over and over again to standing ovations in recent tours, but it is not done justice in this television outing. The more recent video recorded in 1989 certainly captures his live act to far better advantage.

It was with a vastly expanded version of the Knokke performance that Wisdom decided to return to the West End stage for the first time in over 18 years, discounting the special Royal Variety Show. The two-and-a-half-hour show, *A World of Wisdom*, was booked in at the Theatre Royal, Drury Lane, by John Farrow for two weeks in June 1979 after a short out-of-town run-in. It proved a critical and commercial disaster. The opening had Wisdom in full Gump outfit, uncertain where the audience was. Finding them, he goes through most of his famous routines, including 'A Lesson in Rhythm' with Tony Fayne once more as feed. The instruments, a bout of tap-dancing and some acrobatic falls followed, plus an assortment of songs from Newley and Bricusse. Most of the critics thought the show ill-planned and ill-prepared and were saddened by it: 'The entire act is brought off with total professional competence. His clarinet is admirable. He really can dance. His acrobatics are quaint. But his wearisome patter runs into the ground at last. He ends in bungled card-tricks and - last resort of the exhausted comic - community singing.' (*Daily Telegraph*.)

In the meantime, Wisdom made another important decision. In 1977, whilst appearing in *Norman Wisdom - Comedian* at the Gaiety theatre, Douglas, Isle of Man, he fell in love with the island and began making tentative plans to live there. 'I just couldn't believe it and it still amazes and delights me. No racialism, no strikes, and you don't have to put on a tin hat when you go out at night in case you get smashed over the head.' (*Manx Tails*.) Not long after, he was playing his twelfth cabaret season in Australia and suddenly realised that he was mad not to be taking things a little more easily. Semi-retirement was the obvious next step. He sold his Sussex hacienda and his yacht, swapped his Kensington apartment for a large flat in the more congenial climes of Epsom as a London base, and settled down contentedly on the Isle of Man. 'For the first time in my life I am really enjoying a quiet domestic home life. I did not come here as a tax exile, in fact, I don't qualify because I still have property in England. I continue to pay tax in the normal manner.' (*Sunday Express*.) 'I'll be truthful, I'm pretty well-off thank goodness and I want some time at home. I want to ride my motor bike and drive my car, and play golf and have fun. Touch wood, I'm as fit as a fiddle . . . I love Britain but I love it the way it should be, the way it used to be, the way the Isle of Man still is. But I'm not a brilliantly politically minded person. I've just been lucky with my career. I can fall on my arse with ease.' (*Radio Times*.)

The main professional event of this most recent period was being selected to play the part of a man dying from cancer in the television play *Going Gently*. The script was by Thomas Ellice from a book by American author Robert C.S. Downs. Wisdom was at last given a 'straight' role, something he had hankered after for so long. 'It was Innes Lloyd, the producer, who thought of me for the part and I gathered later that director Stephen Frears was against it. Anyway they invited me for lunch where I spoke very little because I wanted to get their ideas, not to let them have mine in case I frightened them. Eventually Stephen invited me to his office and it was obvious that he wanted to question me further so as to make up his own mind. I sat there and he said: "I don't want you to do any comicing Norman, none at all." I told him I could understand that and then I said:

"Look, if I'm in a nightgown I can get out of bed and try to walk away. But the gown gets caught on a spring and as I move away the spring extends. At its fullest extent it'll pull me back suddenly. Now if I put my foot in a chamber-pot, that'd be a scream." Stephen had gone pale! Then I said to him: "Look, why did you ask me in the first place? If you don't think I can act, then sod you - I don't want you or your bloody work because I can act as well as any of your bloody actors. You're a ****." He was a bit taken aback and said: "Norman, don't lose your temper." I put my arm round his shoulders and said: "No, I haven't - but how's that for acting!" And I got the part.'

At that time, Stephen Frears was one of the best directors working in television. He started out as an assistant producer at the Royal Court Theatre during its great days in the 'sixties and the contacts he made there helped him get practical training in the cinema as a directorial assistant. He completed some work for television before, in 1967, making his first feature film, *Gumshoe*, an imaginative thriller with a Liverpool setting, starring Albert Finney. He went on to direct many plays for television, most notably in association with writers Alan Bennett and Peter Prince. The unexpected theatrical success of his TV movie *My Beautiful Laundrette* in 1985 eventually led to Hollywood where he gained international recognition with such films as *Dangerous Liaisons* (1989) and *The Grifters* (1990). In *Going Gently*, made for the BBC2 *Playhouse* slot, Wisdom plays Bernard Flood, a man admitted into hospital for a check-up. Cancer is diagnosed, and a disbelieving Flood is confronted in his ward by Austin Miller (Fulton Mackay), an academic who has long since accepted both his affliction and that he has only a few weeks to live. Flood, too, comes to accept the awful truth and, looked after by day-nurse Sister Scarli (Judi Dench) and the authoritarian night-nurse Sister Marvin (Margaret Whiting), he drifts towards death. Beautifully directed, wonderfully acted by the three principals Wisdom, Dench and Mackay, the play made a huge and memorable impact.

There is a problem in casting a well-known comedian in a serious role which stems from the unusually direct relationship which audiences have with comics. This can be disruptive if casting is against expectations because the sight of the comic suggests a specific frame of reference. Well aware of this, Stephen Frears confronts the problem 'filmically'. The play opens to sombre music with a sharply angled overhead shot down on to a female figure standing on a classically decorated floor. This stark image is then intruded on by two male figures. Still with no explanatory shots, we cut to a shockingly contrasting close-up image of a hand and wrist to which another pair of hands ties a name-tag. Only then does the camera creep up the body to reveal the sombre features of Wisdom, flanked by the worried faces of the two other characters. We are clearly in some sort of institution, though at this stage it's not clear that it is a hospital. What has been achieved magnificently is the elimination of all thoughts of comedy. Then there is a static shot of the figures walking down an ill-lit corridor which is held as the credits go up, George Fenton's expressive melodies continuing over the image. With the completion of the credits the image mixes to a lighter one in which we see the distorted view of Fulton Mackay through a window and the body of the melancholy narrative gets under way. Miller has seen and experienced all this pain before and does not paint a very optimistic picture of the trials and tribulations to come Flood's way. The exploratory operations confirm that they are both terminal cases. Flood clutches to the belief that it is all a mistake, but the more realistic Miller has already embraced his fate with anger and offers Flood no comfort. 'Soon you'll be so angry you won't recognise yourself.' Once he has accepted that his demise is approaching rapidly, Flood fulfils Miller's prediction and becomes alienated from the living including his wife, a part delicately played by Stephanie Cole. The rest of the harrowing film follows the differing paths towards the two patients' institutionalised deaths. 'In company of this quality what Norman Wisdom, as the second patient, had going for him is what he always had: his small talkative body. Toddling down that darkening corridor, dithering at the bed of Mackay, who might be dead, or not, or nearly. Seeming to go two ways at once.' (*Guardian*.)

Sadly no equivalently interesting offers resulted from Wisdom's uniformly praised performance, and other than a dramatic role as a safe-cracker in an episode of the BBC's Channel Island cop series *Bergerac*, Wisdom's appearances have been limited to the occasional celebrity guesting. On stage, Wisdom undertook a rather offbeat musical production called *Jingle Jangle*. *Jingle Jangle* was mounted for charity and staged at the Shaw Theatre in London with the pupils of the Henrietta Barnett school. The show is of as much interest for its financing (featured in BBC TV's *The Money Programme*) as it is for the end result. The music was by Geoff Morrow, who had worked as a record producer with Wisdom in the 'seventies, and who also co-wrote the book in association with the show's lyricist, Hal Shaper. The box-office receipts were promised to the Bud Flanagan Leukaemia fund, and this led to a problem of how to raise the £100,000 production costs for the week-long show. *Jingle Jangle*, as its title might suggest, was set in the world of advertising and the answer to the financing problem was to offer real companies jingles to be sung in the show in return for money. This unusual appeal for sponsorship was highly successful, Morrow only having to approach six companies to get four pledges of £25,000. With the show underwritten, Norman Wisdom gave his services free in the role of the timid, though highly productive, advertising jingle composer. So too, did Bogdan Kominowski, veteran of *Hair*,

Jesus Christ Superstar and *Elvis*, as the blustery and egotistical head of the agency. A pleasant show resulted with Wisdom doing a neat soft-shoe shuffle at the finale, but one which suffered from a lack of songs - most of them being reprised in full to compensate - and from the staging mistakes one would expect from what was essentially a school production. The show was tightened up during the week's sellout run, an original cast album was released and the show was (non-commercially) videotaped. Wisdom still returns regularly to the mainland to do pantomimes, summer seasons and national tours with Tony Fayne. A television documentary has been broadcast, and he has reflected once more on his life for both television and radio. His image has been used in national advertising campaigns for, amongst others, Heineken Lager, British Telecom and British Electronic Transport. At the time of writing Norman Wisdom is recording an LP with Rick Wakeman, and has appeared in another Royal Variety Show (1985), his sixth to date, as well as in the 1988 Children's Royal Variety Show. In 1990 he recieved an award in honour of his Lifetime's Work on the Stage as part of the first British Comedy Awards ceremony.

11. Reflections.

Most of Norman Wisdom's years in showbusiness have been spent at the very peak of his profession. As with most entertainers who have sustained themselves at the top for such a long period, his career is dotted with interesting and intriguing projects which were never completed. Though they shed light on Wisdom's hopes at the time, it is perhaps unfruitful to speculate on the effects had some of them been fulfilled. Who can tell what would have happened had he been acclaimed in a dramatic role early on in his career?

One of the most important proposals Wisdom made in the early days was to make a film based on the life of the boxer Benny Lynch. His first public reference to this idea (as well as to his desire to remake *The Hunchback of Nôtre Dame*) came in interviews given when the success of *Trouble in Store* was apparent. It is perhaps understandable that Rank, at that time, were reluctant to let such a hot property stray too far away from his as yet barely established public image, and the idea was put to one side. Understandable but regrettable: the film would have been a perfect vehicle for Wisdom. 'It would have been a marvellous film. They were raving mad not to do it. Do you know the story of Benny Lynch? He was a boxer, and at that time I was young enough to do it and I knew about boxing. He was a Scotsman who became World Flyweight boxing champion. He started off because one day, after having a few drinks, he went into one of those boxing booths where you try to stand up to a few rounds with a professional to win money. Anyway, he went in there and won - it was unheard of! So they took him on in the booth and he beat all-comers. He soon got picked up to do proper boxing and became British Flyweight champion. The terrible tragedy was that he was on the drink. Even so, it was only because he was overweight that he later lost the World Championship. The National Sporting Club knew he was an alcoholic and they paid for him to go into a home which cured him of drinking after two or three months. On the first fight after coming out, someone got to him in his dressing room with a glass of whisky but he still won semi-drunk. A few weeks later he was fighting this American and he staggered into the ring in a drunken lurch. When the bell rang he had to be helped to his feet and the American thought: "He's out of his brain". When they met in the ring Benny Lynch went boom, boom, boom, bang - and put him away. He wasn't drunk at all! They thought he was pissed out of his mind - he wasn't! There were lots of wonderful stories like that. One time he escaped from a camp where he was kept by his trainers so that he wouldn't go out and get plastered. He came back in a hired car, drunk, and got so angry when the trainers confronted him that he smashed his fist through the windscreen and lacerated his hand. He was fighting the following night, so he went into the ring and knocked the bloke out with one hand - he never even touched him with the injured one! The saddest thing of all was that he was married with two kids whom he loved. But when he went home drunk he always caused quarrels, so his wife never let him in when he was pissed. On Christmas Eve he came home drunk, absolutely broke and he was locked out. He went and got some wood and sat on the doorstep all night in the freezing cold and carved two dolls with his knife as Christmas presents for his kids. He died when he was 33 - it was nothing in his last years to see him on the Glasgow underground going up to people, drunk, and saying: "I'm Benny Lynch, have you got a cigarette?"'

This account may play around slightly with the facts, but it was clearly a splendid subject for Wisdom, full of humour, pathos and a strong part to which he was perfectly tailored. Sadly, it never got off the ground. *The Life Story of Benny Lynch* was resurrected in the talks with Knightsbridge, but the moderate commercial performance - by Wisdom's standards - of *There was a Crooked Man* and *The Girl on the Boat* put an end to the hopes of his fans taking kindly to projects too far from his Gump image. As late as 1966 in his *New York Times* interview with Rex Reed he recalled the project: 'I've tried to sell the idea, but they want to stick to the Norman Wisdom formula. You see the frustrations I face of being a comic.'

If the consequences on Wisdom's career of taking a 'straight' role in his early days would have been interesting, so too would the effect of having made a film in America. *Pleasure Island*, which came in the aftermath of his Ed Sullivan guest spot, has already been mentioned, but another project arose in 1956 when Wisdom was offered *An Englishman in Las Vegas* by Albert Broccoli, who was later to increase his fortune considerably with the James Bond films. The plan was to co-star Wisdom with Edward G. Robinson and Anita Ekberg in one of five films to be distributed in the United States by Columbia Pictures in a deal which would have run alongside the Rank contract and would have brought Wisdom £45,000 per picture plus a percentage of the profits. It is doubtful that Rank were ever entirely happy with the plan, and for whatever reason the project fell through quietly with an announcement about poor script quality. 'That was just for the press, bullshit! I talked for ten days to various people. They just decided not to do that film.' Another proposal which would have been fascinating arose when Jerry Lewis, a superficially similar screen clown, caught Wisdom in *Where's Charley?* and enthusiastically suggested they make a film together. The idea was to co-star Wisdom and Lewis with the Mexican clown Cantinflas, best known for his starring role in *Around the World in 80 Days*, and the Frenchman Fernandel, whose extraordinarily expressive face had launched him into film in 1930 and who was still a top draw in France. In 1960, Wisdom referred to the project again in an interview: 'It was a pipe dream then, but it's become a real proposition now that Jerry's his own producer. He tells me he has writers to work on a story.'

On stage in 1963, there were plans to follow-up Wisdom's triumph in *Where's Charley?* with another musical comedy, this time an adaptation of Arnold Bennett's *The Card*, which had been filmed by Ronald Neame in 1952 with Alec Guinness in the lead. Much later, another musical was posited based on the life stories of Arthur Lucan (Old Mother Riley) and Kitty McShane, written by the author of *The Killing of Sister George*, Frank Marcus. Wisdom dropped out of this project when it was decided to do it as a straight play, and it eventually turned up under the title of *On Your Way, Riley!* at the Theatre Royal, Stratford, with a script by Alan Plater, getting a television outing in Christmas 1984 with Maureen Lipman and Brian Murphy in the main roles. For television, Wisdom considered the scripts for *Some Mothers Do 'ave 'em*, rejecting them for poor quality, paving the way for Michael Crawford to rework them with immense success.

After his great reception in *The Night they Raided Minsky's* plans were afoot for Wisdom to star in another film in America. The two most likely projects were *The Borrowers* and *Adam and Evil*. The classic children's story, *The Borrowers*, was suggested by Hal Prince, fresh from his Broadway blockbuster *Cabaret*, but the plan fell through with the general financial malaise of the industry at that time. The property eventually changed hands and emerged as a 1973 Christmas special on American television, scripted by Jay Presson Allen, with music by Rod McKuen and Eddie Albert in the lead. *Adam and Evil* was an adaptation by Wisdom himself of a J.B. Priestley short story 'Adam and the Tulpa' which he hoped to make with *Minsky* director William Friedkin. Friedkin declared the script the best of its kind that he had come across, but financial arrangements could not be agreed. In the *New York Times* in 1966, Wisdom said of the proposed film: 'The thing I'm most excited about now is this screenplay I bought from J.B. Priestley about a lonely little bass player who creates a woman companion from his imagination and then can't get away from her. She eventually commits murder and steals from him and drives him mad, but there's tremendous comedy in it too.' Wisdom's script is even blacker and harsher than the above outline implies, full of visual humour, and incorporates a perfectly written part for himself. My own belief that it would make a wonderful film was confirmed when I was privileged to witness Norman Wisdom read and mime the entire piece.

And what of the music hall tradition which Wisdom has extended so notably to the present day? Sadly, with the lack of a training ground, the clown tradition is in great danger in all media. There is now no variety circuit to speak of. What was left of the number two and three circuits in the 'fifties was progressively killed off, the revues still touring tried to combat the pull of television with nude shows, but were of little use in sustaining the traditions of variety. One might have thought that the once lucrative circuit of the Northern clubs might have provided a new training ground, but this has not been the case. Lots of money was to be made there in the late 'sixties and early 'seventies. When Wisdom turned to clubs in 1968 he found he could earn more money there than in his peak film days. However, many of the comics that have emerged from them have proved to be of limited adaptability. The best known were those featured in Granada Television's *The Comedians*, and those to have lasted best are arguably Bernard Manning and Stan Boardman. But they still seem tied to an aggressive microphone technique which leaves little room for subtlety or even good verbal timing. The difference between working the clubs and the old variety theatres was put succinctly by Denis Norden: 'A comedian in those days had only seven minutes to come on, register with an audience, win their attention, without breaking any of the traditions or the constraints on the sorts of jokes he could tell, and get off with them wanting to see him again. All in seven minutes. But in the Northern clubs they have forty minutes to get into their act. And there are no holds barred, no constraints, except getting through to the drunks.' The one exception to the disappointing yield from the clubs is, perhaps, Les Dawson. With his wonderful comic looks, this dour and doleful Manchester droll has brought back the art of the monologue, complete with surreal overtones and surprising linguistic inventiveness. Another fine storyteller is the Birmingham-born Jasper Carrott, though his limited abilities in sketches, like that of Irish raconteur Dave Allen, restricts him to the quality of his written material. Like Carrott, Billy Connolly and Richard Digance came out of the folk-music circuit, an underestimated forum which also produced the lesser known hilarities of Noel Murphy's boozy aggressiveness and the contrasting subtleties of Derek Brimstone. The extrovert Glaswegian Connolly looks set to back up his stage and television comedy turns with well-chosen straight roles which exploit his wry incarnation of Scottish thuggery. Two splendid comics have survived appearances on television's talent programme *New Faces* and resulting overexposure to emerge triumphant, Victoria Wood and Lenny Henry, both ensuring that they developed their acts through contact with live audiences.

Perhaps paradoxically, genuine heirs to the music hall tradition have emerged in greatest strength from the rarefied climes of our so-called premier universities, with the emergence of the 'Oxbridge Mafia' via the Cambridge Footlights and their ilk. The links between the music hall and the products of this regime were the postwar radio shows *Take It From Here* and *The Goon Show*. The Denis Norden/Frank Muir scripted *Take It From Here* starred Jimmy Edwards, Dick Bentley and Joy Nichols and ran from 1948 to 1960. The programme sounds tame now, but at the time it marked a new literacy in radio comedy and included influential innovations such as the movie parodies which became a regular feature. *The Goon Show*, which was formulated by people with variety backgrounds - Peter Sellers, Harry Secombe, its writer/co-performer Spike Milligan and initially Michael Bentine - ran from 1951 to 1960. The zany surreality of the scripts and the brilliant use of radio as a medium made the programme compulsory listening at the time, with its anti-establishment attitudes recommending it to the younger generation.

The first major impact made by Oxbridge was the revue to end all revues, *Beyond the Fringe*, which was performed regularly from 1960 to 1962, and which has been revived occasionally since. Its writers/stars were Jonathan Miller, Alan Bennett, Peter Cook and Dudley Moore and it spawned the satire boom of the 'sixties. *Beyond the Fringe* had an enormous influence on British television comedy for many years, with direct descendants *That Was The Week That Was* (1962-1965) and the further collaborations of Cook and Moore, most notably *Not Only, But Also* (1965-1970). The next generation of Oxbridge graduates shone initially on the radio with *I'm Sorry I'll Read That Again* (1965-1973) which included amongst its writers/performers Tim Brooke-Taylor, John Cleese, Graeme Garden and Bill Oddie. 'We had a sort of catch-phrase which was "back to music hall". We were consciously regressing, going against the satirical movement which was going at that time, because that group of people had covered that area so thoroughly.' (Bill Oddie.) It was now a short step to transferring this type of humour to television and giving it a visual dimension. Two series successfully combined the elements of visual wittiness and inspired scripting, building on the efforts of Cook and Moore. Firstly ITV's *At Last the 1948 Show* (1967) which brought non-graduate and prolific scriptwriter Marty Feldman in front of the cameras alongside Brooke-Taylor, Cleese, and another Oxbridge man, Graham Chapman. And secondly, *Do Not Adjust Your Set* (1968/9), which included Oxbridge personnel Eric Idle, Terry Jones and Michael Palin. Feldman went on to make a highly visual series for BBC TV, *Marty* (1968/9), his strange features and physical command indicating the makings of a truly first-rate clown. Sadly, his initially successful transfer to Hollywood led to his tragic death in 1982. The rest of the named members from *At Last the 1948 Show* and *Do Not Adjust Your Set* permuted to create the two most important television excursions into the area enriched by the unlikely combination of the traditions of undergraduate and music hall humour: *Monty Python's Flying Circus* (1969-1974) and *The Goodies* (1970-1978). *Monty Python*, with its cast of Chapman,

▲ A DATE WITH A DREAM. Frame blow-up from Wisdom's first screen appearance in 1948—a thirteen-and-a-half second glimpse of his classic shadow-boxing routine.

▲ Norman in full Gump costume in the cut scene from MEET MR. LUCIFER.

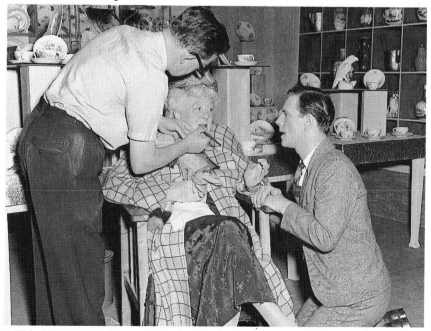

▲ TROUBLE IN STORE. Margaret Rutherford has the final touches applied to her make-up and Norman picks up a few tips from the beloved and experienced actress.

▲ TROUBLE IN STORE. The crew line up with Norman, who is flanked by director John Paddy Carstairs and producer Maurice Cowan, to celebrate the end of the shoot.

▲ ONE GOOD TURN. Norman poses with co-star Shirley Abicair, the popular Australian zither player.

▲ ONE GOOD TURN. Norman and Shirley Abicair pursue their not all too convincing romance.

▲ MAN OF THE MOMENT. Norman, Lana Morris and Jerry Desmonde discuss the niceties of international diplomacy just before the lady is kidnapped by a rival government.

▲ UP IN THE WORLD. Norman admires his handiwork at the opening of one of his finest films for Rank.

▶ UP IN THE WORLD. Norman demonstrates some eccentric dance steps in time to Michael Ward's accompaniment in the mistaken belief that he is entertaining his fellow-workers at Banderville Hall.

▲ JUST MY LUCK. Margaret Rutherford hands over ownership of the racehorse to Norman and Jill Dixon.

▲ THE SQUARE PEG. Norman in the role of General Schreiber interrogates his great screen partner Edward Chapman.

▲ FOLLOW A STAR. Norman about to be given singing lessons by two of his great 'stooges', Jerry Desmonde and Eddie Leslie.

▲ Norman relaxes between takes with his incomparable 'straight-man' Jerry Desmonde.

◄ FOLLOW A STAR. Norman in untypical pose for the revue-style 'You Deserve A Medal For That' performed whilst under the influence of hypnotism!

▲ THE BULLDOG BREED. A welcome bleakness enters the Wisdom screen world as he attempts suicide by drowning.

▲ THERE WAS A CROOKED MAN. Alfred Marks, Timothy Bateson, Norman and Jean Clarke with Reed de Rouen just visible in the background discuss the advantages of a life of crime.

▲ THE GIRL ON THE BOAT. Norman as Sam Marlowe reads Tennyson to Millicent Martin in a seduction ploy foiled, temporarily, by his inability to swim.

◄ ON THE BEAT. Wisdom practises his hilarious wind-up running start as the crew line-up the next shot. Director Robert Asher can be seen behind and to the left of the camera.

▲ ON THE BEAT. Fine portrait shot of Norman in the role of Giulio Napolitani, showing how a minimal use of make-up helped him to produce a completely different and convincing character.

◄ ON THE BEAT. Norman almost convinces doctor Eric Barker that he is tall enough for the force.

▲ A STITCH IN TIME. Out of the frying pan into the fire? Norman eludes his pursuers to cuddle up to the immaculate Jerry Desmonde.

◀ THE EARLY BIRD. Norman as many remember him—taking a spectacular tumble.

▶ THE EARLY BIRD. Norman with his one true love, Nellie the horse.

▲ The unit responsible for many of the Wisdom films have a snack during the making of THE EARLY BIRD. Seated from left to right are the director Robert Asher, Norman, and producer Hugh Stewart. Standing is Robert's brother, distinguished cameraman Jack Asher.

◄ THE SANDWICH MAN. Father O'Flynn takes a nasty blow in this disastrous and fragmented film.

▲ WHAT'S GOOD FOR THE GOOSE. "What's Norman doing that he's never done before?" ran the rhetorical advertising by-line. Work with director Menahem Golan was the answer. Co-star Sally Geeson even appears topless in the continental version. "You didn't see much of me, but it was awful . . . and certainly not at all necessary in a Norman Wisdom film!"

◄ THE NIGHT THEY RAIDED MINSKY'S. Jason Robards and Norman on the burlesque stage. "Norman Wisdom, a Briton, plays burlesque's little fall guy like the ancestor to Chaplin and Marcel Marceau's Bip" (*New York Times*).

▲ Norman sups the famous lager and thus solves the problems of how to erect a deckchair in a lovely TV ad from 1980.

◀ Norman in his other principal costume—the misfit evening suit. A fan photo from the late '40s.

▶ Norman Wisdom as Buttons in CINDERELLA at Birmingham, Christmas 1950.

▲ Norman with his first principal straight man and writing partner, Eddie Leslie.

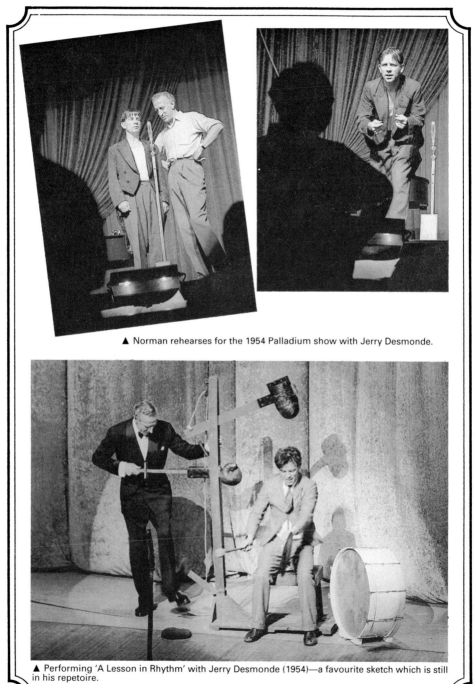

▲ Norman rehearses for the 1954 Palladium show with Jerry Desmonde.

▲ Performing 'A Lesson in Rhythm' with Jerry Desmonde (1954)—a favourite sketch which is still in his repetoire.

◄ TURN AGAIN WHITTINGTON (1960). "As a sort of 'bonus' to his portrayal of Dick, Norman spends 30 minutes or so as Norman, fooling and falling, playing sax, clarinet, trumpet and drums, singing songs old and new . . ." (*Record Mirror*).

▲ The final rehearsal for the stars of the 1954 Royal Performance. Eric Rogers conducts, Norman is in the centre with such luminaries as Max Bygraves, Howard Keel, David Whitfield and . . . and . . .

Cleese, Idle, Jones and Palin, plus cartoons from the American Terry Gilliam (who had worked occasionally on *Do Not Adjust Your Set*), made it to the cinema. Their first film, *And Now For Something Completely Different* (1971), merely reworked favourite television sketches, but the later films have transferred the team's humour with great success to the big screen.

In these days of the writer/comedian or the comedy actor, the presence of the clown on television and film is a rare event; even the portals of variety are being taken over by the stars of situation comedies to often unnerving effect. British television has seen some fine comedy series since *Steptoe*, but they fall into the situation comedy tradition, with such exceptional examples as *Dad's Army; Rising Damp; Till Death Us Do Part; Yes Minister; Auf Wiedersehen, Pet* and *Only Fools and Horses*. Inevitably, though, with television reaching out to a wider and more heterogeneous audience, the clown's essential roots, generally anchored in a working-class culture, are severed and the result tends towards a watering down of talent and commitment. Even the catchment audience of the anti-establishment satirists and their appeal to the youthful intelligentsia gave the university-spawned humorists a focus which is missing from most of today's comics. Now they are often forced in front of a wide audience too early and are strangled by instant acclaim (or criticism) given to an unnurtured talent, which then quickly ossifies or dies. The true clowns shine on television as they do on stage and film, but sadly there are far too few of them, and with the gradual demise of the British film industry, cinema's music hall tradition is in some danger of collapse.

Nevertheless, there are some optimistic signs. The most recent platforms for new comedians have been the alternative cabaret clubs, based on the New York model and pioneered here by London's Comedy Store and Comic Strip. Hopefully, venues like these will thrive as they have already proved invaluable as training grounds. Already Ben Elton has emerged as a stand-up (and writer) of major ability, following Billy Connolly and Victoria Wood in filling large theatres as a top-of-the-bill attraction. John Cleese's scintillating triumph with *A Fish Called Wanda* (1988) must be an inspiration for others to move into the cinema and the commercial success of such films as *The Tall Guy* (1989), *Wilt* (1989) and *Nuns on the Run* (1990) show the game is not yet up. It is interesting to watch the development of the first graduates from the 'alternative' venues now making their mark in television and films and, in particular, the Comic Strip's *The Strike* (1988) augurs well for the future.

Underlying this book has been the belief that Norman Wisdom is not only the music hall tradition's last great cinematic exponent, but also its finest. From *Trouble in Store* in 1953 to *The Night they Raided Minsky's* and *What's Good for the Goose* (both released in 1969), Wisdom was

Britain's top comedy draw. He has certainly garnered the financial rewards of a lifetime of laughter, and there is no mistaking the genuine affection people have for him, and how his fans, some of whom were not even born when he made his last starring film, consider him 'one of us'. However, the personal affection which the public feels for him has never been matched by official recognition in Britain. While other entertainers who came up in his generation have turned up in the Honours List - Morecambe & Wise, Secombe & Sellers and many others - Wisdom has been studiously ignored. It has long been the case that popular entertainers have been slighted by the system, but other factors are at play. His critical reputation has never been high. The bias against slapstick and lowbrow comedy - indeed against most popular British cinema - amongst film reviewers is blatant, and Wisdom's film series failed to run long enough to be accepted as an 'institution' like those of the *Carry On* team. Similarly, though Wisdom's British stage work was highly praised in its time, it has, with the exception of *Where's Charley?*, now been largely forgotten, partly because most of it is in the ignored theatrical forms like pantomime, variety and ice shows. His talent is often taken for granted even by his admirers, and there is little awareness here of the American period of Wisdom's career. This is perhaps not surprising, since *Walking Happy* never came to the West End - plans to bring it over were dashed because of film commitments on *The Night they Raided Minsky's* - and *Androcles and the Lion*, thankfully preserved in New York's Museum of Broadcasting, has, as yet, never been broadcast on British television.

One of Norman Wisdom's most notable characteristics when being interviewed is his habit of never sitting still, leaping out of his chair at the slightest excuse to act out whatever anecdote or story he is relating. There was an extraordinary moment in our first conversation when he was explaining the difference between his comedy and that of Jerry Lewis. To demonstrate he mimed the classic moment in *Press for Time* when he gets the bicycle caught up in the light fitting. With the sketch recalled, he repeated it in the style of Lewis. At the end of the two mimes, both equally hilarious, he had succinctly made his point which depended on how the gag was built. At the end of the talk, he demonstrated some of his ideas for television series, one-off plays and films by acting out various scenes and situations. Some of these may yet be produced, though one gets the impression that contentment with his present lifestyle has tempered the effort required to go out into the financial jungle to get them off the ground. However, he is always contemplating a handful of projects, and at the time of writing he is considering a number of film and television ideas that have a fair chance of backing. It would indeed be wonderful to see him celebrate his fifth decade in showbusiness by starring in another film.

APPENDIX 1

Annotated Film/videography.

Prod=producer; ph=photographer; sc=scriptwriter.
Video availability indicated below is subject to change.

A DATE WITH A DREAM (Dicky Leeman, 1948)
b/w 56 mins.
A Tempean Film for Grand National distribution.
Prod: Robert S. Baker; Associate Prod: ph: Monty Berman; sc: Carl Nystrom. Cast: Terry-Thomas (Terry), Jean Carson (Jean), Bill Lowe (Bill), Len Lowe (Len), Wally Patch (Uncle), Vic Lewis (Vic), Ida Patlansky (Bedelia), Joey Porter (Max Imshy), Alfie Dean (Joe), Julia Lang (Madam Docherty), Harry Green (Syd Marlish), Pat Rose, Pat Doherty, Thelma Tuson, Sydney Bromley, The Vic Lewis Orchestra. Variety Acts: Elton Hayes, Norman Wisdom, The Cox Brothers, Eddie Leroy. Musical Numbers by The Vic Lewis Orchestra: 'Here Comes The Show', 'You Made Me Mad', 'How About Me For You' (with Carson, B. & L. Lowe), 'Unlucky' (with Carson), 'Let Me Dream' (with Carson), 'Now Is The Time For Love' (with Carson, B. & L. Lowe). Others: 'Whose Turn Now?' by Ken Thorne, 'Sombrero' by Elton Hayes, both orchestrated by Ken Thorne.

Norman Wisdom's first film appearance was a fleeting thirteen-and-a-half second glimpse of his shadow boxing routine shot at Collins Music Hall dressed in his misfit evening suit in this low-budget Terry-Thomas vehicle. The director Dicky Leeman, best known for his work at the BBC, was closely associated with WHAT'S MY LINE? *See* Chapter 2.

TROUBLE IN STORE (John Paddy Carstairs, 1953) b/w 85 mins.
GFD/Two Cities. Prod: Maurice Cowan; sc: John Paddy Carstairs, Maurice Cowan, Ted Willis; ph: Ernest Steward. Cast: Norman Wisdom (Norman), Margaret Rutherford (Miss Bacon), Moira Lister (Peggy), Derek Bond (Gerald), Lana Morris (Sally), Jerry Desmonde (Mr. Freeman), Megs Jenkins (Miss Gibson), Joan Sims (Edna), Michael Ward (Wilbur), Michael Brennan (Security Officer), Joan Ingram (Miss Denby), Eddie Leslie (Bill), Cyril Chamberlain (Alf). Songs: 'Don't Laugh At Me, 'I'd Like To Put On Record That I Love You'. Pinewood Studios. Video available UK. See Chapter 4.

'Here at last is the film comedian English pictures have been looking for ever since Elstree first ceased to be merely a London suburb. Unlike so many comics who have come to the screen after making their home in other places, Wisdom hits the bull in one, and gives the impression that he was born for the cinema. He is a natural film comedian. His comedy is entirely visual and independent of words. Like all the great ones, he has the additional (and indispensable) quality that you are fond of him from the moment you first set eyes on him. What rich deep joy it is to find again a master of really top-grade slapstick. This is not in any sense a "grand" picture and it is all the better for that. It is a fast-moving efficient vehicle for the inventive brilliance of this delightful comedian. They have been comparing him with Chaplin, though, if there must be comparisons, I would have placed him closer to Harold Lloyd. But why compare him with anybody. He is good enough to be regarded not as another Chaplin or another Lloyd, but as the first Wisdom.' *Daily Mail.* 'There can be no doubt that Norman Wisdom is what we have been looking for. Unlike other British comedians who have tried to succeed on the screen, Norman does not rely on wisecracks. His devastating humour springs from grotesque and nimble physical movement and from a face which registers half a dozen moods in as many seconds . . . I am not sure that he hasn't more sympathetic appeal than Chaplin. He can repeat the laugh-clown-laugh stuff that Emil Jannings excelled in. He might even be as successful as Alec Guinness in similar but more robust comedy.' *Evening News.* 'All the time Norman Wisdom is hurling himself in and out of situations with a vitality and sureness of touch that keeps the house in uproar. It is impossible to avoid comparisons with the early Chaplin for there is much in common between them . . . Let us come to earth. This picture has the defects of too much slapstick but it establishes Norman Wisdom as potentially the greatest living comic of the screen. There is no one in Hollywood to touch him. Like Chaplin of silent days he can touch the heart with a simple gesture or a change of expression, and again like Chaplin he is indomitable.' *Evening Standard.* 'The mood of the film harks back disarmingly to the innocent world of Harold Lloyd and Buster Keaton and, like those earlier sublimities, it appeals immediately to the day-dreaming clown lurking below the overcoats of most of us. Mr. Norman Wisdom is the new screen comedian who portrays this muffled Galahad . . . To my mind he is a most engaging fool, with his puppy-dog looks and his sudden outbursts of terrible laughter when calamity threatens. We may also note, as he progresses towards his heart's desire, how admirably his personality lends itself to visual comedy . . . I hope we may look forward to a series.' *Financial Times.* 'Like all great comedians, Mr. Wisdom has the seed of tragedy planted firmly in the garden of his soul. In repose his face is, like the traditional clown's, lined with suffering, and the follies he commits, the dire extremities in which he finds himself, are liberally charged with pathos . . . He has real versatility, charm and a delightful singing voice, and it is the greatest pity that *Trouble in Store* devotes so large a part of its attention to his talents as knockabout. For Mr. Wisdom knows how to be subtle, his humour can be polished, and here he is tied to the obvious old routines . . . Mr. Wisdom gives us glimpses of a more delicate approach to comedy, but they are all too brief.' *Spectator.* 'Norman Wisdom is by far the most attractive comic to come along since the lovable and lamented Sid Field . . . *Trouble in Store* is a slap-stick comedy full of old-fashioned laughs but as heavy handed as a Marx Brothers film without the Marx Brothers. However, it establishes Wisdom as a brilliant little man with wit in the corner of his smile and true pathos lurking in his eyes. Given a grown-up script for his next film, he should get a foothold on that deliciously dangerous kind of greatness which at the moment belongs to Charlie Chaplin alone.' *Sunday Express.* 'Norman Wisdom is the name . . . make a point of seeing his film *Trouble in Store.* He's the guy with the gift for both comedy and pathos that British films have been looking for since George Formby stopped 'Cleaning Windows'. If you don't laugh at Norman's antics . . . there is something wrong with your sense of fun. The comedy situations are vintage slapstick . . . This is another Norman Conquest.' *Daily Mirror.*

MEET MR. LUCIFER (Anthony Pelissier, 1953) b/w 83 mins.
Ealing. Prod: Monja Danischewsky; sc: Monja Danischewsky, based on the play *Beggar My Neighbour* by Arnold Ridley; ph: Desmond Dickinson. Cast: Stanley Holloway (Mr. Hollingsworth/Mr. Lucifer), Peggy Cummins (Kitty), Jack Watling (Jim), Barbara Murray (Patricia), Gordon Jackson (Hector), Kay Kendall (Lonely Hearts Singer). Ealing Studios.

Norman Wisdom was to have been a guest artist along with Gilbert Harding, Philip Harben, MacDonald Hobley and David Miller but was cut pre-release. *See* Chapter 3.

ONE GOOD TURN (John Paddy Carstairs, 1954) b/w 90 mins.
GFD/Two Cities. Prod: Maurice Cowan; sc: Maurice Cowan, John Paddy Carstairs, Ted Willis; ph: Jack Cox. Cast: Norman Wisdom (Norman), Joan Rice (Iris), Thora Hird (Cook), Shirley Abicair (Mary), William Russell (Alec), Richard Caldicott (Bigley), Marjorie Fender (Tuppeny), Keith Gilman (Jimmy), Joan Ingram (Matron), David Hurst (Professor Dofee). Songs: 'Take A Step In The Right Direction', 'Please Opportunity' and Abicair performs 'Botany Bay'. Pinewood Studios.

The enormous success of *Trouble in Store* ensured that the same production team would be used in the follow-up. Additional dialogue was provided by Sid Colin, creator of *The Army Game*, and future 'Carry on' writer Talbot Rothwell. The main addition to the team is in the position of assistant director, where Carstair's successor Robert Asher is installed.

Norman works as an odd-job man at the orphanage where he was brought up. Unthinkingly, Norman promises to buy one of the orphans, Jimmy, an expensive toy car, and spends the rest of the film trying to raise the necessary £12. Norman is also in love with Iris, but she is engaged to Alec whose father, Bigley, has plans to redevelop the orphanage and build a factory. In the end all is happily sorted out: the cook and Mary lend Norman the money, the inmates fight off the developers, and Norman walks away happily with the adoring Mary!

'He has a part which enables him to exploit a not unendearing brand of sentimentality, and it is indeed as a "little man" that Mr. Wisdom stakes his claim and bases his appeal. He has a true clown's knack of making a fall a work of art, his indiarubber legs can play amusing tricks and he can enter into a spirit of farcical confusion with the best of humour . . . In *One Good Turn* he is virtually on his own, but Mr. Wisdom still abides the question and remains neither a great comedian nor a popular fashion explicable save in terms of mass hysteria.' *The Times.* 'I have a fancy that he might profit greatly by playing a character part in a "straight" film under some really crack director. It would be an interesting experiment, and might prove astonishingly successful.' *Observer.* 'There's no doubt about Norman, he has the makings of that rare and wonderful creature, a great screen clown . . . I don't think, though, that this film does him justice. Its attitude seems to be that since Norman is sure to get the laughs nothing else matters very much.' *Daily Worker.* 'If you laughed until it hurt at *Trouble in Store* (as most people did) you will probably find the new picture just as mirth-provoking . . . While nipping about in the situations provided for him Norman is excellent. But there are several moments when he tries to be seriously sentimental and I found these embarrassing . . . In the new film nobody has a chance except Norman. The importance of the "stooge" in farce cannot be over-estimated.' *Evening News.*

AS LONG AS THEY'RE HAPPY (J.[JOHN] Lee Thompson, 1955) colour 91 mins.
Raymond Stross/GFD. Prod: Raymond Stross; sc: Alan Melville based on the play by Vernon Sylvaine; ph: Gilbert Taylor. Cast: Jack Buchanan (John Bentley), Janette Scott (Gwen), Jean Carson (Pat), Brenda de Banzie (Stella), Susan Stephen (Corinne), Jerry Wayne (Bobby Denver), Diana Dors (Pearl), Hugh McDermott (Barnaby), David Hurst (Dr. Schneider), Athene Seyler (Mrs. Arbuthnot), Joan Sims (Linda), Nigel Green (Peter), Edie Martin (Elderly Fan), Joan Hickson (Barmaid), Richard Wattis (Theatre Stage Manager), Charles Hawtrey (Irate Fan), Ronnie Stevens (Intruder), Hattie Jacques (Party Guest), Sam Kydd (Milkman), Gilbert Harding. Songs: Wayne performs 'You Started Something', 'I Don't Know Whether To Laugh Or Cry' (reprised by Buchanan), 'Light In Liza's Eyes', 'Be My

Guest'; Buchanan also performs 'If Your Heartaches'; Carson performs 'Quiet Little Rendez-Vous', 'Merry-Mo-Round'; Dors performs 'Hokey Pokey Polka' and Wisdom sings 'Don't Laugh At Me'. Pinewood Studios.

Norman Wisdom appears uncredited as a guest at the finale of this early directorial effort by the maker of *The Guns of Navarone* from the play which ran at the Garrick Theatre in 1953. Only Jack Buchanan and Nigel Green remain from the original West End cast.

A stockbroker's youngest daughter tricks an American singer into visiting their suburban Wimbledon home. Her increasingly disturbed father also receives his two other daughters and their oddball husbands and observes the effect of the entertainer on all his lovesick ·family. His attempts to normalise the situation in league with a phoney psychiatrist only result in more mayhem. Wisdom appears as himself in full Gump suit at the very end in a jokey reprise of the film's opening to sing 'Don't Laugh At Me' in an appropriately sobbing voice.

'But it is pleasant entertainment, with three good interventions as "guest stars" from Diana Dors, Norman Wisdom and Gilbert Harding.' *Daily Express*.

MAN OF THE MOMENT (John Paddy Carstairs, 1955) b/w 88 mins. Group/JARFID. Prod: Hugh Stewart; sc: Vernon Sylvaine, John Paddy Carstairs from a story by Maurice Cowan; ph: Jack Cox. Cast: Norman Wisdom (Norman), Lana Morris (Penny), Belinda Lee (Sonia), Jerry Desmonde (Jackson), Karel Stepanek (Chief Brodnian Delegate), Garry Marsh (Cooper), Cyril Chamberlain (Jennings), Inia Te Wiata (Toki), Evelyn Roberts (Sir Horace), Violet Fairbrother (Queen Of Tawaki), Martin Miller (Tailor), Eugene Deckers (Lift Man), Michael Ward (Photographer), Charles Hawtrey (Play Director). Guests: Ronnie Waldman, Philip Harben, MacDonald Hobley, 'The Grove Family', 'Fabian of the Yard'. Songs: 'Beware', 'Yodelee Yodelay', 'Dream For Sale' and the Beverley Sisters perform 'Man Of The Moment'. Pinewood Studios.

Hugh Stewart replaces Maurice Cowan for the first of his nine Wisdom films. Stewart had been in the film industry since 1932, firstly as an editor and then, during the war, as part of the Army Film Unit, co-directing *Tunisian Victory* with Frank Capra. He was an associate producer with Sir Alexander Korda before coming to Rank where he worked mainly on comedies. Veteran playwright Vernon Sylvaine joined Carstairs as scriptwriter with the intention of bolstering plotting and wit. Sylvaine is best remembered for his farces, particularly those with Robertson Hare and Alfred Drayton. Sylvaine, who wrote the original play *As Long as They're Happy* which provided Jack Buchanan with a starring role on both stage and screen, had been in discussion with Wisdom for some time, even before *One Good Turn*. His script for *Man of the Moment* proved to be one of his last works and he died in 1957 aged 60. Diana Dors, fresh from her dramatic triumph in *Yield to the Night*, was initially offered the Belinda Lee part. Sadly, though not surprisingly, she turned it down.

Norman is now a filing clerk in the Ministry of Overseas Development. Due to illness amongst senior staff in his department, Norman is seconded to go to Geneva to back the British delegation. One of the delegates is involved in an accident and Norman joins the British contingent in the debating chamber. Here, Norman unwittingly vetoes a resolution against the wishes of his superiors when he waves to his favourite film actress, Sonia, who is observing the proceedings. The vote was on the future of one of the Tawakian Islands on which all the major powers wish to set up a strategic base. The Tawakian Queen considers Norman the protector of her subjects' interests because of the veto, and leaves the decision about the island's future in his hands. Thus Norman is courted by all the major powers who shower him with honours and medals, and a Knighthood is conferred on him by the British to give him the necessary status. Eventually, the various ploys come to nothing when the island proves to be actively volcanic and disappears into the sea.

'This, his third film, is probably his best to date: it has a story of sorts, it makes reasonably apposite use of the star's talent for "under-dog" humour and slapstick, and it is put together with some show of unobtrusive competence. All the same it falls a long way short of turning this man of the music-halls into a film comedian.' *Guardian*. 'This isn't a bad plot for a slapstick comedy and Mr. John Paddy Carstairs has directed his third Wisdom film with a much greater professional slickness and dash than was evident in the first two . . . My own grumble with the entertainment is the rather hard-boiled way in which it has sought to assimilate the genuine artless innocence of old-fashioned film slapstick.' *Daily Telegraph*.

UP IN THE WORLD (John Paddy Carstairs, 1956) b/w 91 mins.
Rank. Prod: Hugh Stewart; sc: Jack Davies, Henry Blyth, Peter Blackmore; ph: Jack Cox. Cast: Norman Wisdom (Norman), Maureen Swanson (Jeannie), Jerry Desmonde (Major Willoughby), Ambrosine Phillpots (Lady Banderville), Colin Gordon (Fletcher Hethrington), Michael Caridia (Sir Reginald), Michael Ward (Maurice), Jill Dixon (Sylvia), Cyril Chamberlain (Harper), Eddie Leslie (Max), Lionel Jeffries (Wilson), Edwin Styles (DeMilo). Songs: 'Up In The World' and the White Cockatoo nightclub chorus-line sing 'Talent'. Pinewood Studios with exteriors at Woburn Abbey.

Jack Davies, the writer associated with most of the best Wisdom films, joins the team. Davies, in a long and distinguished career, exerted considerable influence on British Cinema with well over 50 scripts to his name by the 'seventies. Born in 1913, he worked continuously in the movies, initially with B.I.P., graduating to writing the first draft for Will Hay's *Convict 99* (1938). His best remembered film, outside the Wisdom vehicles, is probably *Those Magnificent Men in their Flying Machines* (1963). He is the father of John Howard Davies, the star of David Lean's *Oliver Twist*, who is now Controller of Entertainment at Thames after a spell as Head of BBC Light Entertainment.

Norman is a window-cleaner who manages to get a job at Banderville Park, the country home of Sir Reginald who, still being a minor, is looked after by his mother and two uncles, Maurice and Fletcher. The boy is an overprotected practical joker whose mother is convinced is under constant threat of kidnapping. In this she is right, and the kidnappers strike on the very night that Sir Reginald has 'persuaded' Norman to take him to a London nightclub, The White Cockatoo, to see DeMilo, a famous magician. Unfortunately, the nightclub is also the headquarters of the gang, and though only Maurice is abducted from the country home, they manage to snatch Reginald at the club. The police come to the rescue, only to find that Reginald, who was knocked out in the struggle, has lost his memory. Norman is found guilty of the crime and is sentenced to 25 years' hard labour. He escapes from gaol and treks back to Banderville Park in order to clear his name. The army joins the police to recapture Norman, but during the melée Sir Reginald is again knocked out, regaining his memory in time to clear Norman. Free at last, Norman is able to marry Jeannie, the parlour maid he loves.

'Mr. Wisdom seems to have grown in screen self-confidence and the humour, an artless pantomime season, slapdash affair of hit-and-miss, runs up a reasonable score of unambitious, unsophisticated hits.' *The Times*. 'Norman Wisdom is a man of enormous deftness. His timing is impeccable, those falls and sudden grins are masterpieces of careful planning. But the man's secret lies in his own enormous enjoyment of his part.' *News of the World*. 'In which our Norman ineffectually bill-posts, incompetently jail-breaks and blissfully marries Maureen Swanson. Mr. Wisdom's best film since his first.' *News Chronicle*.

JUST MY LUCK (John Paddy Carstairs, 1957) b/w 86 mins.
Rank. Prod: Hugh Stewart; sc: Alfred Shaughnessy, Peter Blackmore, based on an anecdote by Peter Cusick; ph: Jack Cox. Cast: Norman Wisdom (Norman/Norman's Father), Jill Dixon (Anne), Leslie Phillips (Richard Lumb), Delphi Lawrence (Miss Daviot), Edward Chapman (Mr. Stoneway), Marjorie Rhodes (Mrs. Hackett), Joan Sims (Phoebe), Peter Copley (Weaver), Michael Ward (Cranley), Margaret Rutherford (Mrs. Dooley), Eddie Leslie (Gas Man), Jerry Desmonde (Punter), Cyril Chamberlain

(Gateman), Bill Fraser (Craftsman), Sam Kydd (Craftsman), Michael Brennan (Masseur). Pinewood Studios. Video available in UK.

Just my Luck introduces Edward Chapman into the Wisdom camp. Chapman was born in 1901 and entered films in 1929 with *Juno and the Paycock*, and acted consistently in films until 1970. He died in 1977. He usually took the role of solid, rather dull, family men, best seen in Ealing's *It Always Rains on Sunday* (1947). The casting of Chapman as Wisdom's stooge was an inspired idea, with Chapman's blustery respectability making an admirable foil for the Wisdom characters, and a nice contrast to the more upper-bracket Desmonde. In this film, Chapman has no major scenes with Wisdom, but his character is already fully-formed. The film actually contains a plethora of Wisdom straight-men - Jerry Desmonde and Eddie Leslie appear in brief 'guest' roles, Desmonde uncredited. Bill Fraser, Wisdom's stooge in a special TV show before the Queen to celebrate the Coronation, plays a workmate. Margaret Rutherford returns in a rather over-the-top cameo as a rich, Irish, animal-loving eccentric. Jockey Eddie Diamond is played by Vic Wise, the old 'proprietor' of *Vic's Grill.*

Norman is once again trying to raise money, this time the considerable amount needed to purchase a pendant. He wishes to give this to Anne, a girl whom he admires from afar as she dresses the shop-window across from his workplace. Norman 'borrows' £1 off his overbearing mother in order to place an accumulator bet on all the six Goodwood mounts of jockey Eddie Diamond. The first five horses come in, but Norman finds out that the last, Old Caspar, has no hope and is told that his only chance to win the bet is to buy up the horse and withdraw it. In fact, though he succeeds in the purchase, he fails to get it scrapped. All turns out well when it transpires that Diamond had failed to make the weight and had switched mounts and won on another horse. Despite dealing with the decidedly unscrupulous turn accountants Lumb & Weaver, Norman actually collects his money thanks to the clever machinations of the company secretary and Lumb's girlfriend, Miss Daviot.

'The reason that he is so seldom really funny is that he has not yet the priceless gift of making trite situations look new.' *Financial Times.* 'I found the quieter passages of his performance here not only likeable but even funny.' *Sunday Times.* 'When are they going to make a film worthy of this great comedian? . . . It is a good film and will make you laugh. But I want to see Norman Wisdom as part of a real family, with genuine conflicts. He should make us cry as well as laugh.' *Daily Worker.* 'Carstairs' new comedy is Mr. Wisdom's best since *Trouble in Store.*' *News Chronicle.* 'It is funny for 10 of its 86 minutes, and since this is a definite step forward in the saga of Wisdom films, I thought I'd better record the fact.' *Daily Herald.* 'It is slow, obvious and clearly tailored to the lowest possible intelligence.' *Evening News.*

THE SQUARE PEG (John Paddy Carstairs, 1958) b/w 89 mins.
Rank. Prod: Hugh Stewart; sc: Jack Davies, Henry Blyth, Norman Wisdom, Eddie Leslie; ph: Jack Cox. Cast: Norman Wisdom (Norman Pitkin/ General Schreiber), Honor Blackman (Lesley Cartland), Edward Chapman (Mr. Grimsdale), Campbell Singer (Sgt. Loder), Hattie Jacques (Gretchen), Brian Worth (Henri Le Blanc), Terence Alexander (Captain Wharton), John Warwick (Col. Layton), Eddie Leslie (Medical Officer), Frank Williams (Capt. Ford). Pinewood Studios. Video available in UK.

The last Norman Wisdom for John Paddy Carstairs. There had been some disagreements with producer Hugh Stewart, and Carstairs wished to be given directorial assignments outside comedy, hankering to return to the sort of atmospheric thrillers with which he had excelled earlier. He was also unhappy with Wisdom taking on the dual role. In fact, Carstairs was to direct only four more features, amongst which were starring vehicles for Tommy Steele and Charlie Drake. He worked extensively in television, continued to pursue his writing career and staged a few plays at the Richmond Theatre before his death after a period of ill-health in December 1970.

For the first time Wisdom plays Norman Pitkin, the best remembered of his character names and the one by which Wisdom was known in Russia. The film tells the story of an unsung war hero, Norman, an expert road-digger for St. Godric's Borough Council under his boss, Edward Chapman. Chapman at last embodies the immortal Mr. Grimsdale. While dealing with a road subsidence outside an army camp, Norman clashes with the troops and in revenge the Commanding Officer has him called up along with his pompous boss. Drafted into the Pioneer Corps, Norman and Mr. Grimsdale soon find themselves at the French front - in fact too far forward - and Grimsdale is captured. It turns out that the local German General is Norman's double, and through impersonating him Norman is able to effect the escape of Grimsdale and the local Resistance workers. On returning to England, Norman is rewarded for his bravery by being appointed Mayor.

'He is a competent professional performer with a way of endearing himself to audiences. Here he is fed the right kind of "gags" and there is sufficient substance in the script to prevent him from endlessly repeating himself and relying overmuch on a cloth cap and a wide expanse of mouth.' The Times. 'The best Norman Wisdom film so far: greater range, and the star shedding most of his usual beaming self-approval.' Sunday Times. 'He is given the opportunity to reveal true acting talent as the German Officer . . . I like this sign of progress in Wisdom.' News of the World. 'This film, I am glad to say, presents Norman Wisdom without his funny little suit . . . Despite corn this makes Wisdom's best film so far.' Evening Standard.

111

FOLLOW A STAR (Robert Asher, 1959) b/w 104 mins. Rank. Prod: Hugh Stewart; sc: Jack Davies, Henry Blyth, Norman Wisdom; ph: Jack Asher. Cast: Norman Wisdom (Norman Trustcott), June Laverick (Judy), Jerry Desmonde (Vernon Carew), Hattie Jacques (Dympha Dobson), Richard Wattis (Dr. Chatterway), Eddie Leslie (Harold Franklin), John Le Mesurier (Birkett), Fenella Fielding (Lady Finchington), Joe Melia (Palladium Stage Manager), Richard Caldicott (Conductor), Ron Moody (Violinist), Dick Emery (Inebriated Party Guest), Sidney Tafler (Recording Manager), Edie Martin (Old Lady), Charles Heslop (General), Charles Gray (Taciturn Man At Party). Pinewood Studios. Video available in UK.

The last film to be made under the original seven-year contract. It was also the first time that Robert Asher, who had been first assistant on *One Good Turn* and *Man of the Moment*, was in the directorial chair. Robert's brother Jack, an eminent cameraman most closely associated with the horror films made by Hammer, came in as photographer. The theatre which acts as the Hippodrome was actually the Metropolitan Theatre of Varieties in the Edgware Road, the very place where Wisdom was working in the last week of the touring revue *Let's Make Hey* in August 1947. As the film was being shot, the famous Frank Matcham building was under a death sentence due to road-widening and was finally demolished in 1962. *Follow a Star* also contains a nice cameo from the ancient Ealing stalwart Edie Martin, almost her last film appearance, as the old lady who shows the nervous Norman across the busy road.

This time Norman works in a cleaners, but his ambition is to sing. His hero, old-fashioned crooner Vernon Carew, walks into the shop to have his suit cleaned and pressed, and Norman gets free tickets for the night's performance in return. The sparsely attended show is a disaster, and his attempt to win over the audience on Carew's behalf leads the manager to throw the spotlight on Norman. Carew sees the chance to revive a flagging career and, in cahoots with his agent Harold Franklin, plans to steal Norman's voice while pretending to be giving him singing lessons. The plan is a great success and Carew shoots back into the hit parade. The suspicions of Norman's real tutor, Miss Dobson, and his crippled girlfriend, Judy, are aroused but attempts to expose Carew's fraud go astray because of Norman's lack of confidence - especially when separated from Judy. The news that Carew is to headline at the London Palladium is the final straw and Miss Dobson ties up Carew in his dressing room and sends Norman on stage in his place. Norman is so nervous he is unable to sing, but draws many laughs in his inadvertent comic turn. Carew frees himself and claims back the stage only to be exposed as a fraud when the record of Norman's voice to which he is miming is played at the wrong speed. Norman is revealed as a star and at last feels confident enough to propose to Judy.

'Norman Wisdom's best film yet . . . for 95 out of 104 minutes you don't have to squirm. The little man just fools around, being funny in his own inimitable way and demonstrating once more why he is the only star in British films today who has consistently made a profit for the Rank Organisation.' *Daily Express.* 'The film is full of these crazy laughs.' *News of the World.* 'Starts with Norman Wisdom in one brilliant gag, and has another near the end . . . the going in between is patchy.' *Daily Telegraph.* 'The only comic at present providing a regular scheduled service of clowning in the ancient English music-hall tradition, a tradition worth conserving and adapting to contemporary tastes . . . he does what he does very well, and this film like most of its predecessors, will give its own public a great deal of pleasure.' *Daily Mail.* 'So here you have the absurd situation where you are invited to forget that Norman Wisdom is one of the best comedians of the day, certainly the nearest we have to Chaplin, and to believe that he is a singer of top-of-the-bill potential at the Palladium.' *Daily Star.*

THE BULLDOG BREED (Robert Asher, 1960) b/w 97 mins. Rank. Prod: Hugh Stewart; sc: Jack Davies, Henry Blyth, Norman Wisdom; ph: Jack Asher. Cast: Norman Wisdom (Norman Puckle), Ian Hunter (Admiral Blyth), David Lodge (C.P.O. Knowles), Robert Urquhart (Commander Clayton), Edward Chapman (Mr. Philpots), Eddie Byrne (P.O. Filkins), Peter Jones (Diving Instructor), John Le Mesurier (Prosecuting Counsel), Terence Alexander (Defending Counsel), Sydney Tafler (Speedboat Owner), Liz Fraser (Naafi Girl), Penny Morrell (Marlene), Harold Goodwin (Streaky Hopkinson), Johnny Briggs (Nolan), Leonard Sachs (Yachtsman), Glyn Houston (Gym Instructor), Cyril Chamberlain (Landlord), Sheila Hancock (Doris), Rosamund Lesley (Peggy), Oliver Reed (Teddy Boy), Michael Caine (Sailor). Beaconsfield Studios. Video available in UK.

Though Wisdom's seven-year contract was now over, he stayed with Rank on a film-by-film basis. Relations between the two parties had been remarkably amicable over the years, and though Wisdom had signed a contract with Knightsbridge Films so that he could make features which extended his range, there had never been much doubt that he would remain with Rank in some form. *The Bulldog Breed* utilises the familiar production team and gets off to a lively start by featuring two future superstars in early roles: Oliver Reed and Michael Caine.

Norman begins the film as a delivery boy with Dalton's yacht service, lovesick for the cashier at the local cinema. When she turns his proposal down, Norman decides to end it all. Various suicide attempts prove unsuccessful, but the last of these leads to his joining the navy after he is rescued by a naval officer. Soon Norman is the navy's newest recruit and takes his place on the destroyer *HMS Dorchester* at the time when Admiral Blyth is discussing plans to put a man into space. The Admiral is convinced that any naval recruit is capable of piloting the rocket and Norman is selected. However, Norman proves incapable during training and is reduced to looking after the Admiral's bulldog, Bosun. Things do not go as planned since, during Bosun's nightly stroll, the dog spots a rabbit and gives chase - straight into the rocket. The pursuing Norman is stranded in the spacecraft alone and is mistakenly launched into space. By more luck than judgment, Norman brings the rocket down safely on a Polynesian Island and, by finding himself stranded in the arms of a beautiful native girl, fulfils his naval ambition!

'Near hysteria round me in the stalls showed that Norman Wisdom's contribution was up to standard.' *Sunday Times*. 'Strictly one for the fans.' *Evening Standard*. 'Admirers of Mr. Wisdom will know what to expect. So will non-admirers. Both will be right.' *Daily Mail*. 'Given the few chances he gets in this film, he makes the most of them and is very funny . . . He *is* good. But, there simply isn't a chance for him to float this whole film on his own, and in between the patches of Wisdom, it is a very silly picture.' *Sunday Express*. 'For Norman Wisdom fans, I can unhesitatingly recommend *The Bulldog Breed* . . . it gave me the laugh of the week.' *News of the World*.

THERE WAS A CROOKED MAN (Stuart Burge, 1960) b/w 107 mins. Knightsbridge Films for United Artists distribution. Prod: John Bryan; sc: Reuben Ship from the play *The Golden Legend of Schulz* by James Bridie; ph: Arthur Ibbetson. Cast: Norman Wisdom (Davy Cooper), Alfred Marks (Adolf Carter), Andrew Cruickshank (McKillup), Reginald Beckwith (Station Master), Susannah York (Ellen), Jean Clarke (Freda), Timothy Bateson (Flash Dan), Paul Whitsun-Jones (Restaurant Gentleman), Fred Griffith (Taxi Driver), Ann Heffernan (Hospital Sister), Rosalind Knight (Nurse), Reed De Rouen (Dutchman), Brian Oulton (Ashton), Glyn Houston (Smoking Machinist), Percy Herbert (Prison Warder), Edna Petrie (Woman At Assembly Hall), Jack May (Police Sergeant), Ronald Fraser (Gen. Cummins), Ed Devereaux (American Colonel), Sam Kydd (Foreman Jackson), Redmond Phillips (Padre), Fred Haggerty, Eddie Boyce, Totti Truman-Taylor, William Hutt, John Barrard, John Kidd. Pinewood Studios.

Of the various negotiations which took place outside Rank, two caught the interest of the press. The first were rumours of an American contract involving huge sums of money, but nothing more was heard. The second did yield results and these were with Knightsbridge Films and had started as early as June 1959. Ironically, Knightsbridge was owned by producer John Bryan and director Ronald Neame, the very team which had rejected the opportunity to produce Wisdom's starring debut at Rank. In fact only two of the three intended films materialised: *There was a Crooked Man* and *The Girl on the Boat*, both of which mark important departures from the familiar Gump persona. John Bryan was best known in the industry as one of Britain's most distinguished Art Directors. Born in 1911, he learnt his trade as an assistant on such famous films as *Things to Come* in 1936 before graduating to art director on *Stolen Life* and *Pygmalion* in 1939. From 1943 he spent a period as supervising art director at the Gainsborough Studios before moving on to designing the colour sets for *Caesar and Cleopatra*, for which he was Oscar nominated in 1945, going on to receive that award the following year for David Lean's *Great Expectations*. Here, he became associated with director Ronald Neame and they worked in partnership for many years. Together, with Bryan now working as producer, they made films like *The Card* and *The Million Pound Note* before Bryan became a contract producer with Rank. After the Knightsbridge years, Bryan went on to do the highly acclaimed production design for *Becket*, later forming a company with Peter Sellers to make *After the Fox*. Bryan died in 1969 aged 58. The director, Stuart Burge, is better known for his theatre work, and this was his first venture into the cinema. He started out as an actor with the original Young Vic before moving into stage direction. By the mid 'fifties Burge was working in television, directing the first of the classic novel adaptations, *David Copperfield*. After *The Girl on the Boat* he went on to become director of the Nottingham Playhouse and then for a few years from 1972 took over the Royal Court. In 1981 he made the acclaimed version of *Sons and Lovers* for the BBC, and has in all completed over 100 plays for television, a recent outing being Leonard Rossiter's final television play, *The Moon over Soho*. He has made only three more features for the cinema to date, including Laurence Olivier's *Othello*. See Chapter 7.

'Ninety minutes of hilarious ingenuity. Norman Wisdom has here changed his cloth cap for a battered trilby as a sign perhaps that for once he was adapting himself to a role rather than adapting the role to himself, and he has certainly been helped with unusual intelligence by his fellow-players, his director Stuart Burge and, especially, his scriptwriter, Reuben Ship. The film is, surely, farcical enough to satisfy his steady customers but it is also richly and even satirically inventive.' *Guardian*. 'The best of the Wisdom farces.' *Sunday Times*. 'Take my word for it that this is one of the most inventive and indeed witty combinations of slapstick, sentiment and absurdity.' *Evening News*. 'A sharper, quieter Norman Wisdom discards almost every trace of Gumpery . . . welcome touches of anarchy.' *Daily Herald*. 'Certainly there are some occasional flashes of Norman's impromptu and infectious humour. But they are few and far between.' *News of the World*.

THE GIRL ON THE BOAT (Henry Kaplan, 1962) b/w 91 mins. Knightsbridge Films for United Artists distribution. Prod: John Bryan; sc: Reuben Ship from the novel by P.G. Wodehouse; ph: Denys Coop. Cast: Norman Wisdom (Sam Marlowe), Millicent Martin (Billie Bennett), Richard Briers (Eustace Hignett), Philip Locke (Bream Mortimer), Sheila Hancock (Jane Hubbard), Athene Seyler (Mrs Hignett), Bernard Cribbins (Peters), Noel Willman (Webster), Ronald Fraser (Colonel), Reginald Beckwith (Barman), Dick Bentley (American), Timothy Bateson (Assistant Purser), Peter Bull (Blacksmith), Martin Wyldeck (J.P. Mortimer), William Sherwood (Mr. Bennett). Shepperton Studios.

The second film for Knightsbridge turned out to be the last, the third feature specified in the contract never being completed. Like *There was a Crooked Man*, *The Girl on the Boat* was scripted by Reuben Ship. Ship was a Canadian, born in 1917. During the 'forties and 'fifties he wrote a number of books and plays both for stage and radio in America before finding himself hauled in front of the HUAC investigating committee into Communism. Named as a Communist by several 'friendly' witnesses, Ship was deported to Canada in August 1953. Later he came to England, often working under a pseudonym. One of his most acclaimed works on British television was an adaptation of James Thurber's *The Greatest Man in the World*. *The Girl on the Boat* meant an even bigger change of image for Wisdom. He plays Sam Marlowe, a member of the rich idle classes. A strong cast was assembled with Richard Briers, a pre-*That Was The Week That Was* Millicent Martin, and *The Rag Trade*'s Sheila Hancock. Knightsbridge continued its policy of giving new directors a chance, and *The Girl on the Boat* marked the debut for its director, Henry Kaplan. The film remains Kaplan's only feature outing and he has since worked mainly in television. *See* Chapter 7.

'All credit to Norman Wisdom (as the upper-crust Sam) for trying to break away completely from his more usual knockabout clowning. But he doesn't seem at home in this role which offers him too few opportunities to exploit the simple slapstick talent that has made him so popular.' *Daily Cinema*. 'Outmoded farce, the screenplay not only defies all attempts by Norman Wisdom, one of our most versatile comedians, to raise a laugh, but also hamstrings the hand-picked supporting players . . . Norman Wisdom can sing, dance, mime and is no mean instrumentalist, yet he discards all these gifts to play a run-of-the-mill comedy role as Sam.' *Kinematograph Weekly*. 'Norman Wisdom here attempts something more reticent than his customary over-extrovert style. Despite the convincing enough '20s setting, the Wodehouse story, a few good moments, and a choice piece of character playing here and there, nothing about the film quite comes off . . . Norman Wisdom is essentially an actor whom one either likes a great deal or not at all, but even his supporters might scratch their heads at this and prefer the usual figure with the funny cap.' *Monthly Film Bulletin.*

ON THE BEAT (Robert Asher, 1962) b/w 105 mins. Rank. Prod: Hugh Stewart; sc: Jack Davies, Norman Wisdom, Eddie Leslie; ph: Geoffrey Faithfull. Cast: Norman Wisdom (Norman Pitkin/Giulio Napolitani), Jennifer Jayne (Rosanna), Raymond Huntley (Sir Ronald Ackroyd), David Lodge (Supt. Hobson), Esma Cannon (Mrs. Stammers), Eric Barker (Doctor), Eleanor Summerfield (Sgt Wilkins), Ronnie Stevens (Oberon), Terence Alexander (Chief Supt. Belcher), Maurice Kaufmann (Vince), Dilys Laye (American Lady), Campbell Singer (Mr. Bollington), Lionel Murton (Man In Underground Train), Monty Landis (Mr. Bassett), Alfred Burke (Trigger O'Flynn), John Blythe (Chauffeur), Cyril Chamberlain (Café Proprietor). Pinewood Studios. Video available in UK.

ON THE BEAT reunites Wisdom with Rank and the familiar team of Asher, Stewart and Davies. The film marks a return to Gump territory and a calculatedly safe consolidation of Wisdom's screen popularity, returning to high-flying box office returns. The film provides the star with a meaty double role, a wide variety of routines and a fine supporting cast.

Norman Pitkin works at Scotland Yard as a car-park attendant. His ambition is to join the force and so follow in his father's footsteps. Sadly, he is too short to be accepted, and even gets fired from his car-park job following differences with the Metropolitan Police Commissioner, Sir Ronald Ackroyd. A desolate Norman fails to bluff his way into the constabulary but cannot resist the temptation to wander the streets dressed in his father's oversize uniform - which leads to his arrest for impersonating a police officer. In the meantime, London's crime-fighters have a problem gathering suitable evidence against Italian-born gangster Giulio Napolitani who uses his hairdressing salon as headquarters for his jewel-snatching mob. Napolitani has been offered the beautiful Rosanna as a bride to patch up an inter-gang war, but she is unhappy with the arrangement and throws herself into the River Thames as a more palatable alternative. Back at the Yard, Sir Ronald has noticed the striking resemblance between Napolitani and Norman and, despite misgivings and because of pressure from the Home Secretary, he enrols Norman into the police to do undercover work disguised as Napolitani. Norman succeeds in his task, arresting Napolitani and rescuing Rosanna who had fallen back into the gang-leader's clutches. Now a fully-fledged constable, Norman is free to marry Rosanna.

'Every Norman Wisdom film is dispiriting for the flashes which from time to time suggest that, used with taste and discipline, he might have been a good comic. *On the Beat* rises very slightly above the average of recent Wisdom vehicles. The mawkish self-pity is restrained: the gags are usually visual and sometimes quite inventive.' *Financial Times*. 'This is a Norman Wisdom film, and that, for those who know about these things, is almost enough in the way of explanation and criticism.' *The Times*.

A STITCH IN TIME (Robert Asher, 1963) b/w 94 mins. Rank. Prod: Hugh Stewart; sc: Jack Davies, Norman Wisdom, Eddie Leslie; ph: Jack Asher. Cast: Norman Wisdom (Norman Pitkin), Edward Chapman (Mr. Grimsdale), Jeanette Sterke (Janet Haskell), Jerry Desmonde (Sir Hector), Jill Melford (Lady Brinkley), Glyn Houston (Welsh), Hazel Hughes (Matron), Patsy Rowlands (Amy), Peter Jones (Russell), Ernest Clark (Prof. Crankshaw), Lucy Appleby (Lindy), Vera Day (Betty), Frank Williams (Nuttall), Penny Morrell (Nurse Pudkin), Patrick Cargill (Dr. Meadows), Francis Matthews (Benson), Pamela Conway (Patient), Danny Green (Ticehurst), Johnny Briggs (Teddy Boy), John Blythe (Dale). Pinewood Studios. Video available in UK.

A Stitch in Time is often cited by Wisdom as his favourite film, and his considerable control over its scripting is underlined by the film's emphasis on pathos. Wisdom's scriptwriters had always left gaps in the script for Wisdom to fill in with bits of business, but over the years his contributions were becoming more and more extensive. Jack Davies takes the official credit on *A Stitch in Time*. 'He used to write the original story and then he would come to me and we'd talk about it. I made a lot of suggestions which would be written in. Eventually he said that it wasn't fair that I didn't get a credit and so my name went up as well. Eddie Leslie, of course, was a good writer, and it got so that Jack didn't mind as long as we'd finish it. Eventually, with *A Stitch in Time*, Eddie Leslie and I went off to Spain and wrote the entire script just from an idea of Jack's - and Jack put his name to it! But he was good - and a marvellous bloke.' The film proved an astonishing success, Wisdom's most profitable at the box office breaking records at all 26 cinemas used for the initial London release. With Rank/Odeon admitting to the film taking more money than their previous year's best - the Sean Connery/James Bond *From Russia with Love* - *A Stitch in Time* was probably Rank Distributors' biggest home-market money-spinner to that date. The film also has the considerable bonus of featuring Jerry Desmonde's finest screen performance.

Once more, Wisdom plays Norman Pitkin, now a butcher's assistant to the ubiquitous Mr. Grimsdale. Just before the end of work on early closing day, a teddy-boy (*Coronation Street*'s Johnny Briggs) holds up the store with a gun and in the ensuing panic Mr. Grimsdale manages to swallow his gold watch and chain. At St. Godric's Hospital, to which Grimsdale is finally transported, Norman causes trouble, especially for its chairman, Sir Hector, who is trying to raise money from Lady Brinkley towards a children's holiday homes appeal. Eventually, Norman's well-meaning antics lead him to being banned from the hospital, but not before he has brought a glimmer of happiness to a recently orphaned child, Lindy. Unsuccessfully, Grimsdale attempts to help Norman gain entrance to the hospital, though less for altruistic reasons than to recover his watch which Norman gave to Lindy. In the end, to forestall Norman's threatened resignation, Grimsdale suggests Norman gatecrashes a televised St. John Ambulance fund-raising concert so that he can at least wave to the watching Lindy. On the night, Lindy is not allowed to watch the television, so she makes her way to the Arlington Hotel where the concert is taking place to find Norman making a mockery of the band's precision routines. Finally, with the well-heeled audience laughing at his mishaps, Norman launches into a speech which shames them into donating fulsomely to the appeal. Sir Hector chases after Norman to congratulate him, only for his quarry to misread his intentions and flee, accompanied by Grimsdale, straight under a car! Only then do Norman and Grimsdale get into hospital - as patients.

'This is one of the funniest of all Wisdom comedies.' *Daily Mail*. 'Almost by definition Norman Wisdom is timeless. Regardless of the film, he goes through the same series of gags, grimaces and goo. This time the setting is medical, but it doesn't really make any difference. Mr. Wisdom apparently enjoys great popularity. I can't for the life of me see why.' *Guardian*. 'His kind of comedy is not mine. But a lot of people do find him wildly funny and judging by the roars of laughter at the private showing, his fans will not be disappointed this time.' *Daily Herald*. '. . . most film critics look around at the rest of the audience and ask, bewildered: "What's so funny about that?" But the audience is too busy choking themselves with laughter to tell them.' *Evening News*. '. . . not only unfunny, but in pretty poor taste.' *Sunday Express*.

THE EARLY BIRD (Robert Asher, 1965) colour 98 mins.
Rank. Prod: Hugh Stewart; sc: Jack Davies, Norman Wisdom, Eddie Leslie, Henry Blyth; ph: Jack Asher. Cast: Norman Wisdom (Norman Pitkin), Edward Chapman (Mr. Grimsdale), Jerry Desmonde (Hunter), Paddie O'Neil (Mrs. Hoskins), Bryan Pringle (Austin), Richard Vernon (Sir Roger), John Le Mesurier (Col. Foster), Peter Jeffrey (Fire Chief), Penny Morrell (Miss Curry), Marjie Lawrence (Woman In Negligée), Frank Thornton (Doctor), Dandy Nichols (Woman Swamped By Milk), Harry Locke (Commissionaire), Michael Bilton (Nervous Man), Imogen Hassall (Sir Roger's Secretary), Eddie Leslie (Slater), David Lodge (Arguing Man). Pinewood Studios. Video available in UK.

After *A Stitch in Time*, there was a break of two years before the release of this film. In between there was a public rift between Rank and their star.

Wisdom, with the box office records set by *A Stitch in Time* up his sleeve, demanded a greater say in his films, yearning to be assigned more adventurous projects. Rank would not relent, and after Hugh Stewart rejected the provisionally entitled *Turn Again Wisdom*, a Jack Davies script from a story by Wisdom, no film was agreed for 1964. Both parties probably regretted the decision. Wisdom moved into a stage musical, *The Roar of the Greasepaint - The Smell of the Crowd*, which died during its out-of-town run, and Rank attempted to groom Morecambe & Wise as Wisdom's successors with poor results: witness their debut feature, directed by Asher and produced by Stewart, *The Intelligence Men*. As for *The Early Bird*, it is the film which made Norman's anguished cry of 'Mr. Grimsdale, Mr. Grimsdale' famous.

For the third time Wisdom plays Norman Pitkin to Chapman's Mr. Grimsdale, who this time owns a dairy and employs Norman to do the milk-round with help from the horse, Nellie. Grimsdale's business finds itself a rival in the form of the ultra-modern and ruthless Consolidated Dairies. The combine's man on the street, Austin, does not stop at underhand tactics to thwart Grimsdale's survival. Norman's fight to wrest back control of the streets causes havoc, not least in his rival chief executive's front garden and at Consolidated's headquarters. Rather than face the consequences of a continuation of Norman's activities, the combine agrees to leave Grimsdale's alone - as long as Norman leaves them alone.

'I suppose it will be as popular as all the other Wisdom films have been. People can tell margarine from butter, but they don't always have the energy.' *Sunday Telegraph*. 'Music Hall slapstick, ancient but not vintage.' *Guardian*. 'But this comic has a huge following and for me to say that I laughed only once is perhaps biography not criticism.' *Evening News*. '. . . the only film I have seen which made me feel sympathetic towards monopolies.' *Sun*.

THE SANDWICH MAN (Robert Hartford-Davis, 1966) colour 95 mins. Titan International for Rank. Prod: Peter Newbrook; sc: Michael Bentine, Robert Hartford-Davis; ph: Peter Newbrook. Cast: Michael Bentine (Horace Quilby), Suzy Kendall (Sue), David Buck (Steven), Tracey Crisp (Girl In The Plastic Mac), Norman Wisdom (Father O'Malley). Other guest stars include: Max Bacon, Alfie Bass, Dora Bryan, Earl Cameron, Gerald Campion, Michael Chaplin, Harry H. Corbett, Bernard Cribbins, Diana Dors, Fred Emney, Frank Finlay, Ian Hendry, Stanley Holloway, Peter Jones, John Junkin, Jeremy Lloyd, John Le Mesurier, David Lodge, Michael Medwin, Warren Mitchell, Ron Moody, Anna Quayle, Ronnie Stevens, Sydney Tafler, Terry-Thomas, Wilfrid Hyde White, Donald Wolfit. Various London locations.

Wisdom appears in a cameo in this Titan production, a £250,000 film which constituted part of a co-production deal between Rank and the National Film Finance Corporation, and which provided its writer, Michael Bentine, with his first substantial film role. Titan Films consisted of producer/photographer Peter Newbrook and director Robert Hartford-Davis. Newbrook had worked as a camera operator on David Lean epics such as *The Bridge on the River Kwai* and *Lawrence of Arabia* during his long career which stretches back to 1934. Titan's co-founder Robert Hartford-Davis entered the industry as a teenager before working his way to the States as a photographer on the *Queen Elizabeth*, later taking a university degree in California. Back in England he worked as assistant to John Huston, Basil Dearden and King Vidor as well as directing for television, completing an episode of the embryo *Avengers* series *Police Surgeon* before undertaking a number of episodes of *Upstairs, Downstairs*. His film career never really took off despite such oddities as a Blaxploitation movie in Hollywood, *Black Gunn*. He died, aged only 54, in 1977. *The Sandwich Man* crept before an unsuspecting public without the formality of a press screening and was a total flop.

Horace Quilby, the sandwich man of the title, goes about his daily work. During his day, he bumps into a number of characters while trying to keep tabs on the progress of his prize pigeon Esmeralda, as it flies across the channel. Wisdom's nine-minute cameo is as a priest, Father O'Malley. He is an accident-prone organiser of the All Angels Boys Club who instructs his members somewhat uncertainly in gymnastics, failing to impart much knowledge with his perverse demonstrations.

'Stars or favourite character actors are picked up en route to do a turn . . . Later we have Wilfrid Hyde White talking at cross purposes, Norman Wisdom as an enthusiastic but inept priest in a boys' club gymnasium, and Stanley Holloway as a passionate horticulturist, none of whom is really seen to advantage.' *Daily Telegraph*.

PRESS FOR TIME (Robert Asher, 1966) colour 102 mins.
Titan Films for Rank. Prod: Robert Hartford-Davis, Peter Newbrook; sc: Norman Wisdom, Eddie Leslie from the book *Yea, Yea, Yea* by Angus McGill; ph: Peter Newbrook. Cast: Norman Wisdom (Norman Shields [and family]), Derek Bond (Major Bartlett), Angela Browne (Eleanor), Tracey Crisp (Ruby Fairchild), Noel Dyson (Mrs. Corcoran), Derek Francis (Alderman Corcoran), Peter Jones (Willoughby), David Lodge (Ross), Frances White (Liz), Allan Cuthbertson (Ballard), Stanley Unwin (Nottage), Gordon Rollings (Bus Conductor). Beaconsfield Studios, locations in Teignmouth. Video available in UK.

Wisdom's second film with Titan reunites him with director Robert Asher.

Sadly, this was Asher's last film. He completed much work for television before his untimely death in 1979 after several years of relative inactivity.

Wisdom plays Norman Shields, a newspaper vendor at Westminster Underground station, who can claim the Prime Minister as his grandfather. The P.M. is persuaded that it would be politically astute to place Norman in a job as far away from London as possible, and so he blackmails one of his Conservative backbenchers to employ Norman as a journalist on a provincial newspaper. Once at his new job in the seaside town of Tinmouth, Norman gets caught between the Labour Council, led by Alderman Corcoran, and the Tory M.P. with disastrous results. After a debacle at a beauty contest he has organised, Norman berates both the local politicians for their petty party squabbling. The whole of his outburst is heard by the cheering audience, and when Norman leaves town with the loving Liz, daughter of Alderman Corcoran, he is delighted to hear that dialogue between the two parties has begun.

'. . . the most amusing Wisdom film I can recall for quite a while.' *Evening Standard*. 'As for the scripting and direction of this particular vehicle for Mr. Wisdom's peculiar talents, they make the feeblest Carry On films look like classics of high-comic finesse.' *The Times*. 'I find his sort of vandalism a limited joke.' *Daily Mail*.

THE NIGHT THEY RAIDED MINSKY'S (William Friedkin, 1968) colour 99 mins.

Tandem Production for United Artists distribution. Prod: Norman Lear; sc: Arnold Schuman, Sidney Michaels, Norman Lear based on the book by Rowland Barber; ph: Andrew Laszlo. Cast: Jason Robards (Raymond Paine), Britt Ekland (Rachel Schpitendavel), Norman Wisdom (Chick Williams), Forrest Tucker (Trim Houlihan), Harry Andrews (Jacob Schpitendavel), Joseph Wiseman (Louis Minsky), Denholm Elliott (Vance Fowler), Elliott Gould (Bill Minsky), Jack Burns (Candy Butcher), Bert Lahr (Professor Spats), Gloria LeRoy (Mae Harris). Songs: 'Perfect Gentleman' with Jason Robards. Other songs: 'Take Ten Terrific Girls, 'You Rat You', 'The Night They Raided Minsky's'. U.S.A. Video available in USA. See Chapter 9.

'The film also makes an excellent debut in US-made pictures for British comic Norman Wisdom . . . So easily does Wisdom dominate his many scenes, other cast members suffer by comparison.' *Variety*. 'His pratfalls and his expert knockabout pantomime, as the fall guy for the crooked straight man Jason Robards, is an absolute delight.' *Daily Sketch*. 'Wisdom, long a British Stage star, recalls Keaton in his split-second spills and deadpan pantomime.' *Time*. 'Norman is a great clown and puts over a much better show when being directed than when he tries to run the whole thing himself.' *People*. 'Norman Wisdom has never looked so good on the screen before.' *Sunday Telegraph*.

WHAT'S GOOD FOR THE GOOSE (Menahem Golan, 1969) colour 104 mins. 'A' certificate version; 85 mins: 'U' certificate version. Tigon. Prod: Tony Tenser; Associate Prod: Norman Wisdom; sc: Norman Wisdom from a story by Menahem Golan; dialogue: Christopher Gilmore; ph: William Brayne. Cast: Norman Wisdom (Timothy Bartlett), Sally Geeson (Nikki), Sally Bazely (Margaret Bartlett), Sarah Atkinson (Meg), Derek Francis (Harrington), Terence Alexander (Frisby), Karl Lanchbury (Peter), Paul Whitsun-Jones (Clark), David Lodge (Hotel Porter), Stuart Nichol (Bank Manager), Hilary Pritchard (Disco Cashier), H.H. Goldsmith (Policeman), Thelma Falls-Hand (Bank Clerk), George Meaton (Delegate), Duncan Taylor (Delegate), Jonathan Cox (Son), Sally Begley (Daughter), Patrick Goggin (Son), The Pretty Things (Pop Group). Songs: 'What's Good For The Goose'. The Pretty Things perform 'Blow Your Mind', 'Alexandra', 'Never Be Me', 'Eagle's Sun'. Shot on location in Southport. Video available in UK under title GIRL TROUBLE.

Norman Wisdom's last feature film to date, and the one with which he took most control, being its associate producer and scriptwriter as well as star. The producer was Tony Tenser for his company Tigon British. Tenser had something of a legendary background as a film publicist before forming Compton-Tekli with Michael Klinger, a company which produced Roman Polanski's *Repulsion* and *Cul-de-Sac* amongst its wide-ranging commercial programme. Hand in hand with this production activity, Compton made fortunes through opportunistic exhibition of soft-core sex films. Tenser broke away in 1966 to form Tigon, whose stated production brief was to turn out good family-type action pictures, the most celebrated of which were a series of horror films including *The Curse of the Crimson Altar* and *Witchfinder General*! In 1971 Laurie Marsh took over and Tigon became an entirely different company, though Tenser remained as the group's managing director. The director of the film was another man destined to play an enormous role in the commercial industry in Britain and the rest of the world, Menahem Golan. Born in Tel Aviv, he began in the entertainment trade through being assistant director at the National Theatre in Habima. He studied at the Old Vic School of Theatre Directors and the London Academy Of Music And Drama before returning to Israel as a fully-fledged theatre director. He soon became enamoured of film-making and went to America to study in New York, working for a short time as an assistant to Roger Corman. Back in Israel, he rapidly rose to a position of dominance in his home industry before making his influence felt worldwide. *What's Good for the Goose* was his first of many directorial efforts outside

Israel. For many years he was at the helm of Cannon Films, the company which he set up with his cousin Yoram Globus. He subsequently left Cannon to set up 21st Century Film Corporation. *See* Chapter 7.

'. . .yields far fewer laughs than we have come to expect of him.' *Daily Mail.* 'It is in every way the most embarrassing, horrific and painful film I have seen in many a long year.' *Observer.* 'Crass comedy . . . Just the old complaint, in fact - too unfunny.' *Evening Standard.* 'For ineptitude, obviousness, tepid salacity and squirm-making embarrassment, I have never seen anything to match this story.' *Evening News.* '. . . often repellent film.' *Sunday Mirror.*

TO SEE SUCH FUN (Jon Scoffield, 1977) b/w:colour 90 mins.
Cast: Norman Wisdom, Dirk Bogarde, Marty Feldman, Alec Guinness, Benny Hill, Eric Idle, Spike Milligan, Margaret Rutherford etc.
    Compilation of clips from British comedies 1930-1970 made for the American video market.

HEINEKEN - SHOWREEL OF TV ADS 1973-1983 (1983) colour 20 mins.
Compilation of lager ads issued in association with book *Thirsty Work: Ten Years of Heineken Advertising* (*see* bibliography) which includes Norman Wisdom's 2-minute ad DECKCHAIR (Paul Weiland, 1980) which also features the director as the waiter!

I'M NOT A DENTIST, BUT I RECOGNISE THIS (David Boyce, 1990) colour 15 mins.
Cast: Julie Westwood with guest appearances by Norman Wisdom, Rolf Harris, Leslie Crowther, Boy George, Claire Grogan.
    Student film: a musical satire on advertising and copywriting.

NORMAN WISDOM LIVE ON STAGE (Ross Chadler, 1990) colour 57 mins.
Millenium Productions in association with Conquest Productions and Ravensdale Film & Television. Executive Prod: Vijay Armarnani: Prod: Richard Nicolle; offline editors: Richard Halladay, Elaine Edwards; online editors: Bill Ogden, Michael J. Pearce; musical director: Terry White. Norman Wisdom and Tony Fayne recorded live on stage at the Playhouse, Harlow, Essex, on 28th October 1989. Beckmann Home Video Release.

APPENDIX 2

Stage.

The following is a list of all Norman Wisdom's stage performances so far traced. For more details on individual shows please see text or illustrations where indicated. NW = Norman Wisdom. V = Turn on a Variety bill. RVP = Royal Variety Performance. Where no place name is given, it is a London venue.

1945	Collins Music Hall (V): see illustration.
1946	Basingstoke Grand (V); Portsmouth Coliseum (V); Hastings De Luxe (V). Touring Revue: NEW NAMES MAKE NEWS/SOMETHING TO SHOUT ABOUT (10 weeks): Barrow in Furness, Gateshead Her Majesty's, Blackburn Grand, Burnley Vic, Loughborough Theatre Royal, Leigh, Bolton, Brighton, Harrogate, Hanley.
1946/47	Brighton Grand: ROBINSON CRUSOE Renée Houston (Billy Crusoe), Hugh Rene (Mrs. Crusoe), NW (Mate), Olive Lucius (Robinson Crusoe), Jean Carson (Polly Perkins), Donald Stewart.
1947	Brighton Grand (V); Touring Revue: LET'S MAKE HEY (10 weeks): Derby, Liverpool Pavilion, Leicester, Finsbury Park Empire, Wood Green Empire, Edgware Metropolitan, Brighton Grand; Victoria Palace (V): unbilled place in charity line-up with Laurel & Hardy, Vera Lynn etc.; Skegness Holiday Camp (V); Brussels Alhambra, Belgium: PICCADILLY NIGHTS revue.
1948	Blackpool Palace (V); Brighton Hippodrome (V); Chiswick Empire (V); Knightstone: OUT OF THE BLUE (V); London Casino (V): with Allan Jones, see illustration; Golders Green Hippodrome (V); Bridlington Grand; Scarborough Spa: OUT OF THE BLUE (V) summer season; Leicester Palace (V); Great Yarmouth Windmill (V); London Casino (V); Loughborough Theatre Royal (V); Hull Tivoli; Eastbourne Hippodrome (V); Hastings De Luxe (V); Folkestone Queen's (V); New Cross Empire (V); Brighton Grand (V); Wolverhampton Hippodrome (V); Sheffield Empire (V); Nottingham Empire (V); Glasgow Empire (V).

1948/49	Birmingham Alexandra: ROBINSON CRUSOE NW (Billy Crusoe), Eddie Leslie (Dame), George and Jimmy Paige (Bosun and Mate), Donovan and Byl (Stowaways), Betty Huntley-Wright (Robinson Crusoe), Rosalie Allen (Polly Perkins), Gerald Cuff (Will Atkins), Pauline Williams (Good Fairy).
1949	Swindon Empire (V); Folkestone Pleasure Gardens (V); Bolton Grand (V); Dewsbury Empire (V); Clapham Grand (V); York Empire (V); Blackpool Grand: BUTTONS & BOWS (V) summer season with Billy Russell, George Formby. New York talent contest.
1949/50	Wolverhampton Grand: ROBINSON CRUSOE NW (Billy Crusoe), Eddie Leslie (Dame), Lorna Dean (Robinson Crusoe), Gerald Cuff (Will Atkins), Jerry Jerome (Mate), Dave Jackley (Bosun), Patrick Colbert (Cannibal King/ Father Neptune), Sheila Trigg (Polly Perkins), Donovan and Byl, Danny Lipton. Directed by William Summers.
1950	Cambridge Theatre: SAUCE PIQUANT revue; Brighton Grand (V); Hull Tivoli (V); Chatham Empire: New Cross Empire: Brighton Grand: Northampton New Theatre: Folkestone Pleasure Gardens: Eastbourne Royal: FUN OF THE FAIR (V) with George Pughe.
1950/51	Birmingham Alexandra: CINDERELLA NW (Buttons), Betty Leslie-Smith (Cinderella), Helene Cooney (Prince Charming), Ruthene Le Clerc (Dandini), Betty Nelson (Fairy Queen), Michael Moore (Baron Hardup), Terry Kendall, Nick Nissen (Ugly Sisters), the Three Monarchs. Directed by Oliver Gordon.
1951	Variety Tour: Peterborough Coliseum etc; Empress Hall: LONDON MELODY (7 months) Belita (Catherine), NW (Angelo), Brita Hales (Gisela), Markby Ryan (Napoleon Courmayeur), George Tiley (Felix), Diana Grafton (Mrs. Carlson), Joel Riordan (Carl), Tom Round (Paul), Luise Tranzinger (Lisa), Bruce Gordon (Boris), Lorna Martin, Manfred Felix, Terence Donahue, Guy Massey, Ben Johnson, Richardena Jackson, Laurence Goodwin, Tommy Jover, Raff & Julian, Evelyn Dove, The Allen Brothers & June, Joe & Evie Slack. Sc: Eve Bradfield. Music: Richard Farnon. Lyrics: Patricia Nash. Empress Hall Orch. conducted by Harry Rabinowitz. Produced by Eve Bradfield.

1951/52	Wolverhampton Grand: CINDERELLA NW (Buttons), Ruthene Le Clerc (Prince Charming), Jean Inglis (Cinderella), Stella Holles (Dandini), Terry & Doric Kendall (Ugly Sisters), Fenella Scott (Fairy Queen), The Three Monarchs.
1952	Birmingham Hippodrome: Norwich Theatre Royal: Prince of Wales: PARIS TO PICCADILLY with NW, Eddie Leslie, Bobby Tranter, Mini Gerrard, Medlock & Marlowe. Comedy scenes directed by Charles Henry. Staged by Dick Hurran. NW and Eddie Leslie take time out at Christmas for panto and are replaced by Archie Robbins and Leslie Randall; Deal Regent (Charity V); Adelphi (Charity V); London Palladium: RVP (3/11/1952 - see illustration).
1952/53	Coventry Hippodrome: JACK AND THE BEANSTALK NW (Simple Simon), Julie Andrews (Princess Bettina), Joan Mann (Jack), Eddie Henderson (Dame), Finlay Brothers.
1953	Prince of Wales: PARIS TO PICCADILLY continues run. Coventry Hippodrome (Charity V).
1953/54	Empress Hall: SINBAD THE SAILOR NW (Norman), Andra McLaughlin (Sinbad), Basil Cudlipp-Green (Caliph), Jack Harris (Vizier), Ronald Privett (Allibad), Jane Conlon (Princess), Diana Grafton (Mrs Sinbad), Joan Connell (Armida), John Moss (Magician), Errol Lake (Prince Hassan), Heather Belbin (The Genie), Joe McGuirk (Old Man of the Sea), Larry Barnes (Gorilla) with Joan & Jennifer Nicks. Sc: Eve Bradfield. Lyrics: Patricia Nash. The Empress Orch. and Choir under Leonard Morris who also wrote special music. Produced by Eve Bradfield.
1954	Birmingham Hippodrome: NW in 'Sketches and Variety' with Jerry Desmonde, Joan Regan; PALLADIUM SHOW NW with Jerry Desmonde, Walter Wahl, The Three Monarchs, Gillian Moran, Teddy Hale. Produced by Dick Hurran; The London Palladium: RVP (1/11/1954 - ballet from THE PALLADIUM SHOW with Gillian Moran).
1954/55	Prince of Wales: A GAY MUSICAL SHOW transfer of THE PALLADIUM SHOW with the same cast except

Tony Fayne & David Evans replace The Three Monarchs and Teddy Hale.

1955	Amsterdam (V): Brighton Hippodrome: Birmingham Hippodrome: Liverpool Empire: PAINTING THE TOWN.
1955/56	The London Palladium: PAINTING THE TOWN NW with Jerry Desmonde, Ruby Murray, Pauline Chamberlain, Nanci Crompton, June Ellis. The George Mitchell Singers. London Palladium Orch. conducted by Eric Rogers. Produced by Dick Hurran.
1956	The London Palladium: PAINTING THE TOWN continues run. Weymouth (Charity V); German tour for troops; Brighton Hippodrome (Charity V) with Harry Secombe.
1956/57	The London Palladium: THE WONDERFUL LAMP NW (Aladdin), Sonnie Hale (Widow Twankey), Stephanie Voss (Princess Yasmin), Valentine Dyall (Abanazar), Fisher Morgan (Emperor of China), Ken Wilson (Grand Vizier), Tom Gill (Kamar), Anne Cumming (Chi-Lee), Dave Jackley, Johnny Volant Trio, Ronnie Brodie, Osborne Whittaker, Jope Jackman, David Davenport, Agnes Bernelle. George Mitchell Singers. Orch. conducted by Eric Rogers. Book by Phil Park, Robert Nesbitt. Staged by Robert Nesbitt.
1957	Olympia: guest with Billy Smart's Circus for charity: Eastbourne Pier (V) Sandy Powell's 1000th Pier Show. Shrewsbury Granada (V); Plymouth Theatre Royal (V); Gloucester Regal Cinema (V) with Eddie Leslie. Manchester Opera House: Glasgow King's: WHERE'S CHARLEY?
1958	Stratford Memorial: Palace: WHERE'S CHARLEY? NW (Charley Wykeham), Jerry Desmonde (Sir Francis Chesney), Pip Hinton (Amy Spettigue), Felix Felton (Mr. Spettigue), Marion Grimaldi (Donna Lucia), Pamela Gale (Kitty Verdun), Terence Cooper (Jack Chesney), John Moore (Brassett), Peter Mander (Photographer), Helen Anderson (Patricia), Jill Martin (Agatha), Sheila Francis (Clara), Barry Kent (Reggie). Music and Lyrics: Frank Loesser. Book: George Abbott based on *Charley's Aunt*

by Brandon Thomas. Michael Collins & Orch. Choreography: Hanya Holm. Prod: William Chappell; London Coliseum: RVP (3/11/1958).

1958/59   Palace: WHERE'S CHARLEY? continues.

1959   South African holiday includes many public appearnaces. Stocktown Globe: Liverpool Empire: Hanley Theatre Royal: Newcastle Empire: York: Bristol Hippodrome: Coventry: Taunton Gaumont: Southend: NORMAN WISDOM SHOW with Eddie Leslie, Tony Fayne.

1959/60   Manchester Palace: ROBINSON CRUSOE NW (Norman Crusoe), Elizabeth Larner (Robinson Crusoe), Eddie Leslie (Will Atkins), Billy Whittaker (Mrs. Crusoe), Osborn Whitaker (Bosun), Terry Kendall (Mate), Patricia Stark (Polly Perkins). Staged by Harry Bright.

1960   Victoria Palace: RVP (16/5/1960).

1960/61   The London Palladium: TURN AGAIN WHITTINGTON NW (Dick Whittington), Eddie Leslie (Captain Barnacle), Billy Whittaker (1st Mate), Yana (Alice Fitzwarren), Desmond Walter-Ellis (Jack Allright). Book by Phil Park, David Croft. Produced by Robert Nesbitt.

1961   Blackpool Palace: York Rialto: Bradford Alhambra: NORMAN WISDOM SHOW (V) with Eddie Leslie.

1961/62   Bristol Hippodrome: ROBINSON CRUSOE NW (Norman Crusoe), Eddie Leslie (Will Atkins), Marion Grimaldi (Robinson Crusoe), Billy Whittaker (Mrs. Crusoe), Terry Kendall (Mate), Patricia Stark (Polly Perkins). Produced by Harry Bright.

1962/63   Birmingham Hippodrome: ROBINSON CRUSOE with NW as Norman Crusoe.

1963/64   Liverpool Empire: ROBINSON CRUSOE NW (Norman Crusoe), Stanley Platts (Will Atkins), Marion Grimaldi (Robinson Crusoe), Billy Whittaker (Mrs. Crusoe), Tony Fayne (Bosun), Patricia Stark (Polly Perkins). Produced by Maxwell Wray.

1964   Nottingham Theatre Royal: Liverpool Royal Court: Manchester Palace: THE ROAR OF THE GREASEPAINT - THE SMELL OF THE CROWD NW (Cocky), Willoughby

Goddard (Sir), Sally Smith (The Kid), Cy Grant (The Negro), Dilys Watling (The Girl), Ross Hutchinson (The Stranger), Bruce Wells (The Bully). Urchins played by: Jacqueline Goodman, Sheila White, Gillian Hoyle, Elizabeth White, Diane Dragisic, Roberta Rex, Sonya Petrie, Denise Garvin, Susan Whitnell, Wendy Padbury, Zena Keller, Ann Holloway, Elaine Paige. Book: Music: Lyrics: Leslie Bricusse, Anthony Newley. Choreography: Gillian Lynne. Directed by Anthony Newley.

1964/65   Coventry New Theatre: ROBINSON CRUSOE with NW as Norman Crusoe.

1965   Rank tour to Chile with Eddie Leslie.

1965/66   Birmingham Hippodrome: ROBINSON CRUSOE as above.

1966   Shubert, Philadelphia: Fisher, Detroit, U.S.A.: WALKING HAPPY.

1966/67   Lunt-Fontanne, New York, U.S.A.: WALKING HAPPY - until 16/4/67 Cast: NW (Will Mossop), Louise Troy (Maggie Hobson), George Rose (Henry Hobson), Gordon Dilworth (Tubby Wadlow), Ed Bakey (George Beenstock), Ian Garry (Launcelot Figgins), Sharon Dierking (Alice Hobson), Gretchen Van Aken (Vickie Hobson), Emma Trekman (Mrs. Hepworth), Thomas Boyd (Minns), Casper Roos (Denton), Carl Nicholas (Tudbury), Michael Quinn (Heeler), James B. Spann (Albert Beenstock), Richard Korthaze (Footman), Jane Laughlin (Ada Figgins), Lucille Benson (Mrs. Figgins), Al Lanti (Figgins' Brother), Eleanor Bergquist (Customer), Richard Sederholm (Handbill Boy), Burt Bier (Thief), Chad Block (Policeman). Book: Roger O. Hirson, Ketti Frings based on the play 'Hobson's Choice' by Harold Brighouse. Music: James Van Heusen. Lyrics: Sammy Cahn. Choreography: Danny Daniels. Directed by Cy Feuer.

1967   Michigan: San Francisco, Curran Theatre: Los Angeles, Dorothy Parker Pavilion, U.S.A.: WALKING HAPPY continues on tour (Anne Rogers and Leonard Drum replacing Louise Troy and Ed Bakey).

1968   Extensive provincial cabaret tour, from this date forward, NW usually with Tony Fayne in support; the London Palladium: special RVP for Olympics (13/5/1968).

1969	Glasgow Alhambra (V); Extensive provincial club cabaret tour; 'Ovaltine' Variety tour.
1969/70	Glasgow Alhambra (V).
1970	Bournemouth Winter Gardens: NORMAN WISDOM ENTERTAINS (V); Shekoufeh, Tehran (V); Fisher, Detroit: Brooks Atkinson, New York, U.S.A.: NOT NOW, DARLING NW (Arnold Crouch), Rex Garner (Gilbert Bodley), M'el Dowd (Maude Bodley), Marilyn Hengst (Miss Whittington), Joan Bassie (Miss Tipdale), Jean Cameron (Mrs. Fencham), Ed Zimmermann (Harry McMichael), Roni Dengel (Janie McMichael). Script: Ray Cooney, John Chapman. Directors: Ray Cooney (Detroit), George Abbott (New York).
1971	Great Yarmouth ABC: HOLIDAY STARTIME (V) summer season; Extensive Australian tour; British club tour.
1971/72	Liverpool Empire: ROBINSON CRUSOE NW (Norman Crusoe), Tony Fayne (Bosun), Marion Grimaldi (Robinson Crusoe), Billy Whittaker (Mrs. Crusoe), Patricia Stark (Polly Perkins), Stanley Platts (Will Atkins). Produced by Maxwell Wray.
1972	Coventry: THE SPRING SHOW (V); Bournemouth Pavilion: HOLIDAY STARTIME (V) summer season; Extensive South African tour; British club tour.
1973	Australia/New Zealand tour; British club tour.
1973/74	Chatham Central Hall: NORMAN WISDOM CHRISTMAS SHOW (V).
1974	Skegness Pier Pavilion: SUMMER SHOW (V); Theatre/cabaret tour taking in Teheran, Hong Kong and Australia.
1975	Canadian theatre tour; Kuala Lumpur; British club tour; Margate Lido: NORMAN WISDOM SHOW (V); Wimbledon: AUTUMN SHOW (V).
1976	Tours of Hong Kong, Australia; Skegness Pier Pavilion (V).
1976/77	Bournemouth Winter Gardens (V): Christmas Season.
1977	Douglas Gaiety, Isle of Man: NORMAN WISDOM, COMEDIAN (V).

1978	British cabaret tour; Australian tour.
1978/79	Birmingham Hippodrome: TURN AGAIN WHITTING-TON NW (Dick Whittington), Elizabeth Larner (Sultana of Morocco), Mimi Law (Spirit of the Bells), Tony Fayne (Alderman Fitzwarren), Francesca Boulter (Alice Fitzwarren), Billy Whittaker (Mrs. Whittington), Michael Twain (Captain Barnacle), Stephanie Colburn (Puss). Directed by Ron Richards.
1979	Scarborough Royal Opera House: Coventry: Theatre: Drury Lane Theatre Royal: Bristol Hippodrome: Southsea King's: Norwich Royal: A WORLD OF WISDOM (V); Paignton Festival: SUMMER SHOW (V).
1979/80	Plymouth New Palace: ROBINSON CRUSOE, NW as Norman Crusoe with Tony Fayne.
1980	British club tour; Sandown, Isle of Wight: SUMMER SHOW (V).
1982	Shaw Theatre: JINGLE JANGLE NW (Gerald Frisby), Bogdan Kominowski (Larry Kerasey), Karen Pierce-Goulding (Delores Del Ray), Victoria Finney (Ruth Wilde), Harriet Benson (Miss Fanshaw), Claudia Lloyd (Sabrina). Book: Geoff Morrow, Hal Shaper. Music: Geoff Morrow. Lyrics: Hal Shaper. Director: Sonia Stock.
1983/84	Oxford Apollo: ROBINSON CRUSOE NW (Norman Crusoe), Tony Fayne (Bosun), Dino Shafek (Man Friday), Sandy Warren (Polly Perkins), Tony Scott (Mrs. Crusoe), Samantha O'Brien (Robinson Crusoe). Director: John Redgrave.
1984	Paignton Festival Theatre: THE NORMAN WISDOM SHOW (V) summer season.
1985	THE LEGENDARY NORMAN WISDOM tour: Hanley Theatre Royal, Derby Assembly Hall, Aylesbury Civic Centre, Halifax Civic, Southport, Stockport Davenport, Gloucester Leisure Centre, Lowestoft Sparrows Nest, Peterborough Cresset, Worthing Assembly Hall, Portsmouth Guildhall, Skegness New Embassy Centre, Newark Palace, Blackburn King George's Hall, Sunderland Empire, Llandudno Arcadia, Telford Oakengates Town Hall, Grays, Dorking Halls, Poole Arts Centre, Yeovil

Johnson Hall, Eastbourne Congress, Tunbridge Wells Assembly Hall, Ramsgate Granville, Corby Civic; Drury Lane Theatre Royal; RVP (25/11/1985).

1986   Winter Gardens Margate: THE NORMAN WISDOM SUMMER SPECTACULAR: Separate Sunday dates including Folkestone Leas Cliff Hall, Hastings White Rock, Worthing Pavilion, Wimbledon. Australian tour.

1987/88   Blackpool Grand: TURN AGAIN WHITTINGTON NW (Dick Whittington), Tony Fayne (Alderman Fitzwarren), Billy Whittaker (Mrs. Whittington), Gillian Spibey (Spirit of the Bells), Mimi Law (Queen Rat), Samantha Hughes (Alice Fitzwarren), David English (Captain Barnacle). Director: Pippa Dyson.

1988   Victoria Palace: CHILDREN'S ROYAL VARIETY PER-FORMANCE - see TV 2/5/88. Winter Gardens Margate: THE NORMAN WISDOM LAUGHTER SHOW: separate Sunday dates and tour.

1988/89   Dartford Orchard: CINDERELLA NW (Buttons), Linda Lusardi (Cinderella), Tony Fayne (Baron Hardup), Roy Alvis & David Dell (Ugly Sisters), Paul Reeves (Prince Charming), Jane Lee (Fairy Godmother), Mark Hayford (Dandini). Director: Kevin Wood).

1989   THE LEGENDARY NORMAN WISDOM tour: Wimble-don, Walthamstow, Yeovil, Horsham, Southend, Rams-gate, Richmond, Wolverhampton, Hayes etc.

1990   THE LEGENDARY NORMAN WISDOM tour: similar to above.

1991   Mermaid: THE BERNARD MILES CELEBRATION: all-star fund-raiser to create the Miles Science Scholarship, Pembroke College.

APPENDIX 3

Television.

The following list includes every significant British television appearance traced. Only three overseas programmes - all American - have been included (1951, 1967). V = Variety format with principal guests listed; NW = Norman Wisdom; Sc = Scriptwriter; D = Director; Prod = Producer. Broadcast times for network ITV programmes refer to London area and may vary in some regions.

22/11/47	VARIETY (BBC, 3.0-3.40) V: Gwen Catley, Frank Raymond, Dennis Forbes, NW, The Southern Singers. Introduced by Joy Nichols. Eric Robinson & Orch. D: Eric Fawcett.
18/10/48	WIT AND WISDOM (BBC, 3.0-3.45) V: NW, Bill Reid & Dorothy Squires, The Arngut Brothers, Agnette & Silvio, Andrew Dean, Campbell & Rogerson. Eric Robinson & Orch. D: Eric Fawcett.
20/10/48	WIT AND WISDOM (BBC, 8.30-9.15) Repeat of above.
9/4/49	ROOFTOP RENDEZVOUS (BBC, 8.30-9.30) V: Cavan O'Connor, NW, Leo Fuld, Marion Saunders, Marley & Austin, Toppano, June Elliott, Audrey Wayne, Buddy Raye, The Rooftop Lovelies. Introduced by Jack Buchanan. Eric Robinson & Orch. D: Richard Afton.
13/5/49	CUCKOO COLLEGE (BBC, 8.45-9.45) Declining co-ed college faces rigours of government inspection. Cast: Principal (Dennis Lawes), Resident Staff (NW, Mai Bacon, Stanelli, Diana Morrison, Max Bacon), Pupils (Audrey Wayne, Graham Moffatt, Lillian Ellis, Robert Andrews, Betty Blackler, Anthony Hilton, Beryl McMillan, Andrew Sax, Beverley Cash, Peter Marshall, Christine Finn, Colin Campbell), Intruders (Joe Linnane, Horace Percival). Sc: Ted Kavanagh, Carey Edwards. D: Richard Afton.
8/7/50	MUSIC HALL (BBC, 8.45-9.45) V: The Merry Macs, NW, La Estrella, Chris Sand, Leslie Roberts' Music Hall Maids. Eric Robinson & Orch. D: Richard Afton
30/8/50	WIT AND WISDOM (BBC, 8.45-9.30) V: NW, Sonia

Rook, Veronica Martell, Victoria Campbell. Eric Robinson & Orch. D: Richard Afton.

4/12/50   CRITIC'S CHOICE (BBC, 8.15-9.0) NW shown and discussed by TV critics. D: Richard Afton.

26/3/51   ALL THE FUN OF THE FAIR (BBC, 8.15-9.15) V: Arthur Askey, Elizabeth Welch, NW, Renee Houston & Donald Stewart, Jerry Desmonde, The Keynotes, The Three Oxfords, Victor Platt, The Lucerne Skaters. Eric Robinson & Orch. D: Graeme Muir.

18/4/51   VIC'S GRILL (BBC, 8.55-9.25) V: NW, Eddie Leslie, Beryl Reid, John Hanson, Ernest Maxin, Rae Johnson, Hamish Menzies. Introduced by Vic Wise. Eric Robinson & Orch. Sc: Sid Colin. D: Bill Lyon-Shaw. Series which alternated in this Wednesday slot with Michael Howard in HERE'S HOWARD.

2/5/51   VIC'S GRILL (BBC, 8.55-9.25) same credits as first episode above.

16/5/51   VIC'S GRILL (BBC, 8.55-9.25) same credits as above. Series then continues without NW.

29/5/51   'LONDON MELODY' PREVIEW (BBC, 8.0-8.30) Visit to rehearsals of the Claude Langdon ice show from the Empress Hall starring Belita, NW, Diana Grafton. D: Alan Chivers.

10/6/51   'LONDON MELODY' (BBC, 8.35-10.0) Excerpts from the Empress Hall ice show (see Stage listings). Television D: Alan Chivers.

11/11/51   TOAST OF THE TOWN (in America for CBS, 8.0-9.0 in New York) NW's first appearance on show hosted by Ed Sullivan.

8/12/51   TOP HAT RENDEZVOUS (BBC, 9.0-10.0) V: NW, Arthur English, Freddie Sales, Les Richards, Audrey Wayne, Muriel Young, The Twelve Toppers. Host: Derrick De Marney. Eric Robinson & Orch. D: Richard Afton.

25/12/51   CHRISTMAS PARTY (BBC, 7.30-9.0) V: Ethel Revnell, Terry-Thomas, Jewel & Warriss, Vic Oliver, NW, David Nixon, Rawicz & Landauer, Anne Ziegler & Webster Booth, Petula Clark, The Twelve Toppers. Hosts: Leslie

Mitchell, Jerry Desmonde. Eric Robinson & Orch. D: TV Light Entertainment Department.

25/2/52   WHAT'S MY LINE (BBC, 9.30-10.10) NW is celebrity guest on panel game. Panel: Marghanita Laski, Jerry Desmonde, Elizabeth Allan, Gilbert Harding. Chair: Eamonn Andrews. D: T. Leslie Jackson

27/2/52   THE NORMAN WISDOM SHOW (BBC, 8.15-9.15) V: NW, Eddie Leslie. Eric Robinson & Orch. D: Bill Lyon-Shaw.

2/3/52   *DAILY MAIL* TELEVISION AWARDS (BBC, 8.0-8.30) Presentation and Gala show. With Arthur Askey, Petula Clark, The Ollanders, The Twelve Toppers, Luton Girls' Choir and a cavalcade of famous TV stars including NW, Woolf Phillips with the Sky Rockers Orch. Programme prod: Harry Allen Towers. D: Alan Chivers

27/7/52   NORMAN WISDOM REQUEST SHOW (BBC, 8.25-8.45) 'request programme of something old and something new'. No other credits.

25/12/52   CHRISTMAS PARTY (BBC, 7.30-9.15) V: Arthur Askey, Ethel Revnell, NW, Frankie Howerd, Petula Clark, Betty Driver, John Slater, Eamonn Andrews, Tommy Cooper, Joe Stuthard. Host: MacDonald Hobley. Eric Robinson & Orch. D: TV Light Entertainments Department.

30/5/53   CORONATION MUSIC HALL (BBC, 10.0-12.00) V: Arthur Askey, Winifred Atwell, Michael Bentine, Billy Cotton & Band, NW, Joseph Locke, Medlocke & Marlowe, Tessie O'Shea, Jon Pertwee, Fred Russell. Hosts: Ted Ray, Terry-Thomas. Mantovani & Orch. D: Richard Afton.

1/9/53   THE RADIO SHOW (BBC, 9.50-10.20) NW interviewed by Peter Dimmock. D: Keith Rogers.

28/10/53   FOR YOUR PLEASURE (BBC, 8.55-9.40) V: Terry-Thomas, NW, Bill Fraser, Al Read, Jimmy Edwards, Pat Kirkwood, Helene Cordot, Sally Barnes. Cast presented to the Queen and the Duke of Edinburgh. D: Bill Ward

18/12/53   LET'S HAVE A PARTY (BBC, 5.0-5.55) Visit to Children's Hospital, Paddington Green, with NW, Peter Butterworth, Janet Brown, Gilbert Leaney, Al Stevens, John Hewer. D: Alan Chivers.

19/12/53   JOAN GILBERT'S CHRISTMAS PARTY (BBC, 8.15-8.45) D: Alan Sleath.

25/12/53   CHRISTMAS PARTY (BBC, 7.30-9.15) V: Arthur Askey, NW, Terry-Thomas, Max Bygraves, The Beverley Sisters, John Slater, Shirey Abicair, Chan Canasta, Julie Andrews. Hosts: MacDonald Hobley, Leslie Mitchell. Eric Robinson & Orch. D: TV Light Entertainments Department.

7/2/54   'SINBAD THE SAILOR ON ICE' (BBC, 8.40-9.55) Excerpts from the Claude Langdon show at the Empress Hall starring NW, Andra McLaughlin and Basil Cudlipp-Green. Television D: Alan Chivers.

9/10/55   SUNDAY NIGHT AT THE LONDON PALLADIUM (ATV, 8.0-9.0) V: NW. Host: Jerry Desmonde. Eric Rogers & Orch. D: Bill Ward.

12/9/55   OFF THE RECORD (BBC, 7.45-8.15) NW guests along with Jimmy Young, Barbara Lyon, Radio Revellers, Kim Bennett, The Kirchin Band on show hosted by Jack Payne. Concert Orch. & George Mitchell Singers conducted by Stanley Black. Prod: Francis Essex.

29/1/56   SUNDAY NIGHT AT THE LONDON PALLADIUM (ATV, 8.0-9.0) V: NW, Jerry Desmonde, Bob Bromley, The Arnaul Brothers. Host: Tommy Trinder. Prod: Robert Nesbitt. D: Bill Lyon-Shaw.

5/5/56   IN TOWN TONIGHT (BBC, 7.30-8.0) NW interviewed by John Ellison. D: Peter Duncan.

28/8/56   SHOW TALK (ATV, 7.5-7.15) NW is interviewed by host Clifford Davis in this round up of West End entertainment.

6/10/56   THE NORMAN WISDOM SHOW [SATURDAY COMEDY HOUR] (BBC, 9.0-10.0) V: NW, Marion Keene, Eddie Leslie, The George Mitchell Singers. Eric Robinson & Orch. D: Ernest Maxin.

20/10/56   TELEVISION MOTOR SHOW (BBC, 3.0-4.0) NW interviewed. Host: Raymond Baxter. D: John Vernon.

24/10/56   CRACKERJACK (BBC, 5.0-6.0) Children's V: NW, Joe Baker, Jack Douglas, Mr. Grumble. Host: Eamonn Andrews. Sc: Bill Douglas. D: Johnny Downes.

27/10/56   SATURDAY NIGHT OUT (BBC, 8.0-8.30) NW is one of the guests at party heralding the Royal Film Performance. Presented by Derek Burrell-Davis.

3/11/56   THE NORMAN WISDOM SHOW [SATURDAY COMEDY HOUR] (BBC, 9.0-10.0) V: NW, Marion Keene, Eddie Leslie, Jeremy Hawk, Gay Owen. The George Mitchell Singers. Eric Robinson & Orch. D: Ernest Maxin.

12/11/56   PICTURE PARADE (BBC, 10.0-10.28) NW talks to Peter Haigh about the film UP IN THE WORLD.

17/11/56   IN TOWN TONIGHT (BBC, 7.30-8.0) NW interviewed by John Ellison, Pauline Tooth. D: Peter Duncan.

1/12/56   THE NORMAN WISDOM SHOW [SATURDAY COMEDY HOUR] (BBC, 8.30-9.30) V: NW, Marion Keene, Eddie Leslie, Jeremy Hawk, Gay Owen, June Ellis. George Clouston & Orch. D: Ernest Maxin.

6/1/57   SUNDAY NIGHT AT THE LONDON PALLADIUM (ATV, 8.0-9.0) NW appears as Aladdin in excerpts from THE WONDERFUL LAMP with Sonnie Hale, Valentine Dyall, Stephanie Voss, Fisher Morgan, David Davenport, Agnes Bernell and company. Tommy Trinder hosts Beat the Clock. Television D: Stephen Wade.

24/2/57   SUNDAY NIGHT AT THE LONDON PALLADIUMN (ATV, 8.0-9.0) NW principal guest on show hosted by Tommy Trinder. George Carden's London Palladium Girls. London Palladium Orch. conducted by Eric Rogers. P: Val Parnell. D: Stephen Wade.

4/3/57   OFF THE RECORD (BBC, 9.30-10.0) V: NW, The Beverley Sisters, Grisela Griffel, Edmundo Ros, Lorrae Desmond, Bob Harvey, Don Rennie, Ronnie Aldrich & the Squadronaires. Host: Jack Payne. Concert Orch. and the George Mitchell Singers conducted by Stanley Black. D: Bill Cotton Jnr.

6/6/57   KELLY'S EYE (BBC, 7.30-8.0) Host Barbara Kelly with celebrity guests including NW. Stanley Black & Orch. D: Harry Carlisle.

21/9/57   THE NORMAN WISDOM SHOW [SATURDAY SPECTACULAR] (ATV, 8.30-9.30) V: NW. Jack Parnell & Orch. D: Prod: Bill Lyon-Shaw.

2/12/57	THIS IS YOUR LIFE (BBC, 7.30-8.0) NW's life story told by Eamonn Andrews to sc. by Ken Smith. D: T. Leslie Jackson.
19/2/58	TONIGHT (BBC, 6.45-7.25) NW interviewed about WHERE'S CHARLEY? on show hosted by Cliff Mitchelmore. D: Donald Baverstock.
29/6/58	'WHERE'S CHARLEY?' (ATV, 8.30-9.30) Excerpts from the H.M. Tennant/Bernard Delfont musical comedy at the Palace Theatre starring NW, Jerry Desmonde and Pip Hinton. Television D: Kenneth Carter.
8/7/58	LATE EXTRA (ATV, 11.0-11.30) NW guests in show introduced by Jacqueline Mackenzie, Michael Westmore. Music: Steve Race Four. D: Bimbi Harris.
16/9/58	LATE EXTRA (ATV, 11.0-11.30) Larry Adler introduces jazz band consisting of NW on clarinet with the Duke of Bedford (bass), Humphrey Littleton (trumpet), Peter Sellers (drums), Larry Adler (harmonica), Steve Race (piano). Prod: D: Alan Morris.
3/12/58	PRESS CONFERENCE (BBC, 10.15-10.45) NW interrogated by journalists. Presented by Hugh Burnett.
17/12/58	CLOSE UP ON NORMAN WISDOM (Redifusion, 7.0-7.30) NW interviewed by Macdonald Hobley about films. Sc: Dick Richards. Prod: Ray Dicks. D: Jim Pople.
27/4/59	THIS IS YOUR LIFE (BBC, 7.30-8.0) NW guest on show celebrating Stirling Moss. Prod: T. Leslie Jackson. D: Verr Lorimer.
29/11/59	SUNDAY NIGHT AT THE LONDON PALLADIUM (ATV, 8.0-9.0) V: NW. Host: Bruce Forsyth. D: Albert Locke.
21/12/59	PICTURE PARADE (BBC, 10.30-11.15) NW interviewed by Robert Robinson about film FOLLOW A STAR.
21/3/60	THIS IS YOUR LIFE (BBC, 7.30-8.0) NW guest on show. D: T. Leslie Jackson
22/5/60	ROYAL VARIETY PERFORMANCE (ATV, 8.0-10.30) V: NW performs 'Stolen from the Crazy Gang' with Al Burnett, Diana Dors, Richard Dawson, Jimmy Edwards, Benny Hill, Frankie Howerd, Hattie Jacques, Alfred Marks and Bob Monkhouse as second item on bill at the

Victoria Palace before the Queen and the Duke of Edinburgh. Host: Bruce Forsyth. The Victoria Palace Orch.
under Billy Ternent and Jack Ansell. Show D: Charles
Henry. Television D: Bill Ward.

13/12/60   PICTURE PARADE (BBC, 10.0-10.45) Robert Robinson
reviews THE BULLDOG BREED. D: Christopher Doll.

21/12/60   FILM CLUB (BBC, 5.35-6.0) NW at work on THE BULL-
DOG BREED. Introduced by Alex Mackintosh. D: Leonard Chase.

3/12/61   SUNDAY NIGHT AT THE LONDON PALLADIUM (ATV,
8.25-9.25) V: NW. Host: Bruce Forsyth. Harold Collins
conducts the Jack Parnell Orch. D: Francis Essex.

26/12/62   NORMAN AND BRUCE (ATV, 9.15-10.10) Repeat of
above.

7/7/63   GIVE AT SEVEN (ATV, 6.55-7.0) NW appeals on behalf
of Woodlarks, Farnham, Surrey.

30/11/63   JUKE BOX JURY (BBC, 6.5-6.35) NW on panel with
June Ritchie, Nancy Spain and Jimmy Young. Chair:
David Jacobs. D: Neville Wortman.

25/12/64   ROBINSON CRUSOE (BBC, 5.15-7.15) Cast: NW (Nor-
man Crusoe), Marion Grimaldi (Robinson Crusoe), Eddie
Leslie (Will Atkins), Billy Whittaker (Mrs. Crusoe), Patricia
Stark (Polly Perkins) with Len Lowe, Betty Wheeler, Terry
Kendall, David Fallon, Harold Holness. The George
Mitchell Singers. Eric Tann & Orch. Book: Harry Bright.
TV adaptation by NW, Eddie Leslie, Len Lowe. D: Travers
Thorneloe, Bryan Sears.

23/8/65   THE LAUGHTER-MAKERS (ATV, 10.40-11.10) NW
explains his brand of humour to H.A.L. Craig in fifth programme in series. Prod: James Thomas. D: Rosamund
Davies.

17/12/65   CINEMA (Granada, 9.10-9.40) Michael Scott looks at
films of NW and Jerry Lewis. Prod: John Hampson. D:
Philip Casson.

14/8/66   THE LAUGHTER-MAKERS (ATV, 2.20-2.50) Repeat
from 23/8/65.

26/3/67   THE 23rd ANNUAL ANTOINETTE PERRY AWARDS (in

America for ABC, 9.30- in New York) NW performs 'Walking Happy' from the musical of the same name in this major theatrical awards ceremony. For this show the number was orchestrated by Larry Wilcox and the orchestra is conducted by Julian Stein. Show broadcast from the Shubert Theatre, New York. Prod: Alexander Cohen. D: Clark Jones. Colour.

15/11/67   ANDROCLES AND THE LION (in America for NBC, 7.30-9.0 in New York) Cast: NW (Androcles), Noël Coward (Caesar), Ed Ames (Ferrovius), Inga Swenson (Lavinia), Geoffrey Holder (Lion), John Cullum (Roman Captain), Brian Bedford (Lentulus), Clifford David (Mettellus), Kurt Kasznar (Gladiator's Manager), William Redfield (Spintho), Patricia Routledge (Megaera, Androcles' Wife), George Mathews (Centurion), Bill Hickey, Bill Starr, George Reeder. Sc: Peter Stone from George Bernard Shaw's play. Words and music: Richard Rodgers. Prod: Marc Merson. D: Joe Layton. Colour.

19/5/68   A SPECIAL ROYAL PERFORMANCE (ATV, 8.25-11.0) Variety from the London Palladium before the Queen in aid of The British Olympic Appeal's Fund. V: NW, Ronnie Corbett, Bruce Forsyth, Tom Jones, the King Brothers, Danny La Rue, The New Christy Minstrels, Des O'Connor, Dusty Springfield, Jimmy Tarbuck, Mike Yarwood, Barbara Windsor etc. Stage Prod: Albert Locke. Ececutive Prod: Bill Ward. D: Colin Clewes.

13/7/68   DEE TIME (BBC, 6.35-7.0) NW guests on chat show hosted by Simon Dee. Sc: Joe Steeples. Prod: Colin Charman. D: Roger Ordish.

25/12/68   A SPOONFUL OF SUGAR (BBC1 10.15am-10.45am) NW is a guest in show from Yorkshire Home For Disabled Women in Harrogate. Other guests: Moira Anderson, Simon Woolf. Hosts: Keith Macklin, Sheila Tracy. D: Nick Hunter.

31/12/68   A SHOW FOR HOGMANAY (Scottish, 11.30-) V: NW, Tony Fayne, The Alexander Brothers, The Clancy Brothers with Tommy Makem, Bernadette, Alasdair Gillies, Jimmy Reid. Host: Bill Tennet. Musical D: Dick Holmes. D: Clarke Tait.

21/9/69   MUSIC HALL (ATV, 8.20-9.20) V: NW, Judy Carne,

Frank Gorshin, Jack Haig, Jack Douglas. Hosts: Tony Sandler, Ralph Young. Jack Parnell & Orch. Sc: Sid Green, Dick Hills, Gordon Farr. Prod: Stan Harris, Pat Johns. D: Stan Harris.

28/9/69   MUSIC HALL (ATV, 8.20-9.20) V: NW, Judy Carne, Ella Fitzgerald, Jack Douglas, Valerie Van Ost, Heather Kidd. Rest of credits as above.

5/10/69   MUSIC HALL (ATV, 8.20-9.20) V: NW, Tony Fayne, Kaye Ballard, Lena Horne, Jack Haig, Valerie Van Ost. Rest of credits as above.

26/10/69   THE GOLDEN SHOT (ATV, 4.45-5.30) Quiz show with host Bob Monkhouse. NW guests with Acker Bilk. Golden Girls: Anne Aston, Carol Dilworth. Punster: Len Lowe. Sc: Wally Malston. Prod: D: John Pullen.

9/11/69   MUSIC HALL (ATV, 8.20-9.20) NW returns for last in première series. V: NW, Nancy Ames. Rest of credits as for 21/9/69.

ALL PROGRAMMES NOW IN COLOUR.

31/12/69   THE TENNESSEE ERNIE FORD SHOW (ATV, 8.0-9.0) V: NW, Davy Jones, Harry Secombe, Terry-Thomas. Host: Ernie Ford. The Mike Sammes Singers. Jack Parnell & Orch. Sc: Sheldon Keller, Digby Wolfe. Prod: Digby Wolfe, Bob Wynn. D: Albert Locke.

2/4/70   NORMAN (ATV, 9.0-9.30) Episode 1 of six-part series. Cast: NW (Norman Wilkins), Sally Bazely (Mrs. Tate), David Lodge (Frank Baker). Music: Jack Parnell. Sc: Ray Cooney, John Chapman. Prod: D: Alan Tarrant. Norman leaves his job as a tax inspector to become a musician.

9/4/70   NORMAN (ATV, 9.0-9.30) Ep 2. Norman becomes a pub pianist and gets converted by a pretty Salvation Army magazine seller.

16/4/70   NORMAN (ATV, 9.0-9.30) Ep 3. Norman lands post as music teacher but innocent involvment with a female pupil threatens his career.

23/4/70   NORMAN (ATV, 9.0-9.30) Ep 4. Norman joins an orchestra but only succeeds in creating havoc.

30/4/70	NORMAN (ATV, 9.10-9.40) Ep 5. Norman tries his luck with an amateur opera company.
7/5/70	NORMAN (ATV, 9.0-9.30) Ep 6. Norman attempts to get married before taking up an overseas job.
2/6/70	MUSIC HALL (ATV, 11.0-12.0) V: NW, Judy Carne, Sid Caesar, Lee Delano, Jack Haig, Sheila Burnett, Valerie Van Ost, Miki Iveria. Hosts: Tony Sandler, Ralph Young. NW appears in early episode in second series, rejoining for last three episodes. Jack Parnell & Orch. Sc: Sid Green, Dick Hills, Gordon Farr. Associate Prod: Pat Johns. Prod: D: Stan Harris.
9/7/70	MUSIC HALL (ATV, 11.0-12.0) V: NW, Kaye Ballard, Carol Lawrence, Jack Haig, Valerie Van Ost, Justine Danielle. Rest of credits as above.
16/7/70	MUSIC HALL (ATV, 11.0-12.0) V: NW, Judy Carne, Sid Caesar, Lee Delano. Rest of credits as for 2/6/70.
23/7/70	MUSIC HALL (ATV, 11.0-12.0) V: NW, Judy Carne, Barbara Feldon, Jack Haig, Pat Coombs. Rest of credits as for 2/6/70.
16/8/70	STARS ON SUNDAY (Yorkshire, 7.0-7.25) V: NW, James Mason, The Bachelors, Patricia Cahill. Executive Prod: Jess Yates. D: David Millard.
13/9/70	STARS ON SUNDAY (Yorkshire, 7.0-7.25) V: NW, The Bachelors, Raymond Massey, Maggie Fitzgibbon. Executive Prod: Jess Yates. D: David Millard.
11/10/70	STARS ON SUNDAY (Yorkshire, 7.0-7.25) V: NW, James Mason, The Bachelors, Gillian Humphries. Executive Prod: Jess Yates. D: David Millard.
25/10/70	STARS ON SUNDAY (Yorkshire, 7.0-7.25) V: NW, Ed Hockridge, The Bachelors, Raymond Massey. Executive Prod: Jess Yates. D: David Millard
11/12/70	ASK ASPEL (BBC1, 5.25-5.44) NW interviewed by presenter Michael Aspel. D: Frances Whitaker.
11/4/71	STARS ON SUNDAY (Yorkshire, 7.0-7.25) V: NW, Anna Neagle, Anita Harris, Barry Kent, David Watson, Gracie Fields. Executive Prod: Jess Yates.
18/4/71	STARS ON SUNDAY (Yorkshire, 7.0-7.25) V: NW, James

	Mason, Harry Secombe, Bobby Bennett, Patricia Cahill, Cheryl Grunwald, Violet Carson. Executive Prod: Jess Yates.
24/10/71	STARS ON SUNDAY (Yorkshire, 7.0-7.25) V: NW, James Mason, June Bronhill, Susan Drake, Bobby Bennett. Executive Prod: Jess Yates. D: Len Lurcuck, David Millard.
1/2/72	STARS OF THE YEAR (Granada, 10.30-11.30) V: NW, The Bachelors, Anita Harris, Vince Hill, Danny La Rue, David Nixon, Jimmy Tarbuck, who also presented these *Stage and TV Today* awards. Musical D: Derek Hilton. Prod: John Hampson. D: Eric Prytherch.
23/4/73	MAN OF THE SOUTH (Southern, 11.30am-12.0am) NW recalls his life and career with Barry Westwood. D: Bob Leng.
26/6/73	NOBODY IS NORMAN WISDOM (ATV, 7.5-7.35) Episode 1 of six-part series. Credits for complete series: Cast: NW (Nobody), Priscilla Morgan (Grace), Natalie Kent (Mother). Sc: Watt Nicoll (with Bob Hedley for episodes 4, 5, 6) from idea by Nicoll and John Sichel. Prod: D: John Scholz-Conway. Episode 1. also with Al Garcia (Garrett), Sarah Clee (Miss C), Malcolm Ingram (Brunton), Susan Porrett (Cashier), Peter Glaze (Manager), Neil Wilson (Hopkins). Encouraged by his girlfriend, Nobody begins to display some Walter Mittyesque characteristics.
3/7/73	NOBODY IS NORMAN WISDOM (ATV, 7.5-7.35) Ep 2. also with Windsor Davies (Ruskin), Mike Lewin (Sergeant), Don Henderson (1st Crook), Edwin Brown (Policeman), Harry Fielder (2nd Crook), Peter Penry-Jones (Morse), Angus MacKay (Superintendent), Jean Hilton (Miss Hunter), John Lawrence, Steve Tierney, Ken Tracey. Odd jobs come Nobody's way including singing birthday songs to a parrot via a telephone!
10/7/73	NOBODY IS NORMAN WISDOM (ATV, 7.5-7.35) Ep 3. also with Henry McGee (James), Annette Andre (Moira), John Gattrell (Terry), Melissa Stribling (Daphne), Jean Marlow, Mike Britton. Nobody works for an escort agency.
17/7/73	NOBODY IS NORMAN WISDOM (ATV, 7.5-7.35) Ep 4.

also with David Lodge (Assistant), Paul Whitsun-Jones (Customer), Mike Savage (Louis), Chris Cunningham (Eddie), Richard McNeff, Martin Read, Ted Richards. Nobody becomes a street photographer and gets kidnapped.

24/7/73   NOBODY IS NORMAN WISDOM (ATV, 7.5-7.35) Ep 5. also with Shaw Taylor (TV Announcer), Dan Meaden (Sergeant), Ronnie Brody (Barman), John Wreeford (Kennedy), Philip Marchant (Marshall), Christopher Sandford, Ruth Trouncer, Gabrielle Daye, Ronald Mayer, Hilda Barry, Mike Britton. Nobody investigates the case of an allegedly crooked copper.

7/8/73   NOBODY IS NORMAN WISDOM (ATV, 6.55-7.25) Ep 6. also with Vernon Dobtcheff (Proshnik), Mark Eden (Armitage), Patricia Jordan (Androvitch), Elizabeth Counsell (Anya), Valerie Leon, Carl Rigg. Nobody enters the exciting world of espionage.

9/4/74   A LITTLE BIT OF WISDOM (ATV, 7.5-7.35) In all seven episodes NW plays Norman. Prod: D: John Scholz-Conway. Episode 1: 'The Magic Monkey of Khubla Khan'. Cast: NW, Martin Benson (Sharkie), Stephen Greif (Jacques), Reg Lye, Jenny Lee-Wright, James Greene, Ted Richards. Sc: John Kane. Norman buys a brass monkey and starts winning a fortune.

16/4/74   A LITTLE BIT OF WISDOM (ATV, 7.5-7.35) Ep 2: 'Public Enemy'. Cast: NW, Roddy McMillan (Mr. Big), Tommy Godfrey (Mr. Gamble), Mike Savage (James), George Tovey, John Graham, Derek Deadman, Donald Tandy, John Scott Martin. Sc: Lew Schwarz. Norman goes to an auction with unpredictable results.

23/4/74   A LITTLE BIT OF WISDOM (ATV, 7.5-7.35) Ep 3: 'A Little Bit Of Respect'. Cast: NW, Windsor Davies (Ivor Morgan), Lynda Bellingham (Gwen Morgan), Bernard Martin (Police Sergeant), George Moon (Turnstile Man). Sc: Max Marquis. Norman causes havoc when he joins the police.

30/4/74   A LITTLE BIT OF WISDOM (ATV, 7.5-7.35) Ep 4: 'I Gotta Hearse'. Cast: NW, Patsy Rowlands (Daisy Plummer), Dudley Sutton (Ernie Hadfield), Ann Penfold (Doreen

Newsbitt), Mela White, Richard Beale, Verne Morgan, Barbara Grant, Pamela Denke. Sc: Dick Sharples. Norman gets a job as a hearse driver.

7/5/74   A LITTLE BIT OF WISDOM (ATV, 6.55-7.25) Ep 5: 'Who Was That Lady?'. Cast: NW, Ronald Leigh-Hunt (Reggie), Christine Shaw (Deidre), John Carlin (Smithers), Michael O'Hagan, Paul Haley, Derek Deadman. Sc: Philip Parsons. Norman is an amnesia victim who finds himself unwittingly posing as a member of the aristocracy in a fraud plot.

14/5/74   A LITTLE BIT OF WISDOM (ATV, 7.5-7.35) Ep 6: 'And I Mean That Most Sincerely'. Cast: NW, Henry McGee (Big Jim), Derek Newark (Security Guard), Robert Oates (Floor Manager), Mark Eden, Judy Buxton, Peter Hill, Zena Clifton. Sc: Lew Schwarz. Norman becomes a star performer on a television quiz programme.

21/5/74   A LITTLE BIT OF WISDOM (ATV, 7.5-7.35) Ep 7: 'The Angels Want Me For A Sunbeam'. Cast: NW, Judy Gascoine (Sister Ruth), Frank Williams (Brother Jonas Jackson), Sue Bond (Showgirl). Sc: Dick Sharples. Norman contemplates suicide after destroying a building site.

28/12/74   IT'S NORMAN (ATV, 8.30-9.30) V: NW, David Nixon, Terry Scott, Clodagh Rodgers, The Kaye Sisters. Jack Parnell & Orch. Sc: NW, Jon Watkins, Philip Parsons. Prod: D: John Scholz-Conway.

10/1/75   A LITTLE BIT OF WISDOM. Second series of six episodes. All are (ATV, 7.0-7.30) NW (Norman). Prod: D: John Scholz-Conway. Episode 1: Cast: NW, Sam Kydd (Gentleman Jim), Jackie Pallo (McGurk), Susan Drury (Dolly), Robin Parkinson, Kent Walton, Steve Logan. Sc: Lew Schwarz. An accident with a milk bottle lands Norman in a wrestling match.

17/1/75   A LITTLE BIT OF WISDOM. Ep 2: Cast: NW, Dudley Sutton (Mr. Larkin), Ronald Leigh-Hunt (Mr. Frink), Robert Oates (Dr. Henshaw), Melissa Stribling (Nursing Sister), Ian Talbot, Paul Teague, Deborah Baxter, Mandy Jenner. Norman tries to donate some blood - but ends up a patient.

24/1/75   A LITTLE BIT OF WISDOM. Ep 3: Cast: NW, Roy Kinnear (Butcher), Janie Booth (Mrs. Gott), Peter Hill (Old Smiddy), Mike Lewin, Desmond Jones, Mike Kinsey. Norman tries to return a ring to its rightful owner and nearly ends up in gaol.

31/1/75   A LITTLE BIT OF WISDOM. Ep 4: Cast: NW, Jenny Lee-Wright (Lolita), Henry McGee (Colonel Parker), Bill Dean (Sir Bernard), Ted Richards, Michael Balfour, Derek Deadman, Brett Forrest, Jeanne Doree, Ian Sharp. Norman wins a supermarket competition with unexpected results.

5/2/75   PEBBLE MILL (BBC1, 1.0-1.45) NW interviewed by Donny McLeod. Other hosts: Bob Langley, Marian Foster, David Seymour. Editor: Terry Dobson.

7/2/75   A LITTLE BIT OF WISDOM. Ep 5: Cast: NW, Harold Kasket (Tropovich), Juan Moreno (Dmitri), Mike Savage (Boris), Paul Humpoletz (Knippa). Sc: Jon Watkins. Spies plot to eliminate Norman after he overhears their plans.

14/2/75   A LITTLE BIT OF WISDOM. Ep 6: Cast: NW, Tim Barrett (Nigel), Christine Shaw (Delores), Peter Carlisle (Mr. Bockleberger), Annette Lynton, Philip Jackson, Sarah Porter. Sc: Lew Schwarz. Norman accidentally becomes a 'master' painter.

14/1/76   JUST A NIMMO (BBC2, 9.45-10.15) NW interviewed by presenter Derek Nimmo on Body Language. D: Gareth Gwenlan.

30/3/76   A LITTLE BIT OF WISDOM. Third series of seven episodes. All are (ATV, 7.5-7.35). Cast: NW (Norman), Neil McCarthy (Alec Porter), Frances White (Linda Clark), Robert Keegan (Albert Clark). Prod: D: Les Chatfield. Episode 1: 'The Ladder' also with John Proctor (Window Cleaner). Sc: Ronnie Taylor. Norman is a builder's clerk who gets into trouble when his flatmate Alec borrows a ladder.

6/4/76   A LITTLE BIT OF WISDOM. Ep 2: 'A Present For Linda'. Also with Anthony Dutton (Det-Sgt. Ford), Leonard Woodrow (Customer). Sc: Lew Schwarz. Norman sets out to buy a birthday present for the boss's daughter, Linda.

13/4/76   A LITTLE BIT OF WISDOM. Ep 3: 'Double Trouble'. Also with Lesley Nunnerley (Mrs. Perry), Reg Lye (Porter). Sc: John Kane. Norman is not the person to have around when the company goes into double glazing!

20/4/76   A LITTLE BIT OF WISDOM. Ep 4: 'To Catch A Thief'. Sc: John Kane. When Norman starts to partition his flat, the boss wonders where the materials came from.

27/4/76   A LITTLE BIT OF WISDOM. Ep 5: 'The Party's Over'. Also with Ruth Holden (Gladys), Jennifer Guy (Maisie). Sc: Lew Schwarz. Norman tenaciously chaperones his flatmate's new girlfriend.

4/5/76   A LITTLE BIT OF WISDOM. Ep 6: 'Firebug'. Sc: John Kane. Norman takes an interest in Alec's health.

11/5/76   A LITTLE BIT OF WISDOM. Ep 7: 'Otherwise Engaged'. Also with Ronald Leigh-Hunt (Sir Charles Rathbury). Sc: Jon Watkins. With the boss down with flu, Norman developes a taste for management.

23/11/76   LOOKS FAMILIAR (Thames, 3.20-3.50) Denis Norden chats nostalgically to NW, Margaret Powell, Cyril Fletcher. Compiler: Denis Gifford. Prod: David Clark. D: Robert Reed.

29/12/76   THE NORMAN WISDOM SHOW [GOLDEN SEASWALLOW OF KNOKKE, 1976] (BBC2 8.25-9.0) V: NW, Tony Fayne, Rod Hull & Emu, The Francis Bay Orchestra. Prod: John Ammonds. D: Alan Boyd.

26/3/77   SATURDAY NIGHT AT THE MILL (BBC1, 11.20-12.10am) NW guests with Omar Sharif and Nola Rae in show hosted by Bob Langley and Donny McLeod with the Kenny Ball Jazzmen. Prod: Roy Donnie. D: Roy Norton.

3/8/77   NIGHT OUT AT THE LONDON CASINO (Thames, 8.0-9.0) V: NW, Tony Fayne, Julie Rogers, The Black Abbots, Victor Burnett & June, Roy North, Barry Whitfield. Host: Tom O'Connor. Sc: Spike Mullins, Pat Finan. Music: Alan Braden. Prod: D: Dennis Kirkland.

6/9/77   LOOKS FAMILIAR (Thames, 6.0-6.30) Repeat of 23/11/76.

23/10/77   STARS ON SUNDAY (Yorkshire, 6.45-7.15) V: NW, Olivia De Havilland, Harry Secombe, The Beverley Sisters, Joe Lawrenson, Pat O'Hare, Opus VII, Cliff Mitchelmore. Host: Robert Dougall. Prod: Peter Max-Wilson. D: Lesley Smith.

4/12/77   STARS ON SUNDAY (Yorkshire, 6.50-7.15) V: NW, Anna Neagle, Victoria de los Angeles. Executive Prod: Peter Max-Wilson. D: Lesley Smith.

2/10/78   DES O'CONNOR TONIGHT (BBC2, 8.10-9.0) Host Des O'Connor with guests NW, Elayne Boosler, Dale Gonyea. Colin Keyes & Orch. Prod: James Moir.

26/10/78   PEBBLE MILL (BBC1, 1.0-1.45) Hosts: Bob Langley, Marian Foster, David Seymour, Donny McLeod. NW interviewed by Tony Bilbow. Editor: Jim Dumighan.

26/12/78   BOXING NIGHT AT THE MILL (BBC1, 11.0-12.0) NW, Libby Morris interviewed by hosts Bob Langley, Tony Lewis. Prod: Roy Ronnie. D: Roy Norton.

18/6/79   NATIONWIDE (BBC1, 5.55-6.55) NW interviewed about Royal Court show in programme hosted by Frank Bough, Sue Lawley, Hugh Scully, John Stapleton and Bob Wellings. Editor: Hugh Williams. Prod: David Dickinson, Lino Ferrari.

24/8/79   DES O'CONNOR SHOW (BBC1, 8.5-9.0) Repeat from 2/10/78.

4/1/80   THE MOVING LINE (BBC1: south-west, 10.16-10.47) NW interviewed in arts programme presented by Jackie Gillott. Prod: Brian Skilton.

17/6/80   TELL ME ANOTHER (Southern, 3.45-4.15) Showbiz guests NW, Roy Kinnear, Charlie Drake, Fred Emney, Cardew Robinson recall service days with presenter Dick Hills. D: John Coxall, Paul Bryers.

1/7/80   TELL ME ANOTHER (Southern, 3.45-4.15) NW, Dickie Henderson, Peggy Mount, Sylvia Syms, Derek Batey, Vince Hll, Moira Lister recall high spots/howlers over their 'Big Breaks' to presenter Dick Hills. D: John Coxall, Paul Bryers.

15/7/80   TELL ME ANOTHER (Southern, 3.45-4.15) NW, Acker Bilk, Tom O'Connor, Sydney Tafler, Dave Lee Travis on same topic as above with presenter Dick Hills. D: John Coxall, Paul Bryers.

12/8/80   TELL ME ANOTHER (Southern, 3.45-4.15) NW, Percy Edwards, John Junkin, Roy KInnear, Moira Lister, Cardew Robinson, Sylvia Syms, Sidney Tafler recall magic filmmaking moments which did not appear on screen; with Dick Hills. D: John Coxall, Paul Bryers.

14/10/80   MOTOR SHOW 80 (BBC1, 9.25-10.0) NW, Liza Goddard, Eric Morecambe interviewed about cars in the Motor Show at NEC, Birmingham. Introduced by Noel Edmonds with Jan Leeming, Frank Page, Stuart Hall. Prod: Derek Smith. D: Philip Franklin.

21/12/80   NIGHT OF ONE HUNDRED STARS (LWT, 7.45-9.45) Who's Who of stars perform before Princess Margaret, including NW. Host: Terry Wogan. Staging: Robert Nesbitt. Prod: David Bell, Richard Brewett. D: Alan Boyd.

5/6/81   PLAYHOUSE: GOING GENTLY (BBC2, 9.30-10.40) NW in serious role of man dying from cancer. Cast: NW (Bernard Flood), Judi Dench (Sister Scarli), Fulton Mackay (Austin Miller), Stephanie Cole (Gladys Flood), Peter Attard (George Flood), Margaret Whiting (Sister Marvin), Garry Cooper, Ivan Steward, Edward Lyon, Bill Dean, John Mulcahy, Christian Burgess, Robert Hickson, Ray Hassett, Ann Queensbury. Sc: Thomas Ellice from the novel by Robert C.S. Downs. Prod: Innes Lloyd. D: Stephen Frears.

13/6/81   SATURDAY NIGHT AT THE MILL (BBC1, 10.30-11.20) NW, Cassandra Harris, Sheila Bernette, Frank Finlay guest on show hosted by Bob Langley, Adrian Love. Midnight Folies Orch. Kenny Ball & Jazzmen. Prod: Roy Ronnie. D: Roy Norton.

24/8/82   GOING GENTLY (BBC1, 10.15-11.256) Repeat of PLAYHOUSE production from 5/6/81.

14/11/82   THE MONEY PROGRAMME (BBC2, 6.15-7.0) NW amongst people interviewed by Luke Casey about the financing of JINGLE JANGLE. Show presented by Brian Widlake. Editor: John Reynolds.

19/11/82   NATIONWIDE (BBC1, 6.0-7.0) NW interviewed by Fran Morrison on JINGLE JANGLE.

6/2/83   BERGERAC: ALMOST A HOLIDAY (BBC1, 9.10-10.5) NW plays a safe-cracker in this Channel Islands cop series. Cast: John Nettles (Jim Bergerac), Terence Alexander (Charles Hungerford), Celia Imrie (Marianne), Sean Arnold (Crozier), Annette Badlands (Charlotte), Mela White (Diamante Lil), NW (Vincent), Jeff Rawle, Elvi Hale, Sheila Ruskin, Michael Attwell, Tony Melody, John Carlin, Peggy Ann Wood, Kevin Stoney. Sc: Alistair Bell. Prod: Robert Banks Stewart. D: Laurence Moody.

21/5/83   F.A. CUP FINAL '83: BRIGHTON v MANCHESTER UTD. (LWT, 11.0am-5.15) NW guests in build-up to match with hosts Jimmy Tarbuck, Dickie Davis, Brian Moore. Executive Prod: Stuart McConarchie. Studio D: Patricia Mordecai.

17/6/83   THE TIME OF YOUR LIFE (BBC1, 8.0-8.30) NW recalls Christmas 1953 with presenter Noel Edmonds helped by the Beverley Sisters, Lana Morris. Prod: Henry Murray. D: Pieter Morpurgo.

4/10/83   GOOD MORNING BRITAIN (TVam, 6.25am-9.25am) NW in 'Spotlight' sequence (7.5-7.22) interviewed by John Stapleton. Presenters Nick Owen, Anne Diamond.

6/11/83   AROUND WITH ALLISS (BBC2, 7.15-7.45) NW chats and plays golf with presenter Peter Alliss. Prod: Bob Abrahams. D: Alastair Scott.

25/12/83   THE BOB MONKHOUSE SHOW (BBC2, 10.5-11.0) NW talks about comedy with host Bob Monkhouse. Harry Stoneham Band. Prod: John Fisher. D: Geoff Miles.

27/12/83   VAL PARNELL'S SUNDAY NIGHT AT THE LONDON PALLADIUM (ATV, 9.50-10.50) Truncated version of broadcast from 3/12/61 - 'While Irish Eyes Are Smiling' routine heavily cut. Chatty commentary by NW and Bruce Forsyth is added for Channel Four ITV COMEDY CLASSICS session.

22/8/84   THE BOB MONKHOUSE SHOW (BBC1, 9.25-10.20) Repeat of show from 25/12/83.

6/9/84   THE TIME OF YOUR LIFE (BBC2, 8.0-8.30) Repeat of show from 17/6/83.

6/10/84   A FRAME WITH DAVIS (Anglia for Channel 4, 10.0-

10.30) NW, Max Boyce chat and play snooker with host Steve Davis as referee. Executive Prod: Jeremy Fox. D: Len Caynes.

19/10/84   BERGERAC: ALMOST A HOLIDAY (BBC1, 8.50-9.0) Repeat of episode from 6/2/83.

4/9/85   GOOD MORNING BRITAIN (TVam, 6.15-9.30) NW (from 7.20) chats to presenters Nick Owen, Jayne Irving, Julie Brown, Wincey Willis. D: Peter Webb, Wendy J. Dyer.

1/12/85   THE ROYAL VARIETY PERFORMANCE (LWT, 7.45-10.15) V: NW, Lauren Bacall, Alice Faye, Maureen Lipman, Ron Moody, Anna Neagle, Beryl Reid, Jean Simmons, Elisabeth Welch, Gary Wilmot etc. in performance from Theatre Royal, Drury Lane before the Queen and Prince Philip. Music: Alyn Ainsworth & Orch. Staging: Norman Maen. Prod: David Bell. Television D: Alan Boyd.

16/11/86   THE MAKING OF THE ROYAL VARIETY PEROR-MANCE, 1985 (BBC2, 5.0-5.50) NW featured in documentary about putting on the above event, introduced by Max Bygraves. Prod: Rod Taylor.

15/12/86   WOGAN (BBC1, 7.0-7.35) NW guests on Terry Wogan's chat show. Series Prod: Frances Whitaker. Prod: Peter Estall. D: Tony Newman.

27/12/86   JUST WISDOM (Channel 4, 8.0-9.0) Quasi-documentary on NW's career, with NW, Holly De Jong. Sc: NW, Paul Madden, Laurens Postma. Prod: Paul Madden. D: Laurens Postma.

11/2/87   THIS IS YOUR LIFE (Thames, 7.0-7.30) NW's life story told by Eamonn Andrews. Prod: Malcolm Morris. D: Michael Kent, Terry Yarwood.

25/5/87   WOGAN (BBC1, 7.0-7.40) NW sings 'Don't Laugh At Me' on special British Cinema edition of show hosted by Terry Wogan.

27/5/87   LOOKAROUND (Border, 6.0-6.35) NW interviewed.

29/5/87   GOSLING'S GANDERS (BBC2 Manchester, 8.0-8.30) NW guests.

14/6/87   HIGHWAY (Border, 6.40-7.15) NW performs from the stage of the Gaiety Theatre, Isle of Man, and chats to host Harry Secombe.

▲ THE WONDERFUL LAMP.
Left to right. Tom Gill,
Norman, David Keir, Fisher
Morgan.

◀ The 1956/57 pantomime
THE WONDERFUL LAMP
was Norman's first at the
London Palladium. In it he
undertook an "eccentric act
of usurpation" (*The Times*)
by taking on the role of
Aladdin, to give a
performance which was a
"mixture of jokey bravery
and urchin pathos"
(*Guardian*).

LONDON PALLADIUM

6.15 TWICE NIGHTLY 8.45 MATINEE EACH SAT. AT 2.40

VAL PARNELL & BERNARD DELFONT present

NORMAN WISDOM

IN THE 1954 GAY

PALLADIUM SHOW

JERRY DESMONDE **THREE MONARCHS** **WALTER DARE WAHL** **BOB WILLIAMS**

GILLIAN MORAN

GEORGE MITCHELL SINGERS

SKYROCKETS ORCHESTRA Directed by **ERIC ROGERS**

16 PALLADIUM LOVELIES

SCHALLER BROS. **PEIRO BROS.** **FLORENCE AND FREDERIC** **FAY LENORE**

DANCES BY ALAN CARTER PRODUCED BY **DICK HURRAN** DÉCOR CHARLES READING

▲ Handbill for Norman's first Palladium show which eventually had to transfer to the Prince of Wales to complete its astonishing 11 month run. "Wisdom's art is to show an endearing mugwump battling for his rights" (*Daily Express*).

▼ PAINTING THE TOWN (1956). From which came the duet "Two Rivers" which Norman recorded with co-star Ruby Murray.

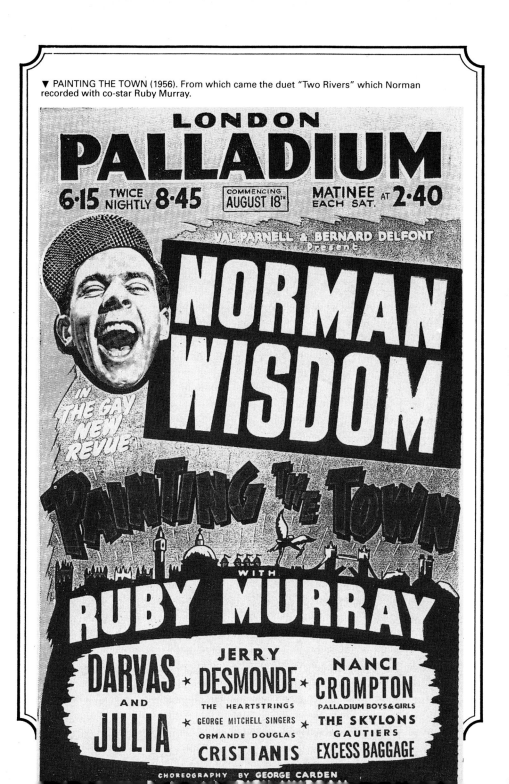

◀ Norman prepares for his first outing on TV's SUNDAY NIGHT AT THE LONDON PALLADIUM (1955).

▼ WHERE'S CHARLEY? Norman's first attempt at a full-scale musical proves a triumph. "It is gay and full of colour. It is admirably cast and directed. And it gives Norman Wisdom a part in which his appealing personality, his quicksilver lightness of foot and his versatility have every chance" (*Daily Telegraph*).

PALACE
THEATRE
Under the direction of CYRIL LITTLER

SOUVENIR
PROGRAMME
ONE SHILLING

At The Famous
LONDON PALLADIUM
Leslie A. Macdonnell
presents

TURN AGAIN WHITTINGTON

Created & Produced by
ROBERT NESBITT

▲ TURN AGAIN WHITTINGTON. The London Palladium's longest running pantomime which played 199 performances and was seen by over 40,000 people.

► WALKING HAPPY. The show which marked Norman's glittering debut on the Broadway stage. Amongst the awards he picked up was Best Actor in a Musical from the *Jersey Journal*: "Wisdom in WALKING HAPPY is the type of comedian a director dreams of for a musical. Wistful, shy, wonderfully amusing in the fashion of Stan Laurel, he captivates us not so much with what he says or sings but with what he does."

▼ WALKING HAPPY. Norman with Louise Troy. "Norman Wisdom is just great as Will Mossop, the Casper Milquetoast of a bootmaker turned into a lion by the love of a good woman" (*Radio WNEW*).

Walking Happy

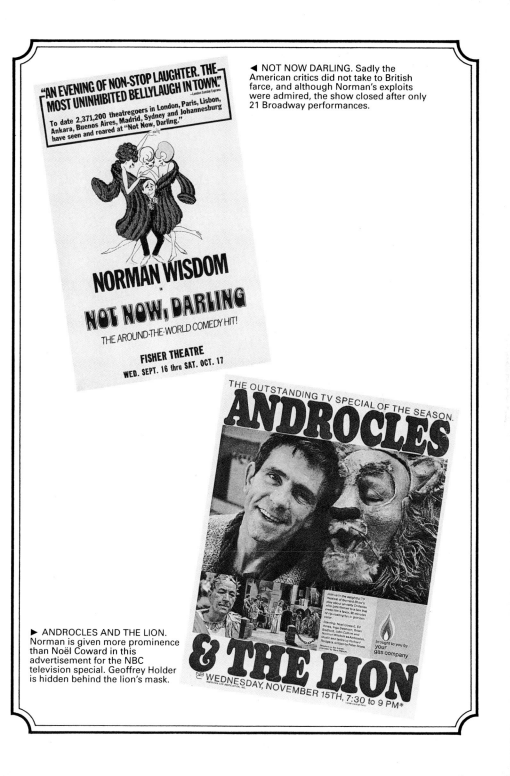

◄ NOT NOW DARLING. Sadly the American critics did not take to British farce, and although Norman's exploits were admired, the show closed after only 21 Broadway performances.

"AN EVENING OF NON-STOP LAUGHTER. THE MOST UNINHIBITED BELLYLAUGH IN TOWN"
—London Sunday Express

To date 2,371,200 theatregoers in London, Paris, Lisbon, Ankara, Buenos Aires, Madrid, Sydney and Johannesburg have seen and roared at "Not Now, Darling."

NORMAN WISDOM
in
NOT NOW, DARLING
THE AROUND-THE-WORLD COMEDY HIT!

FISHER THEATRE
WED. SEPT. 16 thru SAT. OCT. 17

THE OUTSTANDING TV SPECIAL OF THE SEASON.

ANDROCLES
& THE LION

WEDNESDAY, NOVEMBER 15TH, 7:30 to 9 PM*

brought to you by your gas company

► ANDROCLES AND THE LION. Norman is given more prominence than Noël Coward in this advertisement for the NBC television special. Geoffrey Holder is hidden behind the lion's mask.

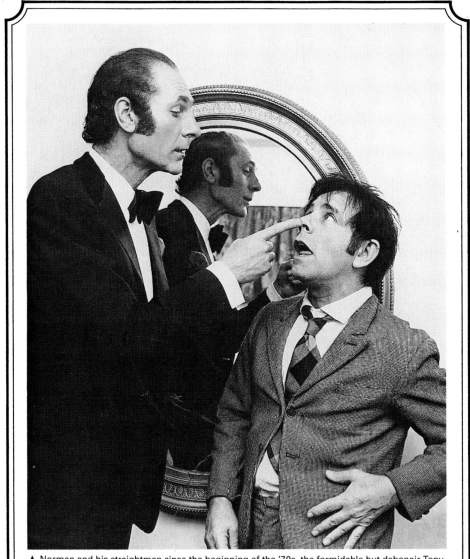

▲ Norman and his straightman since the beginning of the '70s, the formidable but debonair Tony Fayne.

Photograph: Nigel Boonham

15/8/87 THE GOLDEN GONG (BBC1, 9.30-10.45) NW interviewed during documentary on the history of Rank presented by Michael Caine. Prod: Tim Whittingham, Maggie Corke. D: Tom Gutteridge.

18/11/87 IT'S MY PLEASURE (BBC2, 4.0-4.35) NW selects favourite clips and is interviewed by Desmond Lynam.

30/12/87 VAL PARNELL'S SUNDAY NIGHT AT THE LONDON PALLADIUM (Channel 4, 10.0-11.0) Further repeat of broadcast from 3/12/61.

2/5/88 CHILDREN'S ROYAL VARIETY PERFORMANCE (BBC1, 5.45-7.45) V: NW with Nicholas Parsons, Ken Dodd, Michael Barrymore, Roy Castle etc. in performance from the Victoria Palace before Princess Margaret. Music: Ronnie Hazlehurst. Stage D: Brian Rogers. Prod: John Fisher. Television D: Brian Whitehouse.

20/7/88 COAST TO COAST (TVS, 6.0-6.30) NW and Dora Bryan interviewed by Merrill Harries. Editor: Victor Wakeling, Mark Andrews. Prod: Mark Sharman.

6/1/89 GOOD MORNING BRITAIN (TVam, 7.0-9.0) NW interviewed.

28/5/90 ITV TELETHON '90 (Thames, 1.5-5.30; 9.0-10.0) NW makes appearance in Bank Holiday charity appeal show.

25/7/90 WOGAN (BBC1, 7.0-7.30) NW reminisces with guest host Jonathan Ross. Prod: Sylvie Boden.

30/11/90 JONATHAN ROSS (C4, 6.30-7.0) NW interviewed by host Jonathan Ross about lifetime comedy award.

16/12/90 THE BRITISH COMEDY AWARDS 1990 (LWT, 7.45-9.45) Screening of the British Comedy Awards 1990 recorded at the London Palladium featuring NW accepting one for stage lifetime achievement. Presented by Michael Parkinson. Sc. Associate: Neil Shand. TV prod: Dir: Michael Hurll.

1/3/91 SIX O'CLOCK LIVE (LWT, 6.00-6.55) NW meets a fan in programme hosted by Frank Bough, Joanna Sheldon, Danny Baker, Jeni Barnett and Jan Rowland. Executive prod: Simon Shaps. Editor: Vanessa Chapman.

APPENDIX 4

Radio.

Norman Wisdom never made a real attempt to master radio as a medium for comedy, though his regular appearances as a guest on Frankie Howerd's *Fine Goings On* drew the following from the *Radio Times*: 'Norman Wisdom, a delightful clown who can talk gibberish with agonised conviction'. The general response was that Wisdom had to be seen: 'Norman Wisdom again had them laughing at *Henry Hall's Guest Night* - but why I couldn't see. Put him on television please.' Another review of one of NW's *Guest Night* appearances makes interesting reading: 'Frankly I don't think it's his medium. One of his stories was so macabre that I wondered if I had heard him aright' *Birmingham Despatch*. Below are listed all the British radio appearances so far traced. Obviously, many radio appearances are of the quick promotional type, and some of these will have been missed. No recent commercial radio spots have been included. Unfortunately Wisdom's radio listings up to December 1951 seem to be missing from the BBC's files so there could be more significant gaps in the early period. NW = Norman Wisdom; Sc = scriptwriter; Prod = producer; Ed = editor; HS = Home Service (where applicable regional variations are as follows: W = West, N = North, NI = Northern Ireland, M = Midlands, S = South); LP = Light Programme; R1 = Radio 1; R2 = Radio 2; R4 = Radio 4. All listings are for BBC programmes except where indicated.

30/8/49   CHILDREN'S HOUR: BLACKPOOL PIRATES (HS, 5.0-5.40) Charlie Chester, Arthur Hayes, Len Marten, Ken Morris, Henry Lytton, Frederick Ferrari (Pirates); Edwina Carol (Captive); Jimmy Jewel, Ben Warriss (Shipwrecked Mariners); Julie Andrews (Mermaid); Frankie Howerd (Captain Swashbuckle); Donald Peers (Ship Cook); NW (Cockswain). Geraldo & Orchestra. Devised: Alick Hayes. Prod: Nan Macdonald, Alick Hayes.

11/9/49   BLACKPOOL PIRATES (LP, 2.45-3.30) Repeat of above.

5/12/49   HENRY HALL'S GUEST NIGHT (HS, 8.0-9.0) NW guest on show hosted by Henry Hall.

4/1/50   HENRY HALL'S GUEST NIGHT (HS, 7.0-7.45) NW performs with David Nixon on this programme hosted by Henry Hall. Prod: Alastair Scott-Johnson.

9/1/50   HENRY HALL'S GUEST NIGHT (HS, 12.25-12.55) Slightly shortened repeat of above.

22/1/50   BAND PARADE (LP, 5.45-6.30) Variety show with Ted Heath & his Music, Don Carlos & his Samba Band, Skyrockets Dance Orchestra, and NW proves that 'Comedians Sometimes Sing'. Introduced by Jack Jackson. Prod: John Foreman, John Simmonds.

24/8/50   FIRST HOUSE: LOOK WHO'S HERE! (HS, 6.20-7.0) Variety show with Song Pedlars, Jack North & Pat Stoyle, Peggy Ashby, Denis Martin, NW, John Blythe. Rae Jenkins conducts BBC Variety Orchestra. Introduced by David Jacobs. Prod: John Hooper.

26/11/50   PANTOMIME [special programme for overseas troops only, recorded at the RAF camp theatre, Uxbridge]. Cast: Frankie Howerd (Buttons), Joan Greenwood (Fairy Queen), Eric Portman (Wicked Baron), NW (Cat), Jerry Desmonde, Marjorie Holmes, Rosemary Morgan, John Hanson, Bunny Paris. Anton & Orchestra. Peter Knight & Chorus. Sc: Frankie Howerd. Prod: Douglas Moody.

4/1/51   FINE GOINGS ON (LP, 7.30-8.0) Variety show starring Frankie Howerd with Marjorie Holmes, Bill Fraser, NW, Janet Hamilton-Smith, John Hargreaves, The Petersen Brothers, Augmented BBC Revue Orchestra conducted by Robert Busby. Sc: Eric Sykes, Sid Colin. Prod: Bryan Sears.

18/1/51   FINE GOINGS ON (LP, 7.30-8.0) credits as above except produced by Tom Ronald.

1/2/51   FINE GOINGS ON (LP, 7.30-8.0) credits as for 18/1/51.

15/2/51   FINE GOINGS ON (LP, 7.30-8.0) as for 18/1/51.

1/3/51   FINE GOINGS ON (LP, 7.30-8.0) as for 18/1/51.

15/3/51   FINE GOINGS ON (LP, 7.30-8.0) as for 18/1/51 except the music is by Frank Chacksfield and his Orchestra and the script is by Eric Sykes alone.

29/3/51   FINE GOINGS ON (LP, 7.30-8.0) credits as for 15/3/51.

25/7/51   SUNNY SIDE UP (LP, 9.30-10.0) NW guests on show

hosted by Max Bygraves. Paul Fernoulhet conducts BBC Variety Orchestra. Prod: Ronnie Hill.

8/12/51   IN TOWN TONIGHT (HS, 7.15-7.45) NW interviewed by John Ellison. Ed: Prod: Peter Duncan.

10/12/51   IN TOWN TONIGHT (HS, 4.30-5.0) Repeat of above.

8/1/52   Times untraced. A series of 13 weekly shows - 1/4/52 recorded by Radio Luxembourg for Rowntrees' New Cocoa. NW sings four songs in each programme, accompanied by Harry Parry and his Octet. Prod: Gordon Crier.

28/4/52   FRIENDS AND RELATIONS (LP, 8.0-8.30) NW recalls 'Memories Of Service In India' in programme introduced by Wilfrid Thomas. Compiled: Ed: Michael Barsley.

14/6/52   FILM GARDEN PARTY (LP, 4.15-4.45) NW one of guests which include Dirk Bogarde, Petula Clark, Diana Dors, John Mills and Peter Sellers at the *Sunday Pictorial* party in programme presented by Leslie Mitchell. Sc: Bob Black, Bill Harding. Prod: Tom Ronald.

18/12/52   FILM TIME (HS, 1.20-2.0) NW interviewed at the *Picturegoer* Christmas Party. Presenter: Leslie Mitchell. Sc: Michael Storm. Prod: Pat Osborne.

19/12/52   WHAT GOES ON? (M, 7.30-8.0) NW interviewed in 'Personality Spot'.

4/4/53   IN TOWN TONIGHT (HS, 7.15-7.45) NW interviewed in programme hosted by John Ellison. Ed: Prod: Peter Duncan.

17/4/53   DESERT ISLAND DISCS (HS, 6.20-7.0) NW guest with host Roy Plomley.

14/11/53   IN TOWN TONIGHT (HS, 7.15-7.45) NW interviewed at the opening of *Sinbad the Sailor on Ice* by host John Ellison. Ed: Prod: Peter Duncan.

29/11/53   THESE RADIO TIMES (LP, 4.0-5.0) A happy history of everyman's entertainment with Kenneth Horne, Robin Richmond, Anne Shelton, Sir Stephen Tallents, J.C. Trewin, NW. Introduced by Howard Marion-Crawford. Sc: Gale Pedrick. Prod: Thurston Holland.

15/3/54   CHILDREN'S HOUR: FILM NEWS (N, 5.30-5.50) NW interviewed.

26/3/54	FILM TIME (HS, 1.10-2.0) Coverage of the presentation of the British Film Academy awards presented by John Huston at the Odeon Leicester Square. Includes NW receiving his for Most Promising Newcomer. Introduced by Leslie Mitchell. Sc: Michael Storm. Prod: Pat Osborne.
7/6/54	STAGE DOOR JOHNNY (LP, 8.15-9.0) Visits to three West End Theatres with the stars choosing records: The Royal, Haymarket; The London Hippodrome; and to the London Palladium where NW and Jerry Desmonde are interviewed by Brian Johnston.
7/11/54	ROYAL PERFORMANCE (LP, 2.30-4.0) NW is one of many artists appearing in the Royal Variety Performance recorded from 1/11/54. Highlights presented by Alan Melville.
28/6/55	CHILDREN'S HOUR: FILM NEWS (N.NI, 5.35-5.55) NW, John Paddy Carstairs and Belinda Lee interviewed about *Man of the Moment* by the programme's compiler John Stratton.
12/7/55	THE BRIGHT LIGHTS (M, 6.30-7.0) NW interviewed in this entertainments magazine programme.
7/10/55	PARADE (LP, 6.30-6.45) presented by the 'younger generation', includes NW interviewed by Mary Duddy on the advantages of being short.
18/10/55	REVIEW (LP, 6.30-6.45) presented by the 'younger generation', includes a first impression of *Man of the Moment* from John Cohen, Mary Duddy with Norman Ellis in chair. Frank Tilsley guests, NW interviewed.
3/12/55	YOUR PIED PIPER (LP, 11.0-11.50) NW selects music with host Eamonn Andrews.
7/1/56	YOUR PIED PIPER (LP, 11.0-11.50) NW selects music with host Eamonn Andrews.
19/1/56	NORMAN WISDOM'S TOP TEN CHOICE (N.NI, 6.35-7.0)
1/2/56	WOMAN'S HOUR (LP, 2.0-3.0) NW is guest of the week in programme introduced by Jean Metcalfe.
5/2/56	HOME FOR THE DAY (LP, 9.10am-10.0am) The Sunday supplement to WOMAN'S HOUR presented by Marjorie Anderson. Repeat of above.

5/5/56	IN TOWN TONIGHT (HS, 7.30-8.0) NW interviewed by presenter John Ellison on his return from America and Jamaica. Ed: Prod: John Duncan.
17/11/56	IN TOWN TONIGHT (HS, 7.30-8.0) NW interviewed in programme presented by John Ellison, Pauline Tooth. Ed: Prod: John Duncan.
15/12/56	PANTO REHEARSAL (LP, 4.30-5.0) Jean Matcalfe and Brian Johnston go behind the scenes to watch the rehearsals of two West End pantomimes: Emile Littler's *Dick Whittington* starring George Formby to be presented at the Palace Theatre and Val Parnell's *Aladdin* [*The Wonderful Lamp*] to be presented at the London Palladium.
31/12/56	WOMAN'S HOUR (LP, 2.0-3.0) Yearly round-up which includes NW from 1/2/56. Introduced by Marjorie Anderson.
21/2/57	WOMAN'S HOUR (LP, 2.0-3.0) Includes interviews with NW, John Paddy Carstairs, Janette Scott, Bobby Howes by Gordon Gow in 'The Showmakers' slot. Programme introduced by Marjorie Anderson.
22/2/57	THE LAUGHTERMAKERS (HS, 1.10-1.40) 9th in series discussing modern comedians. NW interviewed about 'The Art Of Norman Wisdom'. Sc: Gale Pedrick. Prod: Tom Ronald.
9/6/57	THE WEEK'S GOOD CAUSE (HS, 8.25-8.30) NW appeals on behalf of Pearson's Fresh Air Fund, to send deprived/handicapped children on holidays.
29/6/57	VARIETY PLAYHOUSE (HS, 8.0-9.0) Kenneth Horne introduces a celebration of Cicely Courtneidge's 50th Anniversary in show business. Guests include: Yvonne Arnaud, Noël Coward, Jack Benny, Edith Evans, Robert Helpmann, Robert Morley, NW. BBC Variety Orchestra. Continuity: Eric Merriman. Prod: Tom Ronald.
1/7/57	CHILDREN'S HOUR: FILM NEWS (N, 5.30-5.50) NW interviewed during a visit to Pinewood studios.
28/9/57	IN TOWN TONIGHT (HS, 7.30-7.45) NW interviewed in feature 'Executive Producer For Pinewood, A Young Actress Just 21 And A Comedian' by presenters John Ellison, Pauline Tooth. Ed: Prod: Peter Duncan.

8/3/58	SATURDAY NIGHT ON THE LIGHT (LP, 7.30-10.30) NW interviewed in programme introduced by Charles Richardson, Tim Gudgin. Continuity Sc: Charles Richardson. Ed: Prod: John Bridges.
6/12/58	SATURDAY NIGHT ON THE LIGHT (LP, 8.0-10.0) NW interviewed about *The Square Peg* in programme introduced by Charles Richardson. Continuity Sc: Charles Richardson. Ed: Prod: John Bridges.
15/1/59	WOMAN'S HOUR (LP, 2.0.3.0) Stephen Black interviews NW in feature 'Artist At Work' as part of programme introduced by Teresa McGonagle.
22/2/59	HOME FOR THE DAY (HS, 9.10am-9.45) NW interviewed in feature 'Artist At Work' and talks about his working methods in a programme introduced by Marjorie Anderson. Presumably repeat of above.
11/4/59	IN TOWN TONIGHT (HS, 7.30-8.0) NW interviewed in programme centering on 'London And Its People And Visitors'. Introduced by Franklin Englemann. Prod: Charles Chilton.
26/10/59	CHILDREN'S HOUR: NORTHERN FILM NEWS (N, 5.30-5.50) NW is a speaker.
29/11/59	MOVIE-GO-ROUND (LP, 2.45-3.30) includes a 'Few Words From Norman Wisdom'. Introduced by Peter Haigh. Ed: Prod: Alfred Dunning.
22/12/59	UP IN THE NORTH (N.NI, 8.15am-8.40am) NW interviewed and appears as speaker on this weekly miscellany programme.
7/5/60	IN TOWN TONIGHT (HS.M.W, 7.30-8.0) NW is a speaker in feature 'Famous Film Stars' in programme hosted by Chris Howland, Nan Winton, Tony Bilbow. Ed: Prod: Peter Duncan.
13/5/60	PICK OF THE WEEK (HS, 1.10-2.-0) Gale Pedrick selects above as one of the highlight's of the week's broadcasting in programme introduced by John Ellison. Ed: John Haslam.
17/12/60	IN TOWN TODAY (HS, 1.10-1.40) NW is speaker in feature 'Famous Comedian' in programme introduced by Nan Winton, Tony Bilbow. Prod: Peter Duncan.

6/2/61	CHILDREN'S HOUR: NORTHERN FILM NEWS (N, 5.30-5.50) NW is a speaker.
28/2/61	THE NORMAN WISDOM STORY (HS.M.N.NI.S.W, 7.30-8.30) Narrated by David Nixon with Jack Davies, Joyce Grenfell, Henry Hall, Capt. Walter Hedley, Billy Marsh, Fred Wisdom, Freda Wisdom and NW. George Mitchell Singers. BBC Revue Orchestra conducted by Malcolm Lockyer. Sc: B.D. Chapman. Prod: Charles Maxwell.
3/3/61	PICK OF THE WEEK (HS, 1.10-2.0) Gale Pedrick selects excerpts from above as one of the highlights of the week's broadcasting in programme introduced by John Ellison. Ed: Gordon Williams.
4/3/61	PICK OF THE WEEK (HS, 3.10-4.0) repeat of above.
4/3/61	INTERNATIONAL STAR TIME (LP, 8.0-9.0) NW selects favourite records.
11/3/61	INTERNATIONAL STAR TIME (LP, 8.0-9.0) NW selects favourite records. Possibly repeat of above.
1/6/61	TOPICS NORTH (N, 6.25-6.57) NW speaker in feature 'Film And Theatre Comic'.
7/11/61	ROUND UP (W, 6.25-6.45) NW talks about his Bristol pantomime *Robinson Crusoe*.
19/2/62	ROUND UP (W, 6.25-6.45) NW talks about 'Life And Religion'.
23/2/62	PICK OF THE WEEK (HS, 1.10-2.0) Gale Pedrick selects the above as one of the highlights of the week's broadcasting in programme introduced by John Ellison. Ed: Gordon Williams.
6/1/63	MOVIE-GO-ROUND (LP, 3.0-4.0) Soundtrack of *On the Beat* adapted for radio by Peter Davalle included in programme introduced by Peter Haigh. Sc: Lynn Fairhurst. Prod: Alfred Dunning.
14/12/63	THE WEEK IN THE NORTH (N, 9.30am-9.55am) NW interviewed about *A Stitch in Time*.
19/12/63	WOMAN'S HOUR (LP, 2.0-3.0) NW interviewed about his 'Spanish Retreat In High Street, Kensington'. Programme introduced by Marjorie Anderson.

23/12/63	NORTHERN VIEW (N, 5.30-5.55) NW interviewed about *A Stitch in Time.*
14/5/64	NEWS AND ROUND UP (W, 6.10-6.15) NW interviewed by Brian Moore on joining Brighton directors.
14/5/64	SOUTH EAST NEWS (HS, 6.10-6.15) Identical broadcast as above relayed simultaneously.
5/9/64	SOUNDS TOPICAL (HS, 8.50am-9.0am) Steve Race plays some items from 28/2/1961 broadcast.
22/9/64	TODAY (HS.M.NI.S.W, 7.15am-7.45am) NW interviewed by Keith Macklin in feature 'Newley Musical Runs Aground' about *The Roar of the Greasepaint - The Smell of the Crowd.* Programme introduced by Jack De Manio.
22/9/64	IT'S JOAN TURNER (LP, 10.0-10.30) NW interviewed by host Joan Turner. Prod: Steve Allen.
18/7/65	MOVIE-GO-ROUND (LP, 3.0-4.0) NW interviewed by Lyn Fairhurst in feature 'International Comedy And Laughter' during programme introduced by Peter Haigh. Sc: Lyn Fairhurst. Prod John Dyas.
15/12/65	WOMAN'S HOUR (LP, 2.0-3.0) includes interview with NW by Gordon Gow in 'Showpiece' feature in programme introduced by Marjorie Anderson.
1/12/66	SOUTH EAST (HS, 6.10-6.30) NW's mother Maud interviewed by Tim Gudgin in programme hosted by Bob Holness.
21/4/67	SOUTH EAST (HS, 6.25-6.45) NW interviewed as a 'Name In The News' by David Clitheroe in programme hosted by Derek Parker.
28/1/68	MOVIE-GO-ROUND (R2, 4.0-5.0) NW is star guest and is interviewed by Maureen Bartlett. Host: Peter Haigh. Sc: Lyn Fairhurst. Prod: John Dyas.
2/2/68	PICK OF THE WEEK (R4, 12.10-12.55) Gale Pedrick selects above as one of the highlights of the week's broadcasting in programme introduced by John Ellison.
2/2/68	MOVIE-GO-ROUND (R4, 4.0-4.45) Repeat from 28/1/68.
4/2/68	PICK OF THE WEEK (R4, 11.15am-12.10) Repeat from 2/2/68.

3/10/68   HOME THIS AFTERNOON (R4, 4.45-5.25) NW interviewed by Peter Davalle in 'Going To The Pictures' feature during programme introduced by Ken Sykora.

9/3/69   MOVIE-GO-ROUND (R2, 4.15-5.0) NW is star guest and is interviewed by Nigel Rees in programme hosted by Peter Haigh. Sc: Prod: Lyn Fairhurst.

14/3/69   PICK OF THE WEEK (R4, 12.10-12.55) Gale Pedrick selects above as one of the highlights of the week's broadcasting in programme introduced by John Ellison.

16/3/69   PICK OF THE WEEK (R4, 11.15am-12.10) Repeat of above.

7/4/69   THE LONDON PALLADIUM (R4, 11.25am-12.25) Gale Pedrick tells the story of the top of the bill at this theatre with help from NW, Bob Hope, Ted Ray, Bud Flanagan, Arthur Askey, Joe Davis and others. Prod: Helen Fry.

21/4/69   LATE NIGHT EXTRA (R1, 10.0-12.0) Host Bob Holness talks to NW about *The Night they Raided Minsky's*. Executive Prod: Tony Luke. Prod: Ian Fenner.

25/4/69   ROUNDABOUT (R2, 4.34-6.30) Feature on NW including interview with Frank Salter during programme hosted by Brian Matthew. Prod: Bev Phillips.

17/5/69   JOIN JIM DALE (R2, 8.30-9.15) Insert by NW. Prod: Lyn Fairhurst.

23/5/69   PICK OF THE WEEK (R4, 12.10-12.55) Gale Pedrick selects above as one of the highlights of the week's broadcasting in programme introduced by John Ellison.

30/9/69   TODAY (R4, 7.15-7.45) NW interviewed by Monty Modlyn on 'What Do The General Public Think About Dustmen's Pay?' in programme introduced by Jack De Manio.

10/10/69   ROUNDABOUT (R2, 4.33-6.30) NW interviewed by host Brian Matthew on 'Where Do I Go From Here?'. Prod: Bev Phillips. Ed: Brian Willey.

21/8/70   LATE NIGHT EXTRA (R2, 10.0-12.0) NW interviewed by Christopher Serle in programme hosted by David Hamilton. Prod: Christopher Serle.

2/8/71   START THE WEEK WITH RICHARD BAKER (R4,

9.5am-10.15am) NW interviewed by John Myatt in 'Show Business Summer Scanner' feature. Prod: Richard Gilbert.

30/9/71   BE MY GUEST (R2, 8.2-8.30) NW recalls musical highlights of his career with programme's researcher Tom Edwards. Prod: John Knight.

11/12/71   TODAY (R4, 8.0-8.45) NW interviewed by Denis Frost about his pantomime *Robinson Crusoe* in programme presented by Jack De Manio.

8/3/72   PETE MURRAY'S OPEN HOUSE (R2, 9.2-12.0) NW interviewed by host Pete Murray about above panto playing at the Liverpool Empire.

19/8/72   FILM TIME BRITISH COMEDIANS (R4, 4.0-4.30) NW, Dick Emery, Reg Varney, Benny Hill interviewed in programme hosted by John Bentley. Sc: Lyn Fairhurst. Prod: Bobby Jaye.

8/10/72   THIS WEEK'S GOOD CAUSE (R4, 11.10am-11.15am) NW appeals on behalf of the Independent Adoption Society.

23/11/72   AFTER SEVEN (R2, 7.3-8.0) NW interviewed by Charles Thompson. Prod: Angela Bond.

18/5/73   MEET NORMAN WISDOM (R4, 11.0am-11.20am) Slightly shortened repeat of BE MY GUEST from 30/9/71.

3/6/73   BING (R2, 2.30-3.30) NW takes part in 9th episode entitled 'Going My Way' in 14-part serialisation. Research: Sc: Charles Thompson. Prod: Brian Willey.

18/12/73   PETE MURRAY'S OPEN HOUSE (R2, 10.2-12.0) NW guest.

27/12/73   LATE NIGHT EXTRA (R2, 10.2-12.0) NW guest on programme hosted by Peter Latham. Prod: Geoff Dobson.

17/3/74   THE HENRY HALL STORY (R2, 2.30-3.30) NW takes part with Al Read, Ted Ray, Bob Monkhouse, Elizabeth Seal and Henry Hall in Chapter 2 entitled 'The Show Man' of 4-part serialisation. Narrator: Michael Flanders. Sc: Gavin Blakeney. Prod: John Browell.

31/3/74   THE HENRY HALL STORY (R2, 2.30-3.30) Last part of above entitled 'The Man'. Taking part: NW, Anne Rogers, Mike Hall, Ted Ray, Al Read, Albert Marland, Henry Hall. Rest of credits as above.

22/2/75   THE HENRY HALL STORY (R2, 12.2-1.0) Repeat of Chapter 2 from 17/3/74.

8/3/75   THE HENRY HALL STORY (R2, 12.2-1.0) Repeat of Chapter 4 from 31/3/74.Í

2/10/75   JACK DE MANIO PRECISELY (R4, 3.50-4.35) NW and De Manio in discussion. Prod: Michael Raper.

8/12/75   HARRY CARPENTER'S OPEN HOUSE (R2, 9.2am-11.30am) NW guest. Prod: Angela Bond, Peter Chiswell, Jack Dabbs.

4/1/76   THE JULIE ANDREWS STORY (R2, 2.30-3.30) NW takes part with Lillian Stiles-Allen, Barbara Andrews, Peter Brough, Dilys Laye, Beryl Reid, Sandy Wilson, Dennis Main Wilson in Chapter 1 entitled 'From Walton On Thames To The Great White Way' of 3-part serialisation. Narrator: Ian Carmichael. Interviewer: Sc: David Rider. Prod: Bobby Jaye.

24/2/77   PM REPORTS (R4, 5.0-5.50) NW interviewed by host Brian Widlake on why he wants to change his knockabout style and play serious roles in the theatre.

11/9/77   THIS WEEK'S GOOD CAUSE (R4, 11.10am-11.15am) NW appeals on behalf of the Sailor's Children's Society.

8/12/78   HARRY POWELL'S OPEN HOUSE (R2, 12.30-2.30) NW guests. Prod: Angela Bond.

25/1/79   JOHN DUNN (R2, 4.47-6.45) NW interviewed by Liz Daniels about looking for a secretary.

5/5/79   SPORT ON 2 (R2, 1.30-6.0) Includes item on 'The Brighton Story' with Peter Brackley interviewing NW, Mike Bamber, Jack Aldridge, Dora Bryan, Alan Mullery. Introduced by Jim Rosenthal.

12/6/79   PETER MURRAY'S OPEN HOUSE (R2, 12.30-2.30) Guest artists include NW, Mick McManus, John Quinn. Prod: Angela Bond.

18/6/79   THE WORLD AT ONE (R4, 1.0-1.40) NW interviewed by

John Parry on his Theatre Royal show *A World of Wisdom* in programme presented by Brian Widlake. Ed: Derek Lewis.

2/7/79   WOMAN'S HOUR (R4, 2.2-3.0) NW, Robin Ellis, Lee Remick, Derek Jacobi interviewed by Gordon Gow in 'Entertainment Roundup' feature during programme hosted by Sue MacGregor. Ed: Wyn Knowles.

5/7/79   STAR SOUND EXTRA (R2, 10.30-11.0) NW interviewed in programme presented by David Bellan. Compiled: Sc: Lyn Fairhurst. Prod: Tony Luke.

7/7/79   AWAY FROM IT ALL (R4, 12.2-12.27) NW tells 'Traveller's Tales' to Maxwell Boyd in programme presented by Joan Bakewell. Prod: Jenny Marshall. Ed: Roger MacDonald.

9/7/79   STAR SOUND (R2, 10.30-11.0) NW interviewed in programme hosted by David Bellan. Compiled: Sc: Lyn Fairhurst. Prod: Tony Luke.

12/7/79   TODAY (R4, 6.30am-8.35am) Hannah Buckle screeches loudly at jokes told by NW and Pat Coleman in programme presented by John Timpson.

24/12/79   STAR SOUND SPECIAL (R2, 10.2-11.0) Includes interviews with NW, Gemma Craven, Yul Brynner, Carol Channing, Glenda Jackson etc. in programme introduced by David Bellan. Compiled: Sc: Lyn Fairhurst. prod: Tony Luke.

15/10/80   GOING PLACES (R4, 7.20-7.45) Interviews with NW, Lord Montagu and Sue Baker from Birmingam Motor Show. Presenter: Clive Jacobs. Prod: Stephen Phelps. Ed: Roger MacDonald.

24/11/85   THE COLOUR SUPPLEMENT (R4, 11.15am-1.0) NW chats with presenter Margot MacDonald and recalls 'A Year Of My Own: 1950'. Prod: Ian Gardhouse, Simon Shaw, Vanessa Harrison.

22/4/87   A WEALTH OF WISDOM (R2, 10.2-10.15) NW talks about his life to interviewer and researcher Michael Pointon in first of 8-part series. 1: Treble Top. Series produced by Edward Taylor.

29/4/87   A WEALTH OF WISDOM (R2, 10.2-10.15) Credits as above. 2: The Fastest Errand-Boy In Deal.

6/5/87	A WEALTH OF WISDOM (R2, 10.2-10.15) Credits as above. 3: The Horizontal Flyweight.
13/5/87	A WEALTH OF WISDOM (R2, 10.2-10.15) Credits as above. 4: A Passage To India.
20/5/87	A WEALTH OF WISDOM (R2, 10.2-10.15) Credits as above. 5: Skating On Thin Ice.
27/5/87	A WEALTH OF WISDOM (R2, 10.2-10.15) Credits as above. 6: Marilyn And Margaret.
3/6/87	A WEALTH OF WISDOM (R2, 10.2-10.15) Credits as above. 7: Gone To The Pictures.
10/6/87	A WEALTH OF WISDOM (R2, 10.2-10.15) Credits as above. 8: Newley, New York And Noël.
14/2/91	A WEALTH OF WISDOM (R2, 9.45-10.0) 1: Treble Top. Repeat of above series.
21/2/91	A WEALTH OF WISDOM (R2, 9.45-10.0) 2: The Fastest Errand-Boy In Deal. Repeat of above series.
28/2/91	A WEALTH OF WISDOM (R2, 9.45-10.0) 3: The Horizontal Flyweight. Repeat of above series.
7/3/91	A WEALTH OF WISDOM (R2, 9.45-10.0) 4: A Passage To India. Repeat of above series.
14/3/91	A WEALTH OF WISDOM (R2, 9.45-10.0) 5: Skating On Thin Ice. Repeat of above series.
21/3/91	A WEALTH OF WISDOM (R2, 9.45-10.0) 6: Marilyn And Margaret. Repeat of above series.
28/3/91	A WEALTH OF WISDOM (R2, 9.45-10.0) 7: Gone To The Pictures. Repeat of above series.
4/4/91	A WEALTH OF WISDOM (R2, 9.45-10.0) 8: Newley, New York And Noël. Repeat of above series.

APPENDIX 5

A: Discography.

Singles (78s and 45s)

BEWARE/LONDON MELODY (Wisdom/Farnon:Nash) Bob Farnon & orch. & The Eight Stars. Decca F9738 1951
BEWARE/DREAM FOR SALE (Wisdom/Toff) Norrie Paramor & orch.
Columbia DB 3654 1955
DO YOU BELIEVE IN CHRISTMAS/ALL OVER THE WORLD (David W.Webster) Arr. by Pete Jeffries.
Genie RWS 0372 1965
DON'T LAUGH AT ME/ONCE IN LOVE WITH AMY (Wisdom:Tremayne/Loesser) Norrie Paramor & orch.
Columbia DB 3133 1952
FOLLOW A STAR/GIVE ME A NIGHT IN JUNE (Wisdom/Miller:Green) Accomp. arr. and dir. by Malcolm Lockyer.
Top Rank JAR 246 1959
HAPPY ENDING/THE WISDOM OF A FOOL (Park/Silver:Alfred) Eric Jupp & orch. Columbia DB 3903 1957
HEART OF A CLOWN/BEWARE (Kane:Rollins:Nelson/Wisdom) Norrie Paramor & orch. Columbia DB 3084 1952
I'D LIKE TO PUT ON RECORD/MY LITTLE DOG (Mischa:Spoliansky/Wisdom:Tremayn) Wally Stott & orch & chorus.
Philips PB 223 1954
IF YOU BELIEVE IN ME/YER GOTTA GET AHT (Ornadel:Croft/Saroney) Geoff Love & orch.
Columbia DB 4601 1961
THE JOKER/WHO CAN I TURN TO? (Bricusse/Newley) Accomp. directed by Peter Knight.
Columbia DB 7352 1964
ME AND MY IMAGINATION/UP IN THE WORLD (Hoffman:Merrill/Wisdom) Philip Green & orch.
Columbia DB 3864 1957
NARCISSUS (THE LAUGHING RECORD)/I DON'T 'ARF LOVE YOU (Nevin arr Paramor:Grenfell/Mortimer) with Joyce Grenfell. Norrie Paramor & orch. Columbia DB 3161 1952
Columbia SCD 2160 1960

PLEASE OPPORTUNITY/YOU WERE MEANT FOR ME (Wisdom/ Freed:Brown) Wally Stott & orch.
Philips PB 372   1954
SUSSEX BY THE SEA (trad:Wisdom) Theme done for Brighton F.C. No more information traced.
1965
TAKE A STEP IN THE RIGHT DIRECTION/I'LL ALWAYS LOVE YOU (Newell/Wisdom:de Rance) Wally Stott & orch.
Philips PB 381   1954
THEY DIDN'T BELIEVE ME/SO NICE TO DREAM (Rourke:Kern/ Park:Wilkinson) Wally Stott & orch.
Philips PB 299   1954
TWO RIVERS/BOY MEETS GIRL (Roberts:Hennesey) with Ruby Murray. Ray Martin & orch./Norrie Paramor & orch.
Columbia DB 3715/SCM 5222   1956
WHITE CHRISTMAS/IS EVERYBODY HAPPY? (Berlin/Arnold:Martin:Morrow) arranged by Geoff Morrow.
EMI 2098   1973
YODELEE, YODELAY/IMPOSSIBLE (Fishman/Julien) Norrie Paramor & orch.
Columbia DB 3700   1955
YOUNG AT HEART/JUST TO BE WITH YOU (Leigh:Richards/Spencer:Nelson) Wally Stott & orch.
Philips PB 259   1954

EP recordings

BEWARE/DREAM FOR SALE/DON'T LAUGH AT ME/ONCE IN LOVE WITH AMY (Wisdom/Toff/Wisdom:Tremayne/Loesser) Norrie Paramor & orch.
Columbia SEG 7612   1955
FOLLOW A STAR/GIVE ME A NIGHT IN JUNE/I LOVE YOU/THE BATH SONG (Wisdom/Miller:Green/Wisdom/Wisdom) Accomp. arr. and dir. Malcolm Lockyer.
Top Rank JKP 2052   1960
NORMAN AND RUBY: with Ruby Murray: BOY MEETS GIRL/UP IN THE WORLD/O'MALLEY'S TANGO/ME AND MY IMAGINATION (Roberts:Hennesy/Wisdom/Carter:Mitchell/Hoffman:Merrill)   Norrie Paramor & orch./Ray Martin & orch./Norrie Paramor & orch./Philip Green & orch.
Columbia SEG 7687   1957
'WHERE'S CHARLEY?' SELECTION: with Terence Cooper, Pamela Gale, Excerpts: MY DARLING, MY DARLING/MAKE A MIRACLE/ LOVELIER THAN EVER/THE WOMAN IN HIS ROOM (Loesser) Michael Collins & orch.
Columbia SEG 7844   1958

YOU'RE GETTING TO BE A HABIT WITH ME/SKYLARK/YOU MUST HAVE BEEN A BEAUTIFUL BABY/BY THE FIRESIDE [IN THE GLOAMING] (Dubin:Warren/Carmichael:Mercer/Warren:Mercer/ Noble:Campbell: Connelly) Geoff Love & orch.
Columbia SEG 7856 1958

LP recordings: For show recordings, only songs performed by Wisdom are listed.

ANDROCLES AND THE LION: 'Velvet Paws', Strength Is My Weakness', 'The Arena Pantomime', 'Don't Be Afraid Of An Animal'. (Richard Rodgers). Soundtrack from NBC TV special in USA. Orch. cond. by Jay Blackton.
RCA Victor LSO 1141 1967
CINDERELLA AND DICK WHITTINGTON. Charity LP for Stars Organisation for Spastics. Spoken Word, with musical backing. NW is the Newsboy in Cinderella and provides additional voices for Dick Whittington. (Words: Martyn Pedrick. Music: Malcolm Lockyer).
Polydor 2478 093 1975
I WOULD LIKE TO PUT ON RECORD: 'I Would Like To Put On Record';, 'Young At Heart', 'I'll Always Love You', 'You Were Meant For Me', 'So Nice To Dream', 'Take A Step In The Right Direction'. 'Just To Be With You', 'My Little Dog', 'They Didn't Believe Me', 'Please Opportunity'. For composer/orchestra credits see singles releases.
Wing WL 1216 1956
ONE MAN'S MUSIC [A TRIBUTE TO NOEL GAY]. Compilation LP with Des O'Connor, The Mike Sammes Singers and Beryl Reid. Wisdom performs 'Leaning On The Lamp Post', 'Lambeth Walk', 'Me And My Girl' (Noel Gay).
Columbia SCX 6299 1969
JINGLE JANGLE. Original Cast Recording: 'C.C.C.C.C.C. Cola', 'Me, Myself And I', 'Allied Carpets Jingle', 'Jingle Jangle', 'Vox All De Fuss', 'You've Come To The Right Place', 'Goodtime', 'The Missing Years', 'Delores', 'I'm Wilde, You're Kerasey' (Morrow/Shaper). Orchestra cond. and arr. by John Altman.
Class JJ001 1982
THE NIGHT THEY RAIDED MINSKY'S. Film Soundtrack. 'Perfect Gentleman' (Strouse:Adams). Conducted and orchestrated by Philip J. Lang.
United Artists SULP 1235 1969
WALKING HAPPY Original Broadway Cast Recording: 'How Do You Talk To A Girl?', 'If I Be Your Best Chance', 'What Makes It Happen?', 'You're Right, You're Right', 'I'll Make A Man Of The Man', 'Walking Happy', 'I

Don't Think I'm In Love', 'It Might As Well Be Her' (Cahn:Van Heusen). Orchestra and Chorus conducted by Herbert Grossman.

Capitol VAS 2631 (USA) 1966

WHERE'S CHARLEY? Original London Cast Recording: 'Better Get Out Of Here', 'Make A Miracle', 'Once In Love With Amy', 'My Darling, My Darling' (Loesser). Michael Collins and Orch.Columbia SX 1085 1958

Monmouth Evergreen MES 7029 (USA) 1970

Norman Wisdom also guests on Tony Fayne's LP, TONY FAYNE'S BACK, on track 'Traffic Warden'.

Rosie Records RR 008 1983

Norman Wisdom's most popular songs have been included on many compilation LP's and cassettes. A few are listed below:-

DOWN MEMORY LANE (Australia, EMI AX 1108): 'Lambeth Walk', 'Narcissus'

FAVOURITES OF THE 1950s (MFP DC 41 10509): 'Don't Laugh At Me'

HAIL VARIETY! (Oriole MG 20033/ZCHRH4): 'Don't Laugh At Me' extract

HMV GOLDEN GREATS (EMI TC IDL 19): 'Don't Laugh At Me'.

JUST FOR LAUGHS (EMI One Up OU 2079): 'Narcissus'

MUSIC HALL FAVOURITES (Pickwick DTO 10210): 'London Melody'.

SAVILLE'S TIME TRAVELS 1957 (TC MFP 41 5648 4): 'The Wisdom Of A Fool'.

SMILE (EMI BIRDS1): 'Narcissus'.

THE SOUNDS AND SONGS OF LONDON (EMI EMS 1055881): 'Lambeth Walk'.

THEY PLAYED THE EMPIRE (Decca RFLD 23): 'Beware'.

THEY PLAYED THE PALLADIUM (Decca RFLD 30): 'London Melody'.

THIS IS LONDON (EMI TC THIS 12): 'Lambeth Walk'.

B: Composing Credits.

Songs written by Norman Wisdom

THE BATH SONG [aka THE SQUARE SONG]	Francis Day & Hunter	1960
BEWARE	Chappell & Co. Ltd	1951
CINDERELLA MAN	ATV Music Ltd	1951
DON'T LAUGH AT ME (with June Tremayne)	Northern Songs	1954

FOLLOW A STAR	Filmusic Pub.	1960
I LOVE YOU	Francis Day & Hunter	1960
I WANT TO BE LOVED	unpub.	1965
TONIGHT [aka KISSED AND CUDDLED]		
I'LL ALWAYS LOVE YOU (with De Rance:Hero)	Francis Day & Hunter	1954
I'M HUNGRY	unpublished	1954
MY LITTLE DOG (with June Tremayne)	Northern Songs	1954
NOBODY	ATV Music Ltd	1973
PLEASE OPPORTUNITY	Northern Songs	1954
SHE'S MY NO GIRL (with June Tremayne)	unpublished	1954
UP IN THE WORLD	Barry Music Co.	1956

BIBLIOGRAPHY

There has been little serious writing on Norman Wisdom's work, a notable exception being a chapter in John Fisher's invaluable *A Funny Way to be a Hero*. The three newspaper/magazine serialisations of Wisdom's life-story provided much useful information, but should be approached with caution as they can be misleading.

Bevan, Ian	*Top Of The Bill*	Frederick Muller	1952
Brown, Geoff (ed)	*Walter Forde*	British Film Institute	1977
Busby, Roy	*British Music Hall*	Paul Elek	1976
Dacre, Richard	*Wit & Wisdom*	Primetime 6/7 magazine	1983
Davies, Hunter	*The Grades*	Weidenfeld & Nicholson	1981
Fisher, John	*Funny Way To Be a Hero*	Frederick Muller	1973
Fisher, John	*What A Performance!*	Seeley Service	1975
Gifford, Denis	*The British Film Catalogue*	David & Charles	1973
Gifford, Denis	*The Illustrated Who's Who in British Films*	Batsford	1978
Langdon, Claude	*Earl's Court*	Stanley Paul	1953
Lee, Norman	*Money For Film Stories*	Pitman	1937
Mayle, Peter	*Thirsty Work: Ten Years of Heineken Advertising*	Macmillan	1983
Midwinter, Eric	*Make 'Em Laugh*	George Allen & Unwin	1979
Montgomery, John	*Comedy Films* (with preface by Norman Wisdom)	George Allen & Unwin	1954
Morecambe, Eric & Wise, Ernie with Holman, Dennis	*Eric And Ernie*	W.H. Allen	1972
Nathan, David	*The Laughtermakers*	Peter Owen	1971
Nobbs, George	The Wireless Stars	Wensum	1972
Palmer, Scott	*Who's Who of British Film Actors*	Scarecrow	1981
Salberg, Derek	*Once Upon A Pantomime*	Cortney Publications	1981
Secombe, Harry	*Goon For Lunch*	M.J. Hobbs	1975
Staveacre, Tony	*Slapstick!*	Angus & Robertson	1987

Wilmut, Roger	*From Fringe To Flying Circus*	Eyre Methuen	1980
Wilmut, Roger & Rosengard, Peter	*Didn't You Kill My Mother-In-Law?*	Methuen	1989
Wisdom, Norman, with Jympson Harman	*The True Story Of Norman Wisdom*	Evening News 9-part series from 28/12/53	
Wisdom, Norman	*Up In The World*	John Bull 4-part with uncredited writer series from 10/11/56	
Wisdom, Norman	*My Fight For Life*	Evening News 5-part with Reg Gutteridge series from 18/11/63	
Wisdom, Norman with Rex Reed	*Me Life, Me Wife And Me*	New York Times	11/12/66
Wood, Alan	*Mr. Rank*	Hodder & Stoughton	1952

INDEX

Mackay, Fulton 93–94
MAN OF THE MOMENT (film) 28, 39, 42–44, 46, 70, 107–108 (plot), 112, [30]
Mann, Hastings 13
Manning, Bernard 99
Marceau, Marcel 77
Marcus, Frank 98
Margaret, HRH The Princess 63, [15]
Marks, Alfred 55, 59, [39]
Marsh, Billy 15, 16, 20, 23, 69
Marsh, Laurie 123
Martin, Edie 112
Martin, Ernest 75
Martin, Mary 75
Martin, Millicent 56, 59, 116, [40]
MARTY (tv) 100
Marx Brothers, the 83, 105
Mason, James 88
Matcham, Frank 112
Matthews, A.E. 26
Maxin, Ernest 67
McCarthy, Neil 90
McGill, Arthur 47
McKuen, Rod 98
McLaughlin, Andra 63
McShane, Kitty 98, [5]
'Me and My Imagination' (sketch) 70
MEET MR LUCIFER (film) 25 (plot), 105, [25]
Merrick, David 73
Merson, Billy [1]
Metropolitan Theatre, Edgware Road 14, 112
Miller, David 105
Miller, Jonathan 100
Miller, Max 3, 4, [8]
Milligan, Spike 100
MILLION POUND NOTE, THE (film) 115
Mills, John 46, 75
MIRAGE (film) 78
Misfit Evening Suit 16, 18, 35, 39, 54, 65, 70, 103, [52]
MISS ROBIN HOOD (film) 27
Mitchell, Guy 67
MONEY PROGRAMME, THE (tv) 94
Monkhouse, Bob 18, 69, 71
Montague, Bert 13, 15
MONTY PYTHON'S FLYING CIRCUS (tv) 87, 100–101
MOON OVER SOHO (tv) 115

Moore, Dudley 100
Moran, Gillian 65, [15]
Morecambe, Eric 1, 6, 87, 102, 120, [14]
Morgan, Fisher [61]
Morgan, Priscilla 88
Morley, Robert 69
Morris, Lana 27, 28, 31, 33, 35, 37, [30]
Morrow, Geoff 94
Moscow Film Festival [1965] 73
Moss Empire Theatre Circuit 4, 15
Muir, Frank 99
Murphy, Brian 98
Murphy, Noel 99
Murray, Barbara 25
Murray, Ruby 65
Music Hall Tradition early days 1–2; definition 1–2; radio 4–5; early sound films 3–4; postwar 5; television 5–7; TV situation comedy 6–7, 101; contemporary revival 98–99; university humour 99–101; 'alternative' comedy 101
MUSIC HALL [1969/1970] (tv) 87–88
MUSIC HALL [1950] (tv) 19
MY BEAUTIFUL LAUNDRETTE (film) 93
MY FAIR LADY (stage) 78
Nadel, Norman 77
'Narcissus [The Laughing Record]' (song) 43
National Film Finance Corporation 121
Neame, Ronald 24–25, 98, 115
Nesbitt, Robert 66, 71–72
NEW FACES (tv) 99
NEW NAMES MAKE NEWS (stage) 12–13
Newbrook, Peter 121
Newley, Anthony 72–73, 92
Nichols, Joy 15, 100
Nicol, Watt 88
NIGHT THEY RAIDED MINSKY'S, THE (film) 46, 50, 79–82, 79–80 (plot), 83, 98, 101, 102, 122–123, [50]
Nixon, David 16
NO STRINGS (stage) 78
NOBODY IS NORMAN WISDOM (tv) 88–89
Norden, Denis 99
NORMAN (tv) 87, 88
NORMAN WISDOM – COMEDIAN (stage) 92